A TIGER'S TALE
...of a born loser

by Ralph Spencer

TURNER PUBLISHING COMPANY
Paducah, KY

TURNER PUBLISHING COMPANY

Publishers of America's History
412 Broadway • P.O. Box 3101
Paducah, KY 42002-3101
(270) 443-0121

Copyright © 2002 Ralph Spencer
Publishing Rights: Turner Publishing Company
All rights reserved.

Turner Publishing Company Staff
Editor: Tammy Ervin
Designer: M. Frene Walker

Library of Congress Control No. 2002116942
ISBN 978-1-63026-936-4

Additional copies may be purchased from
Turner Publishing Company. Limited Edition.

About the Author

Born on Sept. 26, 1918 in Kenosha, Wisconsin, Ralph Spencer has had an interesting life. At age 24, he was drafted into the Army and promoted to Private First Class. After passing all the tests for the OCS board, Spencer decided he did not want to be an officer. He spent  3 years in the Army (1 of which was in Europe). As a tank driver, he fought all through the Battle of the Bulge.

Upon returning home, Spencer set up his own business. He was married four times, divorced three times and had two children, an adopted daughter and a son.

Spencer has moved 36 times and worked over 100 different types of jobs. He now resides in Wellington, Texas at the age of 83.

Acknowledgements

My many thanks to Beth Motsenbocker and Patricia Melton for their patience and expertise as typists and computer operators. I also wish to thank my friend, Ed Wehnes, for making the suggestion that I should write the story of my life.

Table of Contents

A Tiger's Tale of a Born Loser

I was born in Kenosha, Wisconsin on September 26, 1918 to Ernest Raymond and Mata Bherns Spencer. I weighed 10 pounds and two ounces. I was born in an upstairs apartment where my folks were living on South 36th St. This was at the time of the flu epidemic in 1918. My mother was caught up in the epidemic and died three weeks after giving birth.

My father left my sister, Vinetta, who was two, and I with my mother's folks in Hebron, Illinois until after the funeral. When he came to pick us up, they refused to let him have us. In order to regain custody, he had to go to court and sue for custody. So I lost not only my mother but my grandparents on her side, too, as my father would not let us visit or even talk about them.

I can just barely remember my grandfather on my dad's side. When I was about three years old, he was sick in bed for a year before he died. He had a little bell that he rang when he wanted something. Answering the bell was a job for Vinetta and me.

Grandpa had been a farmer, a milkman on a route in Rockford, Illinois, operated a dairy and cheese factory before I was born, but my only memory of him was answering his bell.

When I was four years old, I was staying with my aunt and uncle and I was in the field with my uncle while he was husking corn. In those days, the corn was all husked by hand. He had a grain wagon there with a buckboard on one side of it. As he husked the corn, he would throw the corn, and it would hit the buckboard and fall into the wagon. The team was trained so that when the husker moved forward, they would move along with him without any driver. I got tired of walking, and thought I would get up in the wagon and ride for a while. I did not say anything to my uncle, but just climbed up onto the rear wheel. Before I could get into the wagon, the horses started up, going ahead, and threw me down in front of the wheel. The ground was fairly soft. The wagon ran over me, across the left side, over my left leg and shoulder, just missing my head. When I came to, I was back in the house. My uncle said when he first saw me; I was curled up around the wheel like a big worm. Fortunately, I had no broken bones and no other effects.

When I was about four years old, my grandmother took my sister and me on a trip to Ohio to visit my great-grandmother, Hannah Hawk. I don't remember much about the trip except for two or three highlights. One of which was we stayed overnight in a rooming house somewhere in Ohio. I was just about eaten up by bed bugs. The next morning when we had breakfast, the woman served us pancakes, and I had a nice, great big bed bug right in the center of my pancake!

While we were at my great-grandmother's house, she would get up early in the morning and bake an apple pie so we could have hot apple pie for breakfast. The first time I took a bite of mine, it was so hot that it burned the roof of my mouth and tongue. Ever since then, I have not been able to eat any hot fruit pies.

We took a hike one day over to an apple orchard to gather some apples. On the way, we had to cross a small creek with no bridge. We pulled our shoes and socks off to wade across the creek. My sister was almost across when I saw a snake going downstream away from us. I said, "Oh, look, there's a snake." My sister took off and made about four or five attempts to get up the bank on the other side of the river while I was standing there laughing at her. After we got to the apple orchard, there was a wood rail fence around it. We were told to get up and sit on top of the fence. I got up on the fence and my sister did not. In three or four minutes, a little baby black snake wiggled across the top of her foot. You never saw anybody run so fast in your life as she did, and never moved an inch! After that, she got up and sat on the fence with me.

When I was about five years old, my Dad remarried. Lela Hopkins was her name. We lived in an upstairs apartment. I slept with my grandmother, and one night I got up to go to the bathroom. I saw her sitting on my dad's lap. I wondered why she wanted to do that! She was good to me. My sister and I both liked our new step-mother. She worked in a clothing factory. The lady that worked next to her was Don Ameche's mother. We got to know Don before he became a movie star. At one time, her factory was out on strike. In those days, strikers got pretty violent sometimes. The strikers bombed out the side of the building where she worked. Fortunately, it was at night, and the building was empty so no one was hurt. We lived about two miles from the factory, and the blast woke us up at about 4:00 a.m.

We went to the McKinley school, about a mile from where we lived. We walked, as there were no school buses at that time. One winter evening when it got dark early, my sister and I saw a man following us about a half a block back. Scared, we got home as quickly as we could. Then we learned that it was our Dad, following us to make sure we came directly home from school.

We lived in a poorer section of the town. There was a gang of boys that were two or three years older than me who were always getting into trouble. They wanted me to join the gang, which I did not want to do and did not do so two or three times a week, they would gang up on me and beat the daylights out of me after school. There were about six or seven of them who would form a ring around me. If I started to get the best of one, he would step out and another would step in so I did not stand a chance! My nose would bleed so badly that they had to take me to the doctor to get it stopped. The doctor advised my dad to get me a blackjack with a leather thong on it to wear up my sleeve, and for me to use it! He never did!

At the age of eight, I entered into the life of crime! There was a junkyard about four blocks away from our home. With another boy, I would go to the junkyard at night, sneak through a hole in the fence and each of us would swipe an old tire. We would roll them home and the next day when the junk man came around, we would sell the tire back to him for a dime. We each made fifty cents one week, and then my dad almost caught us, so we decided we had better give that up!

One day, a friend of mine took me into a drug store, and bought me an ice cream sundae for fifteen cents. I really thought that was something as I had never been in a drug store before, and had never had an ice cream sundae, nor had fifteen cents to spend. I marveled at how he could have thirty cents to spend!

It was about that time that I got my first job. That was selling the *Saturday Evening Post* and *Ladies Home Journal*. I did fairly well with it! My second job was a school crossing guard. We had hand held stop signs, and each boy was stationed on a street corner to stop the traffic so the children could cross the streets. One year, our class put on a pageant of *Snow White and the Seven Dwarfs*. I was one of the dwarfs.

When I was seven years old, I had a little friend the same age that lived about four houses away from us. His parents were avid card players, but had no one in the neighborhood to play with, so they taught him and me how to play 500. (This was not 500 Rummy.) And the four of us would play almost every day. I have always loved that game. He also had a bicycle that he taught me how to ride. I done pretty good riding it straight ahead, but always when I went to make a turn, I would wind up on the ground. If I were going to make a right hand turn, I would lean toward the left in order to balance the bicycle, or if I were going to turn to the left, I would turn to the right. Finally, he saw what I was doing, and told me that when you make a turn, you lean in the direction that you are turning, which I tried, and it worked.

If we were bad in school, the teacher would keep us after school and make us report to Shorty. Shorty was the school janitor. I don't remember his name. Everybody called him Shorty. He would give us a piece of broken glass and put us to scraping inkblots out of the floor. You had to be mighty careful not to cut yourself on that piece of broken glass. After two to three times of scraping inkblots, you just naturally tried to be a little better in school.

Every year, we would go out to my aunt and uncle Fuller's to spend Christmas. They did not have electricity on the farm, but we did have electric lights on the tree. Dad would pull the battery out of the car and hook the lights up to it.

My sister and I always spent every summer at the farm with the Fullers. One day I had a birdhouse that I was going to put up in a tree. I guess I thought that since the birds always flew high, the birdhouse had to go high. I was about thirty feet up in the tree.

I intended to go higher, but there was a large dead limb. Although I knew I should not put my weight on a dead limb, it looked to be big enough so that it would hold me, so I stepped up on it, and naturally, the limb broke and I went down! Fortunately, about six or seven foot off of the ground, the tree split into a crotch and my left leg caught in the crotch of the tree. There I was hanging upside down about two-foot from the ground. After I got my senses back, I doubled up, but I could not get my foot loose! I untied my shoe and managed to work my foot out of the shoe. When I got to the ground, I got a stick. About that time, my grandmother and aunt came around the corner of the house, and found me trying to pry my shoe out of the tree. Both almost passed out when I told them what had happened!

Another time, I thought I would help my uncle out tearing out an old barbed wire fence. He was out in the field working, so I thought I would go ahead and tear the fence down for him. I got a section of the barbed wire loose, and gave it a fling to throw it away from me, but it hit my arm and ripped it open right down to the bone! I could see two or three inches of white bone! I went to the house and my aunt doctored it up for me, but did not take me to the doctor to have it sewed up. It took about three months to heal, so I have a nice big scar on my arm from it. The neighbors about a half-mile down the road had four children about our ages, so we always played together. My uncle had an old buggy, so they would come up at night and we would hitch up one of his horses and go buggy riding. We really enjoyed that! It was a lot of fun!

My uncle had half a dozen cows, which he was selling, and had to get them into Richmond to the stock yard, which was about seven or eight miles from the farm. He had no truck, so we had to drive the cows by hand. With one of the neighbor boys who had his pony and me on my uncle's horse, we got to play cowboy and drove the cattle into Richmond, which took us all day.

Farm life was not all play! We had our chores to do, such as slopping the hogs, feeding the chickens, gathering the eggs, hoeing the corn, and shocking the grain at harvest time. They had a threshing crew that serviced about fifteen farms. All of the farmers went from one farm to the next. There was a huge old threshing machine, and I do mean it was huge, and when it was at my uncle's we would play hide and seek in it!

My uncle moved to a new farm, and the tenant before him had a whiskey still set up in the basement of the house. When he left, he left two barrels of corn mash in the basement. We had to clean that out, because you could smell it throughout the whole house. We took it out and buried it, but we did not bury it very deep, just a couple of inches of dirt over the top of it. The chickens, which were not caged, could smell the corn mash, and they scratched it up and were eating it. Also, there were a couple of pigs that got loose, and they got into it. We really had a circus there! Two pigs and about a dozen chickens as drunk as they could be! I mean they were drunk!

Also, he had a very good orchard there with about four different types of apples, three cherry trees, some peach trees, plum trees, which kept us busy in the fall picking fruit. Thirty years later, I went back to paint the buildings on that farm for the new owner. There was not a sign of a fruit tree anywhere. I asked the owner, "Whatever happened to that beautiful orchard that was here? I used to spend my summers here, and there was a beautiful orchard!" He said, "Well, the fellow who owned this farm before me went out and got drunk one night, and when he came home, he ran into one of the apple trees and wrecked his pickup. The next day, he got his tractor out and pulled up every fruit tree on the place! He was not going to run into any more trees!"

I wanted to join the Boy Scouts, but my dad would not let me. My grandmother took me and I joined the Boy Scouts secretly. My dad found out, and was mad, but he said since I was already in, I could stay in!

We lived in Kenosha where my father worked as a welder in the Nash automobile plant. He always took us out to the farm of my Aunt and Uncle, Chloe and Jim Fuller, near Richmond, Illinois, where we stayed for the summer months.

I was five when they entered me into a kindergarten. The teacher thought I was so bright that at mid-semester, in January, she promoted me into first grade, where the first grade teacher promptly failed me, so I was right back with my original class! I was tongue-tied, and had a bad lisp, unable to talk plainly. Work was oral, and since I was hard to understand, the teacher never called on me to recite.

That summer, my dad took me to the doctor, had my tonsils and adenoids removed, and had my tongue clipped so I could talk plainly, and had me circumcised all at one time. Half of the summer was spent recovering!

My folks named me Fazell Ralph Spencer. The Fazell (pronounced fa ZELL') came from a religious book of some kind. I always wished they had never seen it, as that name has plagued me all of my life. They were Methodist, and entered me into the Methodist Sunday School, where they promptly registered me as Hazel Spencer. After five years, I was given a diploma for perfect attendance for five years, which was registered to Hazel Spencer! I still have that diploma!

My first experience with playing baseball came when I was in the third grade. Nobody wanted to play the position of catcher, so that job was given to me. Nobody told me how to play that position, so I squatted down behind the batter, and on the first ball pitched, the boy took a swing at the ball and caught me square in the mouth with the bat, as I was sitting much too close to him! Fortunately, no teeth were knocked out, but it did cause a big, fat lip for the next two weeks!

I don't recall too much of my grade school years. One thing I'll never forget was a plague of head lice! I had my head shaven to get rid of the lice. Vinetta had long hair so my grandmother sat for hours every night picking the lice out of her head. There was one Italian boy in my class that was named Stinkerino. He really smelled up to his name! Sitting across the classroom from him, one could see the lice crawling in his hair!

Once when I was about eight years old, I was out at my uncle's farm. There were railroad tracks that ran through his farm, and there was a nice big patch of wild strawberries on the edge of the tracks. I was out picking those strawberries. It was in the summer, and I was barefoot. I started to take a step, and something made me stop with my foot up in the air. I looked down, and there was a big, old rattlesnake coiled up. If I had stepped down, I would have stepped right down on him. I just froze. Then, after a short period, I started easing my foot backwards real slow. I think it must have taken me five minutes to get far enough away from him, that if he decided to strike at me, he couldn't reach me. Then, I turned and really made tracks out of there. That was one animal that I wasn't about to argue with.

I learned to read early on! By the time I finished third grade, I was a good reader, and have read throughout my life. For my eighth birthday, my dad bought my first pair of sidewalk roller skates! They were the clamp-on types. The day he gave them to me, I was mad at him for some reason, so I ran away from home. I headed out to my aunt and uncle's house, about 35 miles away. I put my skates on and started skating. By the time I was three or four miles out of town, the skates were completely worn out, so I started hitch hiking. Along about dusk, I was about 10 miles from my destination, and confused in my directions, so I stopped at a farmhouse and asked the lady there for directions. She wanted to know who I was so I told her my name was Fuller and I was a Boy Scout making a hike. After thanking her, I cut across a field to the next road over, which would take me into Richmond, Illinois. The first car that came along I thumbed, and it was the lady who had given me the directions at the farmhouse. She was worried about me and came after me to give me a ride home. After picking me up, she stopped at the next farmhouse and used their phone to call the Fullers. In those days, operators handled the phone calls. As she went through the telephone exchange in Richmond, my folks were calling the Fullers to see if they had heard anything about me. The operator put two and two together and connected the woman to my Dad. The lady took me on in to Richmond and stayed with me there until my folks got there to pick me up. When we got back to Kenosha I expected a good whipping, which I dreaded, because Dad used a razor strap. I was surprised when I did not get a whipping. In fact, I did not even get a scolding! I guess they were so glad to find me and that I was okay!

The following summer, at the Fuller farm, I got mad at my uncle because he made me hoe corn when I wanted to play! I ran away again! Leaving my hoe in the corn field, I cut across the rail road tracks, hiked into Richmond, about three miles away, went to the train depot, and talked the agent into giving me a ticket on the milk train into Kenosha since I had no money to pay for the ticket by promising that my Dad would reimburse him. I got back home and found myself locked out! My folks were out at Richmond trying to locate me! I went to a neighbor who fed me and called the Fullers, where my folks had just arrived.

When I was twelve, we moved from Kenosha to Delavan, Wisconsin, where my Dad opened up a welding shop. I remember my first day of school that year. We had a new principal, E.G. Lang, who was a short, small man. He called a general assembly of the whole school, where he gave a little speech. He had six of the biggest football players up on the stage with him. We all wondered what they were doing up there! When he got through with the speech, in which he told us just exactly how he was going to run the school, and exactly what he expected of the students, and what could be expected of him.

He called the six boys up and told them (almost any one of those boys would have made two of him), "I understand that you fellows like to fight. I'll tell you what I'll do. Tonight at 4:00 o'clock, I'll meet you all across the street, off of school property, and I'll take you all on, one at a time or all at once, any way you want it!" At 4:00, he was on the street corner waiting, but not a one of them showed up. We found out later that he used to be a boxing instructor in the Army, and were the Army's welterweight champ! One time in boxing in gym class, I had just put on a pair of gloves when E.G. came along and said, "Here, Spencer, I'll show you how to box." He put on a pair of gloves and we started in. I'll bet he hit me twelve times while I was just thinking about where I was going to hit him, and then I could not do it. Everybody liked E.G. He was tough and strict, but very fair. He would not stand for any booing at ball games. Anyone who booed was put out and not allowed to attend the games for the rest of the season. That also applied to the visiting fans.

The state school for the deaf and dumb was there at Delavan. We used to play them in basketball and football. They were invited to our dances, and we were invited to theirs. Their school gym, instead of being on the ground floor, was on the third floor of the building. The reason was that the children, being deaf, could not hear the referee's whistles, but they could feel the vibration in the floor, which worked out pretty well. At their dances, the drummer was always the loudest instrument in the band. The girls could feel the vibrations of the drums and keep time to the music, so they were really good dancers.

In sixth grade, I got my first paper route for the *Milwaukee Journal*. It was a real big route. I had seven daily papers and ten Sundays. I kept the route for five years. When I finally gave it up, I was delivering 135 dailies and 165 Sunday papers. It brought in a pretty fair income for those days. I got one cent per daily paper and three cents for each Sunday paper. I had three customers who paid me by the year. I collected from them on the first of December, which gave me my Christmas shopping money. I also had six that paid every six months, and about twelve that paid every three months. About 50 paid monthly and the rest by the week. That gave me a pretty good start in bookkeeping, just to keep track of all of those payments.

I went to work once in a meat market. I thought I had a real good job! It paid five dollars a week! After the first week of putting in sixty hours for the five dollars, I began to think it was not such a hot job, and I quit!

I went out to Lake Lawn, a big golf course three miles out of town, and started caddying out there. We got seventy-five cents for eighteen holes. If we could double up and carry two bags, that was a dollar and a half. One day, on a big tournament, there just was not enough caddies to go around, so we all got to carry four bags. We carried those four bags for seventy-two holes! We started at six in the morning, and it was dark when we got through. I made twelve dollars for the day's work, plus about another fifteen dollars in tips, which was a small fortune for a boy! Two of my favorite golfers were the men that played Amos and Andy. They were white men who played colored men on the radio. They always tipped pretty well. Our policy was "first one out in the morning got the first job." Oftentimes, we would sleep out at the golf course in order to be there first in the morning. I caddied out there for four years.

My stepmother always prepared a lunch for me. It was always two peanut butter sandwiches. I got so sick of them that I would not even look at my lunch! I would throw it out into the cornfield about half way to the golf course. I asked her several times to fix some other kind of sandwich, and she always said she would, but she never did! That was the only complaint I ever had about my stepmother! She was always very good to me! In fact, I got along better with her than I did with my Dad.

My sister and I both had small savings accounts in a bank in Woodstock, Illinois. During the depression, Roosevelt declared a "Bank Holiday" when all of the banks in the country were closed for about two months. All accounts were frozen. When they finally opened up, those accounts were still kept frozen, and it was as if they had opened up a new bank. After five or six years, the banks started paying off on those accounts. I received one check from the bank for ten dollars, which was about twenty five percent of my savings, as I had forty dollars in the account, with the promise to repay the account in full over a period of four years. This winter, I belonged to the youth group of the Methodist church, and they were having a special meeting in Whitewater, Wisconsin, which I wanted to attend. My sister, Vinetta, was going, and my folks could not afford to send both of us, so I could not go. One morning I woke up, heard my grandmother and sister going downstairs, and they were talking. I heard my grandmother say, "We can pay Bud back later, and he will never know the difference." That set me to thinking! What would they pay me back? They had not borrowed anything. Then I realized that they had borrowed something from me that I did not know about. The more I thought about it, I figured out what it was! They had received my ten-dollar payment from the bank, and they were using that to send my sister to Whitewater. When I went downstairs, I started asking questions. I wanted to know, "When do we get another payment from the bank in Woodstock? The last one was about a year ago, and they are supposed to make one every year." They hemmed and hawed around, but I kept after them, and finally, they had to admit that they had received the payment, and they were using that to send Vinetta to Whitewater. I said, "Let's just wait a minute! That is my money, and I want to go to Whitewater, too. I'll just take my money and go, and let Vinetta stay at home." That is what happened! I took my money and went to Whitewater, but they managed to come up with the ten dollars so Vinetta went to Whitewater, too.

I decided to go out for the football team in High School. At that time, we had a family by the name of Reed in the town that had five boys who were all natural athletes, all big six footers or better, 180 to 220 pounders. At one time, all five were on the first string team, which did not leave much room for anybody else. They were all good athletes, and they all made sixteen letters in high school, four in football, four in basketball, four in baseball, and four in golf. Little old me, I managed to make one letter in my junior year in football. I played center and guard, switching back and forth between the two positions. The first time the coach put me into a game as center, I was so excited that on the first pass, when I passed the ball back to the quarterback, it went a little high, over his head! We lost fifteen yards on that play! So the next play, the same thing happened again, and we lost another fifteen yards. Then the coach yanked me out! And I couldn't blame him! After that, I settled down and did a pretty good job. In fact, I once made the winning touchdown while playing center! We had the other team backed up on their two-yard line. They were going to kick, but one of our fellows blocked the kick, and I was there to fall on the ball! There was another fellow who played center and guard, too, and we switched back and forth, center half of the game and guard half of the game. The following week, the same thing happened to him! He got through and managed to fall on a fumble for a winning touchdown! With the Reed boys playing, we had a football team that was unscored on for two years! Also, we had some excellent basketball teams. One year, we were unbeaten, taking the local championship, and went to state where we were heads on favorite to win the state. The boys won all of their games up to the final game, and the final should have been a shoo-in, but the night before, the whole team went out and got drunk! The next day, they couldn't play period! They were beaten by about forty points! Talk about having a mad coach!

In my freshman year, I took a course in ancient history. At that time, ancient history was a senior subject. There were two freshmen in the class, myself and Charma Davies in the class with thirty-five seniors. The first six weeks, when we got our report cards, Charma had a 96 and I had a 95. The next highest mark in the class was an 89. Two freshmen out of a class of seniors got the highest marks! I decide that if I could get a 95, and Charma a 96, I certainly could beat her! The next six weeks, I went all out. At the end of the six weeks period, the teacher gave us an assignment to write a fictional story about ancient times. Our grade was going to depend strictly on that story. I wrote about Nebuchanezzar and his hanging gardens. I had twenty-seven sheets of notebook paper, hand written on both sides. For extra credit, to boot, I made a chart, which took forty hours to make. When we handed the stories in, and she returned them after grading them, she had two marks on mine. One was one word that she had underlined because I misspelled it, and the other was a big F for Failure! Naturally, I did not like that at all! After school, I took it up to her and asked why she had failed me on the paper! Rather snottily, she said, "I don't have to tell you! You failed, and that's it!" I argued with her a little bit, but she refused to tell me, so I asked where my chart was. She said, "I'm keeping that. I'm going to put that on school exhibit next spring." I happened to know the chart was in a small room just off of her room where the teachers could take a break. I knew that all of the charts were up in that room. The students were not supposed to go into that room, but that did not stop me! I went in and got my chart and went back down to the history room and stood there and tore the chart and my story up into little pieces, as small of pieces as I could get it covering the school floor, and then I told her, "Now, let's see you put that on school exhibit! Anything I fail in is definitely not going on exhibit!" That incident ruined me in high school! After that I never did any homework, or took lessons home. Anything I could not do in class just did not get done!

I made sure that I had a class under that teacher every semester that I was in high school. Miss McCoy was her name, and her Father had been a tinner there in town, and naturally, our nickname for her was Tinner McCoy. I was "Peck's Bad Boy" in her class. For four years, I gave her a very hard time! History was my favorite subject, and I had read all of the history books that she had from cover to cover even before I got into high school. I forget the exact circumstances, but one time, she did admit in front of the whole class that I knew more history than anybody in that room! As a second thought, she added, "Except myself." At the end of my freshman year, I was so sick of my first name Fazell that I decided that I was just going to drop that name and go by my middle name, Ralph. The first day of my sophomore year, I informed all of my teachers and the principal that my name was no longer Fazell. It was Ralph, and Ralph was the only name that I would answer to! In Tinner's class, I would be doing my algebra. She would pick out a particularly hard question and call on me to answer. I would not even look up from my algebra; just rattle the answer off to her, which would burn her up, as she was hoping to take me unaware. When she called on me, she could never remember that I was Ralph, and she would call me Fazell, and I would ignore her. She would call me again in a little louder voice, "Fazell!" and I would still ignore her. She would call me again practically shouting the third time, and I would ignore her. She would get so red in the face that I thought she was going to burst a blood vessel. Finally, she would remember and say, "Ralph," and I would answer her. As she was sort of a nervous individual, and she always would fiddle with her buttons until they came off. By the end of the day, she would have worried off all of her buttons and had her blouse all pinned up with safety pins.

One day she had my pal Joe and I, to clean the erasers for her after school. She left and went home. We opened the windows and cleaned the erasers on the red brick under the windows. When she came to school the next morning there was a white patch about ten feet long on the red brick under the windows. She was as mad as all get out, and she told me and Joe to get some buckets, water and a step ladder and get out there and get all of the chalk dust off of the side of the building, which we were glad to do, as we were outside having a good time while the rest were inside having class!

One semester, I was taking civics under Tinner when two weeks before the end of the semester; she kicked me out of class. I suppose I could have gone to the principal and got back into class because her reason for kicking me out was for something that I had not done. Instead, I just took the class over again the next semester.

Tinner always had her blackboard full of writing. She had two ancient history classes, one in the morning, and one in the afternoon that were the same class. She gave the same test to both classes. Usually, the tests only took about half of the period, and the second half of the period, she would spend correcting the tests, and she would write the answers out on the blackboard. I came in to the afternoon class one day and she passed out the test papers. I noticed right away that she had the answers all written out on the black board. I did not need the answers, but there were several other students that did. I know that they all noticed the answers, too. Everything went fine until about five minutes before the end of the period when Charma raised her hand and said, "Miss McCoy, you have all of the answers to the test on the blackboard!" She had just noticed them! The whole class was mad at Charma. Miss McCoy gave us a different test the next day! As I said, the black boards were always covered with writing, so on the day of the test, some of us would slip into the room while others kept her out of it, and we would write all of our notes in between her writing on the black board. That went on for three years, and she never did get wise to it!

We always had a six weeks test, which usually counted for about two thirds of our grade. I would be carrying an average of about 50 or 60 for the six weeks, and then I would get a 98 or even a 100 on the six weeks test, which would bring my average up to just passing. About two years after I graduated from high school, I was back in town and I called Tinner up, made a date with her, but I did not tell her who I was. I told her that I had met her at the golf course at Lake Lawn, and that I would meet her out there. Naturally, I did not show up!

We had a chemistry and physics teacher, who was so small that we called her Minnie Mouse. She wore a size two shoe, and she had to go to a children's shoe to find them to fit, so she never had any pretty shoes. She was a good teacher, who knew her chemistry and her physics. In the physics lab, there was a big electric shock machine. It was broken, and had been broken for two or three years. It had two big brass balls on it, and when it worked, you could spread the balls about two feet apart, and it would shoot a spark from one to the other. We all knew what it was for, but if we would come in after school for an hour or so every day, we could tear that machine down and rebuild it. Then she would show us what it was for rather than tell us! So we did. There were seven of us. Under her direction, we tore the machine down and rebuilt it. It took about two weeks. We had it all reassembled. We reminded her, "You promised to tell us what this machine is for." She said, "No, I said I would SHOW you what it is for, and I will!" She lined us up in two groups of three, having the first man take hold of the brass ball, with the second and third holding onto him. She said, "Fred, go over and start turning that big wheel over there." Fred went over and took hold of the wheel and as he started to turn it, I reached over and took hold of her arm. Fred was turning the wheel, and she was sitting on the floor! That was mean of me, I know, but after all, she was going to do that to me!

One night after school, some of us boys went into the chemistry lab, disconnected the water and gas lines, and reconnected the water to the gas lines, and the gas to the water. There were twelve sinks in the lab, sitting back to back, six in a row. The next morning, just before the teacher got into the classroom, we went into the lab, turned all of the water faucets on, and lit them. When she came into the lab, there were twenty-four spouts of flame coming out of the water faucets! Well, she did not like it, but she was a good sport. We reconnected everything, as it should be for her!

There was one fellow, a country boy, named Ralph, who was just naturally dumb. We always paired up in the chemistry lab for an experiment. One day, for our experiment, we were to distill water. Before the teacher came in, the other Ralph came up to me and asked me, "Would you mind having me for a partner for this experiment?" Nobody else wanted to partner with him, because he always loused things up. He asked, "Would you mind if I did this experiment by myself?" He never had done one alone. I said, "Go ahead!" I knew something would happen so we could have a little fun! He set up the equipment, doing pretty well. He had a big bulb there, which was to be filled about two thirds full of water, mixing in enough powdered ink just to color it good. Then, he was to distill the ink out of the water. He mixed in about fifty percent powdered ink, fifty percent water. The Bunsen burner was then started to bring it to a slow boil. There was a rubber cork in the distiller with a Centigrade thermometer so the temperature could be checked. He put the Bunsen burner under it, and brought it to a fast boil. "If I had known what was going to happen, I would have stopped him right there!" I knew the thing was going to blow its top, but just as it reached the point when it was going to blow, the teacher came out of the class room into the Chemistry Lab and stepped up beside Ralph. Just as she stepped up, it blew out! We had a twenty-foot ceiling in the Chemistry Lab. It not only covered Ralph and the teacher from head to foot, and the black board, but hit the ceiling and left a spot about six foot in diameter! She never said a word to Ralph, but she turned around and really chewed me out, because she knew that I knew better than to let him do something like that by himself. She said, "I want to see you in here after school!" I reported to her after school, and she said, "I want you to go to the janitor, get yourself a bucket and a big step ladder, and I want that whole mess, including the ceiling, cleaned up before you go home tonight!" I got the bucket, the ladder and the scrub brushes, set the ladder up in the lab, and she saw that I was willing to work, so she went home. As soon as she left, I hightailed it over to the other part of the school, got hold of Ralph, and told him that the teacher had made me get the equipment together, and she wanted him there to clean that mess up. He went over and worked until after midnight, while I went home. He never could get it cleaned up. Twenty years later, we went through the lab at a school reunion, and even though the ceiling had been painted at least six times, you could still see the dark spot.

This incident happened when I was a junior. There was a girl named Elizabeth there. She was a rather large blonde, and was four years older than any of the rest of us. She had dropped out of school when she was a sophomore, and then, had come back that year to finish her schooling and to get her high school diploma. I was going with her younger sister at the time. We were in the Physics Lab, and she came past and poured a test tube full of water down my neck. I grabbed up a small glass of water, and took off after her. Well about that time, the Physics teacher came in, and just as she did, I poured the glass full of water on Liz's head. She collared me, and said, "That's enough of that. If you can't behave yourself, I won't have you in the lab class." I said, "Fine, I need another study hour anyway." This teacher was an excellent teacher, and this was her first year teaching in the Delavan School. When school opened that fall, for some reason all of the girls signed up for the physics class, which is really a boy's class. There were almost twice as many girls in the class as there were boys. But, as we got started, the girls began to realize that physics was not for them. There had been nine or ten girls that had dropped out of the class. The principal had warned her that if she had any more dropouts, they wouldn't renew her contract. I knew this, as I had happened to overhear a conversation about it. So, I waited for about six weeks (I was still in the chemistry class; she had only kicked me out of the lab class). I asked her one day, "Teach, how am I doing in class here?" She said, "Well, you are doing pretty good in class. But there is no way that you can pass without the Physics Lab, and I'm not about to let you back in there." I said, "Oh? Well, if I can't pass without taking the lab class, and you won't let me back in there, I guess I'll just have to drop out of the class. There is just no use in going on." She said, "Oh, you can't do that." I said, "Oh yes I can. You just watch me." I knew she couldn't afford to have another drop out. So, the result was, she let me back in the Physics Lab.

One day, one of the boys was sleeping underneath a tree with his mouth open, when a bird dropped square into his mouth. He woke up in a hurry!

One day, the other boys decided they were going to initiate me. They were going to throw me into the lake! I was a pretty good runner, and kept ahead of them, managed to pull my shoes off, rolled up my pants legs, and waded out into the lake before they caught up with me. That made them mad! They did not want to get out into the water themselves, so they started throwing stones at me. After I got hit once or twice, I decided that the best thing that I could do was to duck myself in the lake, and that satisfied them. I caddied all day long in some squishy shoes!

There was one foursome that I caddied for regularly. They always had two or three bottles of whiskey with them, and they did more drinking than golfing. After about the third hole, when they were feeling pretty good, we would start betting them. We would bet they could not make par on the hole, or make a birdie on it. Naturally, we won! We sometimes took as much as $25 or $30 in bets in a day off of them! One day, one was so drunk that he tipped his caddy with a $100 dollar bill. When the caddy master found out about it, he made the fellow give the man back his hundred-dollar bill, but the guy still gave him a $10 tip.

One of the boys lost his golfer's ball in the middle of the fairway. The golfer started berating him, "What kind of caddy are you? Why didn't you line that up with something so you would know where the ball was? The boy said, "I did line it up with something!" The golfer said, "What?" He said, "I lined it up with a bird sitting out in the middle of the fairway." The golfer said, "Where's the bird?" The caddy said, "Heck, the bird flew away when the ball landed!" The golfer did not have much of anything more to say!

My friend Joe, lived about a block away from me, and their house sat back about a 100 feet from the road, and was built so the house faced the road. They had a basement to the house. The basement was built so that about half of it was above ground. That put their front door about six feet off of the ground. They had never built a porch to it. In the summer they would leave the front door open with the screen door hooked shut. One day, I went down to pick Joe up and as I came into the yard, here came Joe out the front door, and he didn't bother to open it. He just came right through it. He hit the ground and here came his mother right through the door after him. She had a broom in her hand and was chasing him. He ran around the garage, and the second time around, he got tired of that, as he went around the corner and ducked back against the building, and his mother came around the corner, and he grabbed the broom out of her hands, and started chasing her. I figured I had better go on home. Well, I never did find out how that argument ended.

My dad ran a welding shop, but he really was not a businessman, and did not know how to charge for his work. He was afraid that people would not come back if he charged too much. He just barely made a living. We never had any money to spare. I always had to wear secondhand, Salvation Army clothes that were ragged and patched, and I was always ashamed of my clothes. One year, I saved my money up from caddying, and in the middle of August, I had saved up $75 so I could buy myself some decent school clothes. My dad came to me and said the taxes were due on the house, and if he did not pay the taxes, they would take the house away from us. I loaned him the $75 to pay the taxes, and I wore my hand-me-downs for another year. He never was able to repay the loan.

One year, there was a Boy Scout Jamboree at the City Park, called The Springs. About three hundred Boy Scouts from all over the country attended it. I lived about three blocks from the campgrounds, and although I was camping out with the other scouts, it only took me about five minutes to get home. I got the bright idea for a business venture! I took and made popcorn balls, and they really went over big! I sold about a hundred a night at ten cents apiece. So rather than the Jamboree costing me money, I made money, since it lasted seven days, and I was making about $10 a day!

Once, when I was in the seventh grade, our teacher was out of the room for a while. Most of the boys were cutting up and acting up, but for once, I was behaving myself. When I saw the teacher watching the other fellows through the doorway, I was glad that I had been a good little boy! She came in and quieted them down, took six into the hallway, lined them up, and went down the line slapping each one. A buddy of mine who was about second from the end decided he was not going to be slapped! When she came up to him to slap him, he ducked! She caught the last fellow full force and sent him head over heels!

I used to take a sack and walk down the railroad tracks, picking up coal. When a train came by, I would razz the fireman, make him made at me, and he would start throwing coal at me, which is what I wanted. I would do that two or three times a week during the summer. I would manage to collect enough coal to last us about a month anyway.

Once my friend Joe and I were snooping around in the attic of the school when we found an opening going up onto the roof. We were the only ones who knew about it. None of the teachers or the janitor had ever been up there for years, and it had been entirely forgotten. We got together with a couple of other kids who were pretty good artists and drew a full sized calf on a big piece of cardboard, painted and cut it out. We took it up through the outlet in the roof and set it up in the bell tower, which was four stories high. The next morning when we came to school, there was the principal, half of the teachers, chief of police, and fire chief standing there wondering how we got the calf up in the bell tower, as from the ground, it looked just like a real calf. Finally the fire department got some ladders out and managed to get up to the bell tower and they rescued the calf. They were pretty well put out by it. They never did find out "who did it."

We had some good Halloween pranks! One fellow had an old Model T car. On Halloween night we disassembled it, and reassembled it on top of his garage roof. He was pretty upset the next morning when he found his car on top of his garage. He couldn't figure out how it got up there, or how he was going to get it down.

Once, a bunch of us was going to go over to the neighboring town of Darien and upset outhouses for Halloween. When I arrived at the meeting place the others had gone on without me, and I was pretty put out! The next day, I was very happy they had! They had gone over and upset about six outhouses, and one of them shattered completely when they pushed it over. They were picked up by the police, had to spend the night in jail, and the next day, the police took them back over to Darien where they had to set all of the outhouses back up properly and buy new lumber and build a new outhouse to replace the one that was shattered. I was really glad that I missed out on that one!

The first year we moved to Delavan, there was an old civil war cannon sitting in a little triangular park about a half a mile from downtown. Some of the older boys got together, cleaned it up, loaded it up, and managed to fire it off. It broke windows for two or three blocks around. They never did find out who did it.

It got so that on Halloween night, they had so many special deputies out that we just could not do a thing! They had about one deputy to every block. The next year, we went out the night before Halloween. The year after that, they had the deputies out on both nights. We thought, "That's enough of that foolishness!" Most of the school kids got together and while the stores were all open the night before Halloween, we scattered out, two or three kids in each store on both sides of the street, and at a given signal, one fellow came down each side of the street, went into a store, and come out with two or three other kids, and they would assemble in the middle of the street in a snake dance. By the time we got to the third block of the business district, we had about sixty kids in the line, just whooping it up and having a good time. We headed for the East End, which was the small business district about three quarters of a mile from downtown. We took our time and wandered our way down the streets, blocking traffic, naturally, and what we hoped would happen, did. They pulled all of the deputies from all over town to follow us down to the East End. When we got down there, we just milled around for about a half-hour, then we broke up and all went home. When the chief of police and the deputies got back uptown, they found an outhouse sitting in the doorway of the police station and another one on the steps of the library. There had been a second group of about ten boys that did the dirty work while the big crowd of us pulled the deputies away from downtown.

My friend Joe lived about a block away from us. We decided we would learn Morse code and set up a telegraph line between our houses so we could talk back and forth. For several months, we scrounged all of the copper wire we could find, and strung it up between the two houses. Meantime, we were studying Morse code. After we had the line set up and hooked up, we never used it the first time. Neither of us had learned the code well enough to send a message.

One year Joe and I decided that we would run away and bum our way out to San Francisco, and find work on a freighter going down to South America. In preparation for the trip, we each bought a new pair of work shoes and immediately took them to a shoe repair shop and had a second sole put on them, then had the bottoms covered with hobnails. We figured if we got in any fights along the way, we would be able to do a little damage with our feet. Neither of us said a word to our folks or anyone else about what we were going to do, knowing they would never let us do it if they knew. We set out and hitchhiked to Jamesville, twenty miles away, where we caught a freight train going to Minneapolis. There must have been about a dozen other bums on the train with us. We managed to get to Minneapolis and stay overnight in a hobo jungle. The next morning when we got up, Joe had had enough of the hobo life, so we turned around and went back home. That took care of our South American adventure!

The folks did not even realize that we had been gone for three days. My folks figured I was with Joe, and his just thought he was with me. We looked like a couple of hobos, black with the soot from the train engine. They wanted to know where in the devil we had been and what we had been up to! They could not say too much to us because it was all over and done with and no harm done.

When I was a sophomore, the state gave an intelligence test to all sophomores in the state. We were allowed one hour to complete the test. I breezed through it, and handed my papers in at the end of a half-hour. The results of the test were kept secret. We were never to know how we did on the test. Two weeks after the test, the principal, E.G. Lang, made a visit to my dad and talked to him for half an hour or so, which was very unusual. The more I thought about it, the more I knew that he was talking to my dad about the intelligence test, and what my grade had been on it. I asked my dad. He said, "No" and refused to tell me what they were talking about. That convinced me that I was right, and I was more determined than ever to find out what my grade had been on that test. I kept badgering my dad about it. It took me about a year, but one day I got him so mad that he just blurted out, "I don't see how somebody that got the second highest mark in the state could be so damned dumb!" For having that high of grade on an intelligence test, you would never know it by my marks in school. I graduated at the very bottom of my class. However, I think if I had known what my grade on that test had been at the time I took it, I would have perked up, and probably have graduated in the top ten of my class, which I could have easily done.

We had two French and Latin teachers, both were very good in their own ways. My friend Joe and I took Latin under Miss Parkinson. She was a very good-looking woman. She had spent two years in Paris, studying French. She was soft hearted, and could not bear to flunk anybody; even if you had a fifty or sixty grade, she would pass you anyway. Joe and I had been acting up in class, and she kicked us out of class. She was a very nearsighted person. She had the thickest lens in her glasses of anybody I had ever known. Without her glasses, she could not see her hand in front of her face. After school let out, she always had a lot of students in her room, batting the breeze. We stood outside the door until we saw her take off her glasses. When she did, we went in, picked up her glasses and hid them in one of her desk drawers. The other kids all knew that we were up to something, but never said anything to her. She had an old portable phonograph that had not worked for two or three years. We took the phonograph, tore it to pieces, every screw, nut and bolt was laid out, there must have been fifty or sixty pieces lying out. She finally found her glasses. She saw what we had done and really raised cane! She was going to make us buy a new phonograph for the class and pay for it with our own money. Well, we put the phonograph back together, and don't ask how we did it, but the damned thing worked when we got through with it! We were back in her good graces and back in class again.

She taught first year Latin, and when we went into the second year Latin, we had Miss Hargas, the other Latin teacher. The first day, she gave the whole class a test to see how much we had learned under Miss Parkinson. Then, she started the whole class out at the very beginning. That year under her, we learned Latin! We not only picked up the first year, but we completed the second year!

The first day of our junior year, we had a study class, which was held in the auditorium. Miss Wold, our biology teacher, supervised it. The first day, she picked out six boys and separated us, one in each corner of the room, and a couple in the center, but not together. We could not leave our seats, we could not use the library for our study purposes, and we could not talk to anybody. (Everybody else had those privileges.) That was the first day of school, and none of us had done anything to deserve that treatment! We tried talking to Miss Wold, tried to get permission to use the library, but nothing doing! We all got together, the six of us, with no ring leader, and we brought anything that would roll to class: golf balls, marbles, ball bearings round stones, and we started rolling them from front to back, back to side, side to center, etc. That went on for about three days. Of course, nobody got any studying done, neither us nor nobody else. About the middle of the class on the third day, I looked around and could not see Miss Wold anywhere. I pulled out a golf ball and rolled it back to Fred Deckert in the back seat. About the time I let loose of the golf ball, I felt somebody grab me by the shirt collar. There she was, sitting in the seat right behind me! It was the first time that she had been able to catch anybody in the act. Of course, she knew who was doing all of the dirty work. Then she told the six of us that she wanted to see us after school in the teacher's room. After school, all six of us reported over there. She took us one by one up into the teacher's room. She left me until last! I never did find out what she said to any of the others. When I entered the room with her, the first question she asked me was, "Why were you the ringleader of this bunch?" I told her, "I'm sorry! There was no ringleader! We were all in it together." Oh, yes, you were the ringleader!" I said, "No, I was not the ringleader!" She said, "No don't lie to me!" I said, "I'm not lying! I'm telling you the truth." She said, "You're lying!" and she started to slap me. When she slapped me, I started to laugh. When I started to laugh, that made her madder yet, and she slapped me again harder, so I laughed a little harder yet! After about six slaps, I got tired of that, turned around and stalked out the door. Said goodbye to her in a very loud voice, slammed the door behind me, went down the two steps, and there was Miss Jacobson, the assistant principal standing there. She said, "Ralph, you go back in there and apologize to Miss Wold!" I said, "Apologize for what?" She said, "For the way you said goodbye and slammed that door. I said, "Oh, no, I'm not about to go apologize to her for anything. She is accusing me of something that I didn't do, and she would not listen to anything I had to say." That made Miss Jacobson mad! She hauled off and slapped me. I really had to laugh then! Although she slapped me as hard as she could, her hand was so soft and puffy, that I hardly felt the slap. I just said goodbye to her in a normal voice and went home. Nothing more was ever heard of it!

The next day, we met with Miss Wold, and we told her if she would restore our privileges to us, we would all behave ourselves. She agreed to that. We did behave ourselves. But I had a little deck of cards. They were only an inch and a half by two and a half inches. We would go into the library and play cards back there. She never did catch onto that. The study hall was always in the auditorium. The stage was at the front of the room. It had two little dressing rooms, one on each side of the stage. There were four of us that got permission to go back there and do our studying in one of the dressing rooms. There were two doorways to each room. One opened onto the stage, and the other into the auditorium. We would lock the door to the stage, so nobody could come through that way. We would hang a coat hanger on the door handle of the other door in such a fashion that when someone would go to turn the knob, the coat hanger would fall off. We weren't studying we were playing cards. As someone started to come in the stage door, it was locked, and they would have to come in the door off of the auditorium, and by the time that they got in there, there wasn't a card to be seen; we were all studying away. The principal actually came through twice, checking on us, and complimented us on doing such a good job of studying.

One year, a couple of the other fellows had been barred from the Senior Prom. They were pretty put out about it. On prom night, they got hold of a half-grown pig, sneaked into the gym with the greased pig through the back, and when the Grand March was on, turned the pig loose. That was the end of the prom! Everybody tried to catch the pig, but could not do it. Boys and girls both wound up with grease all over their clothes!

Miss Currie was our English teacher. We had individual movable seats in our classroom. One day, one of the boys brought a small snake into the classroom. When all were seated, he turned the snake loose on the floor. Of course, the girls were all shrieking, yelling, and jumping on their seats. Miss Currie came back to see what was causing all of the trouble. One of the boys picked up the snake and put it in his pocket. That went on for the whole period. She was standing by her desk, so everybody had to pass in front of her when we went out. The fellow that brought the snake had it in his hand when he went past her. He held out his hand and said, "I've got something for you, teach!" She said, "Is that what has been causing the trouble all period long?" He said, "Yes." She held out her hand, and he dropped the snake into it. She stood there and looked at it for a minute, handed it back to him, and said, "Take it outside and turn it loose." The same boy, one day put a thumbtack on her seat. When she sat down, she came up in a hurry, pulled the thumbtack out of her, and never said a word! She knew who had done it! A little later on, she called him up to the blackboard to do some writing. While he was doing that, she put the thumbtack on his seat! When he came back and sat down, he came up with a yelp, too. That cured him of playing around with thumbtacks! English was not exactly my favorite subject, but I did fairly well in it. One year, we were studying "The Poem of the Ancient Mariner." I happened to like it, so I memorized the whole poem, all four hundred and thirty verses of it. I had it down letter perfect! She gave us a final test at the end of the season, based entirely on "The Ancient Mariner." I breezed through that test in about half the time it took any of the others. She collected the tests, corrected them overnight, and gave them back the next day. I took a look at mine, and she had about thirty or thirty-five questions marked wrong with a big "F" for failure on it. The more I looked at that test; I could not believe my eyes. The first question she had marked wrong, I knew was right. I checked every other question, and they were all right. I got up, took my paper up to her, and said, "Miss Currie, I think you have made a mistake in grading these papers!" She said, "Oh, no, I have a master sheet to go by, and I checked them all off it." I said, "Then your master sheet is wrong!" She said, "It can't be. It was put out by the publishers!"

I said, "Well, the publishers are wrong! You know I know this poem! You know I have memorized every verse of it!" She said, "Yes, I know you have. I said, "Take your text book and open it up to "The Ancient Mariner." She did, and I started reciting it as she read. I came to the first question that she had marked wrong. I said, "Just look at that close right there." She did, she stopped and thought for a second, and said, "You know, you are right." I said, "Just check the rest of these questions." She did and she kept saying, "You're right! You're right! You're right!" She had to take up all of the test papers and go through and remark them. When she handed the papers back the next day, I had a 98. A couple of the other kids were mad at me, because they had a 95 or 96 the first time on the test. After she remarked the papers, they failed. One of my other high school accomplishments was to hold the school record for being late! One whole semester, I was late for school every morning and every afternoon. Not only that, I was late to every class.

I had a good friend named Arnold Klebs who was a little older than me and graduated two years ahead of me. During my junior and senior years, I practically lived out at his house. His mother was like a second mother to me. She was also a chiropractor, one of the first in that part of the country. She was a graduate of the Palmer School of Chiropractic's in Des Moines, Iowa. At that time, I would have a cold from the first of October, all the way through the winter, until the middle of May, going around with handkerchiefs to my nose ninety percent of the time. She took pity on me, stretched me out on her worktable, and went to work on my sinuses.

After three treatments, my cold was gone, my head and nose cleared tip, and I was not bothered with a cold for the rest of that year. Since then, whenever I feel a cold coming on, I head for the nearest chiropractor, and invariably, with one or two adjustments, they would get rid of the cold for me.

So far, I have said nothing about the social activities. There were all of the usual parties, birthdays, Christmas, Halloween, school proms and dances. In the six years that I attended Delavan School, I was invited to just one girl's birthday party. She lived out in the country. When we got out to her house. The party was started, and I was totally ignored. I never did figure out why she invited me, because all of the usual party games they had, I was excluded from. I guess that was because I was from about the poorest family in town, and I lived on the wrong side of the tracks.

My folks gave me one birthday party. They invited two boys that lived next door. One was three years older than I was. He spent all of his time talking to the folks. The other one was a homosexual that I hated and I couldn't wait until he got out of there and went home. That was quite a party! My sisters all had nice birthday parties that they invited all of their friends to.

As for the first prom that I attended, my junior year, my sister drafted me to take one of her girlfriends that didn't have a date. The girl was three years older than I was. She came over the night before the prom and taught me how to dance. I surprised myself by doing fairly well at the prom. There was only one girl out of my class that I ever dated. She was a Mormon and was trying to convert me. There was one other girl that I was in love with. Her name was Charma Davies. Socially, she was about the most elite girl in town. Her father was president of the bank. He had at one time been principal of the school. She lived about a mile away from us. Even in the winter, in freezing weather, I would walk up past her house and wish I could get up the nerve to go to the door and ask to see her. Finally, after about a dozen trips, I got real brave, so I went to the door and asked to see her. She came to the door and greeted me, asked me in, took my coat and hat and hung them up, and said, "Why don't we go down to the basement to the den." When we got down to the den, I was surprised! I had never seen a room like it before. It was full of all kinds of recreational equipment. She asked, "What would you like to do? We can play checkers, or play the Victrola so we can dance, or play cards, or just sit and talk." I said, "Let's play a game of checkers." I think that was the best evening of my life! When I left, she saw me to the door. I wanted to kiss her, but did not have nerve enough to try, so I just said goodbye. She said, "Be sure to come back and see me again." A week later, I saw her in school, asked her if she would like to go to the movies with me. She said, "Why, yes! I would be delighted!" We set a date, and when I called at her house to pick her up, she said, "You know, Ralph, why don't we just go to the basement and do a little dancing and talking. I've already seen the movie." She was just being kind to me, because she knew that I really didn't have the money to take her to the movies. She was a very good musician. In fact, she wrote her first opera before she graduated from high school. She tried to explain music to me, telling me what all of the notes was and what they were for. It was useless, as I have absolutely no music in me. From then on, we usually had about one date a week. The only time I ever did take her to a movie, she met me at the door when I went to pick her up, and asked me which coat I thought she should wear, the cloth or fur coat. That kind of flabbergasted me! Me telling her which coat I thought she should wear! I said the fur coat. I did not have a car, so my friend Arnold played chauffeur for me. We went to Elkhorn, the neighboring town, to the movie. After her freshman year, her parents pulled her out of school and sent her out east to Wellesley, where she finished high school and college. We corresponded while she was there, and we would have dates when she was home for a holiday break. Her whole life was centered around her music. She went on to become a professor of music, and taught music at Nebraska State University for several years. She finally married a minister who was a missionary to Bangladesh, where they lived for ten years.

Arnold had graduated from high school, but did not have a job. His folks were well enough off that they gave him a Model A coupe with a rumble seat and an allowance that covered most of his gas, oil, and spending money. He lived a mile and a half out in the country, and he would come in every morning, pick me up, and take me to school. I lived three blocks from the school! At noon, he would be there to pick me up and take me home for dinner, and then he would go out and eat his own dinner at home, then come back and pick me up to take me to school again in the afternoon. He would be there when school was out to pick me up and take me home again. It got to the point where nobody referred to him by his name, just called him "Spencer's chauffeur."

The winter of 1935-36 was a really bad one. We had one spell of weather for thirty-one days in a row when the temperature never rose above 15 degrees above zero. We had so many blizzards that winter that the entire town of Delavan was snow bound for over a week! I mean, nothing went into or came out of that city. There were several people who had wood burning stoves for heat who ran out of firewood and burned their wooden furniture and knocked walls out of the house to burn the lumber for heat. The snowdrifts were so high that we had a picture of my baby sister, who was about four years old at the time, sitting on top of a telephone pole. When we finally got a break in the weather so the snowplows could get out, they had to send a crew out in front of the snowplows to break the crust on the snow before the plows could operate. My friend Arnold's brother was at home and needed to get to Jamesville, (twenty-one miles away). We took him over to Jamesville and it took almost three hours to make the twenty-one miles. We put him on the train to Madison, where he was going to college. At 10:30 at night, we headed for home. Twenty-one miles to go! We got home at 7:30 the next morning. We got in behind a huge snowplow and just stayed there. Otherwise, we would never have made it! The plow hit a snowdrift going full force, and it would stop it dead. He would have to back up and hit the snow bank three or four times before he could break through. At one point, we passed a large semi truck that was stuck in the snow. All we could see of it was a little of the rear end that was sticking out. I often wondered if the driver was still in the truck. We never found out. If he was, he was a dead man, because it was a week before they got the truck out of the snow bank.

I had another friend, whose name was William Nelson. His father was a professional troubleshooter. He went around the country, and would take control of a company that was on the verge of bankruptcy, and put it back on its feet, so it was making a good profit again. He had come into Delavan and took over the Borg Warner plant, which was about to go under. He was getting it re-organized and back on its feet again. Bill was a gun enthusiast. He had two rifles, a shotgun, a pistol and a revolver. One day we were in his parent's car, and I was driving. We were going through the east end, which is a small business district. He was in the back seat with his shotgun. He rolled the window down, stuck the shotgun out of it, and shot off both barrels into the air. He said, "Now, let's get out of here. Let's make them think that Al Capone is in town." Well, I got away from there in a hurry. I didn't have any idea that he was going to do anything like that. Then another time, we were in a theatre at night, and without warning me, he pulled out a pistol, which he had loaded with blanks, and fired two shots at the floor. If you ever saw a theatre clear out in a hurry, that was it! And, we were on our hands and knees between the seats, searching for the side door. We got out of there, and never got caught. When his dad finally got Borg Warner back on their feet, he moved into Milwaukee to take over a plant there. They were renting a nice apartment, in a large hotel and apartment complex. His father bought him a membership in two different gun clubs, and arranged for the hotel to set up a firing range in the basement for him. That wasn't enough, for him however. One night, he sat in their apartment, shooting lights out in the apartment across the street, and he hit a preacher's wife in the elbow. There was a big spread about that in the *Milwaukee Journal*. Then, you never heard anymore about it. I imagine his father bought him out of it somehow. But, after that I never did hear from him again.

Churches

My friend Joe was a Catholic. I used to attend church with him occasionally, even though I was a Methodist. One Sunday, I sat there and listened to the priest give a sermon on drinking and smoking, and all of the evils that they could cause. I was quite impressed with the sermon. The next day, I was in the back room of the drug store folding my papers and stacking them in my delivery sack, when in came the priest, and he sat down in a chair, and opened a bottle of wine that he had with him, and poured out a water glass full of it. He lit a big cigar, and sat there smoking and drinking the wine. That kind of disillusioned me about him. Now this was back in the 30s during the tail end of the depression. He decided that the church should build a school, so that the Catholic children could go to a Catholic school rather than, a public school. Well he just assessed every member of his congregation $1,000.00. Now there were a few in the congregation that could afford that $1,000.00 assessment, but the big majority could not afford it. I personally know of about six families that had bought small homes out around the lake. They had their homes paid for, and were retired. And when the church assessed them the $1,000.00, they had to mortgage their homes to get it. Then, they couldn't keep up their mortgage payments, and consequently lost their homes.

He got the school built, and it was a grade school for grades one through eight. He charged $500.00 per child tuition. Several of the younger families with three, four, or five children, had an awful time paying the tuition. But pay it they did, even though some of them were going hungry. In my junior and senior years in high school, I practically lived with my friend Arnold Klebs. I looked on Mrs. Klebs as my second mother. Mrs. Klebs had some

Catholic friends who had a seventeen-year old daughter, who after graduating from high school, decided to become a nun, and entered a convent to take her training. She did just fine in the convent, until she learned that in order to become a full, fledged nun, she had to have a child, and that the priest would be the father, She couldn't take that, so she ran away from the convent, and came out to the Klebs's. We hid her out there for three weeks, until the search for her had quieted down. Then her folks managed to pick her up and took her up to northern Montana, and settled down there with her under a different name, so the church couldn't find them. Catholic nuns are married to the church; they go through a traditional marriage ceremony with wedding rings, and the wedding vows. What happens to their children is a different story.

At the same time that we were hiding the girl from the church, there was a big piece in the paper one day. A company in Philadelphia had bought an old church from the Catholic's and had demolished it, and was going to build a large apartment house on the site, and while they were excavating for the basement, they uncovered a lime pit with about fifty skeletons of babies in it. That appeared in the papers one day only. After that, you never heard another word about it. And, about six months later, the same thing happened in Pittsburgh. That story appeared in the paper just one day, and there was never a follow-up story on it. Years later when I was driving a cab in Kenosha, I had three nuns that were fairly regular passengers of mine, and in the summertime when it was hot, I would be soaking wet with sweat, and they would be sitting in the back of the cab there just as cool as could be. They wore black habits all the time, and as everybody knows, black absorbs heat. So, once I asked them, "How can you be so cool, when I'm just drowning in sweat?" One of them laughed and said, "Well, I guess we can tell you. We just don't wear anything underneath these." Every Friday night, I would pick them up at the church and take them to an address in the center of town. There was a big, old, building that they would go into. After taking them to that building twice, I wondered what the dickens was they doing in there. So the next time, I picked them up and dropped them off there, I just sat there in my cab and watched them. When they went into the building, they held the front door open long enough for me to see that there was a pretty wild party going on in there.

Another church in Delavan hired a new minister. He was a young fellow and everybody thought the world of him. They thought that he was just a wonderful minister. I was caddying out at Lake Lawn at the time, and I would see him out there every night, getting drunk. About six months after he started work in Delavan, he was arrested for molesting four of his young choirboys. That was quite a scandal. And of course he was fired. And the last I ever heard of him, there was a piece in the *Milwaukee Journal* about him. He had been arrested there for accosting two sailors.

We had two colored girls in our class all through high school. They were nice girls and everybody liked them. But, there were no colored boys in town for them to date. So, when the school prom came along, they were not going to attend. But, we all got together and told them that the prom was for them as well as it was for us, and that we all wanted them to attend. They came to the prom and we made sure that they never sat out a single dance, as everyone of us boys danced with them.

My senior year in high school, I was going to school just a half a day in the afternoon. I had secured a job with Henry Hanson, a German cabinetmaker. Most all of the high school boys had worked for him at one time or another, and none of them lasted more than two or three weeks. He was a master craftsman, and expected everyone to be as good as he was, so he was very hard to get along with. I rather enjoyed the work, and I got along with Henry pretty well. He was paying me the big sum of twenty cents an hour, which at that time, was a very good wage. I was going to school half days in the afternoon. I would get up at five and go to work at six o'clock in the morning, worked until twelve, went home, had dinner, changed clothes and went to school, slept most of the time, got out of school at three thirty, went home and changed clothes and went back to work at four, and worked until midnight, or even one or two in the morning. At twenty cents an hour, I was bringing home paychecks of twenty, twenty-one, twenty-two, and once, even twenty-three dollars a week. I lasted for a little over a year with Henry, and was really beginning to learn something about the business. For example, a lady brought in five antique chairs to be refinished, and wanted a sixth one made to match. I did most of the work on the sixth chair. When the chair was finished, Henry lined them up and asked me to pick out the one we had made. So help me, I could not do it, but he could. He was so good that he even had people from Europe sending him work. I remember that someone sent him an antique grandfather clock that was broken. The works were made completely of wood, no metal in them whatsoever, and three of the cogwheels were broken. Henry made three new cogwheels, reassembled the clock, and it worked well. While he let me do some of the refinishing on the clock, I was not allowed to touch the inside works.

One day Henry came to work all smiles and just as happy as could be! I said, "Hey Henry, what is the good news?" He said, "Well, my wife owns some property out in California, and they just struck oil on it." I said, "Wonderful!" Two days later, he came to work with a long face and grouchy as could be. I said, "Hey Henry, what is the bad news?" He said, "Well, you know that property that I told you about that they struck oil on?" I said, "Yes!" "Well," he said, "they struck oil all right, but it was a pipeline they hit!"

For a year, I had gotten along well with Henry. With no real problems, my work was okay. He gave me a big raise of a nickel an hour, a twenty-five percent raise! About two weeks after I got my raise, things kind of blew up! I could not do anything right, and it got so bad that I could not take it! I asked Henry, "What in the heck is wrong? For a year I've worked for you and now I can't do anything right. You are jumping down my throat every five minutes about something!" He hemmed and hawed for a few minutes, and finally he said, "Your dad came over and had a talk with me. "And what did he say?" I asked. Henry said, "Well, he said he could not trust you with anything. He said you got very poor marks in school. He was thinking about coming over and collecting your wages." I replied, "He would collect my wages one time and one time only! After that there would not be any wages to collect! I cannot go on under these conditions! I am giving you two weeks notice so you will have time to find someone else to take my place. But do me a favor. Just don't tell my folks that I am quitting." He said, "Okay." Two weeks later, I quit my job with Hanson, packed my new suitcase that my folks had given me for a graduation present, a five-dollar pasteboard suitcase, and took off without saying anything to my folks. I went into Kenosha to look for work. I went to a cousin of mine who had told me that I could stay with him anytime I wanted to. It was about six in the evening when I got to his house. There was nobody home and I sat outside waiting for them until about nine. Mosquitoes were eating me up. He told me that they never locked the house, so if I came when they were not there, I could go in and make myself at home, so I decided that it was time for me to go inside. I took a chair and sat down by the kitchen door, thinking that I would sit there in the dark and surprise them when they got home, It was not long until I heard a Model A Ford in the driveway. I thought to myself, they are home. In a minute, they came in, turned the lights on in the kitchen, and there were a woman and a girl I had never seen before. I looked at them and they looked at me. and I said, "Who are you?"

And they said, "Who are you?" I told them who I was and they told me who they were, and they told me that they had bought the house from my cousin two months before. I told them why I was in their house. They were nice people, and offered to put me up overnight, but I did not want to impose, and went out into Forrest Park and found a good tree to sleep under, and went to bed.

I could not find any work in Kenosha, so I went into Chicago, and the first day there, I found a job there. I found a job in a sheet metal factory, making metal cabinets of all types, It paid forty cents an hour. I had a friend who had been in Chicago a while, so I looked him up. He had a room with a double bed in it. He agreed that I could stay there with him and share the room expenses. It was about ten miles from our room to the factory where I was working, and I did not have carfare, so I hitchhiked to and from work. My friend Ralph Baumguard, was a short order cook in a small cafe about two miles from where we lived. At night, to have something to do, I would walk down to the café for a cup of coffee, which was all that he could give me. He could not give me a hamburger, because the boss had them all counted, and he had to account for every one. After about three months in the sheet metal factory, I saw an ad in the paper for a furniture factory. Because they were on strike, they had a little office opened away from the factory where they were hiring scab workers. I signed up to go to work for them at a dollar an hour. We would meet every morning in an underpass somewhere, a different place every morning. They would pick us up in a covered truck and run us through the picket line into the factory. We were taken home at night the, same way.

As I had done quite a big of lathe work in manual arts at school and for Henry Hanson as well, they put me on a big automatic lathe. It could turn out a table leg every five minutes. A stock of wood was in place, turning one way, while the preset metal knives were above it, turning the other way against the wood stock, carving the wooden leg all in one operation. It had a quarter inch metal shield at the top, which enclosed everything while the lathe was operating. When it was changed over to make a different leg, the knives all had to be reset. One day, I was starting to reset the blades for a new leg, when the foreman came by and stopped me. He said, "You can't do that. We have an expert who does the setup work for us. It has to be done just exactly right." I said, "I know what I am doing here." He said, "Nothing doing! I'll have the expert over here to set it up for you." Which he did. On the first leg that I started to carve, one of the blades came loose, and came through the quarter inch shield, leaving a gash in the metal shield about a foot long, and embedded itself in the twenty foot ceiling. If I had been leaning two inches further over the machine, the blade would have taken the front half of my face right off! I shut the machine down and the foreman came running down, yelling, "What happened here?" I said, "So much for your expert! The blade came loose, and is sticking in the ceiling up there! If I am going to operate this machine, I'll do my own setup work from now on. Then if I get my face cut off, I will have nobody to blame but myself." I did my own setup work from then on, and had no further trouble.

I worked in the furniture factory for about two months. When the strike came to an end, I was out of a job. I answered a sales ad in the paper, and became a Fuller Brush man. I did not have a car, but my territory was right in the west side of Chicago, and I could ride a street-car out to it and back. I did fairly well. I was not getting rich, but I made enough to pay my room rent, car fare, buy my meals, and have a couple of dollars to spend. I stayed with that for about four months. When things started easing up, I started going in the hole, so I was forced to quit that.

I went down to Manteno, Illinois, to my stepmother's folks, and stayed with them that winter. It was a fairly large family. There were three boys, and three girls at home, and I made number seven. Lela's (my stepmother) father was working for the W.P.A. and of course that did not pay very much. With nine people to feed, we ate beans! Beans for breakfast, beans for dinner, beans for supper, with not even any bread to go with them. We were thankful to have those beans to eat, but after three months of a steady diet of soup beans, I have not been much of a bean eater for the rest of my life. That was corn country that they lived in. Everybody raised corn. We would go out and contract with a farmer to clean up his cornfields. When he harvested his corn, he used a corn picker, and there was always a lot of corn knocked to the ground. We got to pick up the corn that was left on the ground. We would get one wagonload, and give the farmer one wagonload of what we picked up. I had gotten a Monopoly set for Christmas that year, and I took it down to the Hopkins with me. We practically wore that Monopoly game out. It was about the only game we had to play, and there was somebody playing it day and night.

My stepmother had a married sister Luella. She and her husband lived about two miles from us. He was a no good drunk, and was always beating up on her, so my stepmother's brother Raymond and I would take turns staying with them, in order to keep him from beating up on her. One day, as I entered the yard, I noticed a bee hive sitting out in the front yard. Bill had never had any bees before, so I knew it was something that he had just gotten. It was summer time and I was wearing a short, sleeved shirt. I had barely got into the house, when Bill said, "Hey Ralph, come out in the yard with me. I want to show you something." I said, "Okay." I knew it was the beehive that he wanted to show me. He took me out to the beehive. I guess he thought that I wouldn't know what it was. He said, "Just open the lid a couple of inches and stick your arm in there." I raised the lid a little bit, and slowly eased my forearm into it. I held my arm inside the beehive for about three minutes, until I knew that my arm was fully covered with bees. I pulled my arm out and held it up so he could see that it was completely black with bees. I said, "Is this what you meant for me to do?" He just stood there with his mouth open. He couldn't say a word. I raised the lid on the hive and slowly brushed the bees off my arm, back into the hive. He never mentioned bees to me again.

My stepmother's brother, Eldy, was working on a farm about a mile from my uncle's. He had a '32 Dodge straight eight with double side, mounts, which I have always considered to be the most beautiful car that I have ever seen. I borrowed it from him one day to go to Delavan. It was about nine o'clock at night when I started out. The trip was only thirty miles. I got just west of Lake Geneva, about eight miles from home, and I guess I was doing about seventy miles an hour when a tire blew out. I made an abrupt about face in the car, and headed back toward Lake Geneva and on the other side of the road. I got the car stopped, pulled off of the road, got the jack out, and the head was missing off of the jack. I had to jack the car up just on the rod. It took about ten tries before I got the car jacked up. I would get it part of the way up, and it would slip off of the rod! I got the wheel off, got the tire irons, and after about forty-five minutes, I managed to get the tire off of the rim. The tire and the tube were shot. There was a spare tire and tube in the trunk. The tire was okay, but there was not an air nozzle in the tube. I thought I would try to take the one out of the one that blew, and try to put it in the good tube, but when the tire blew, it blew the air nozzle out somewhere along the side of the road. I got a flashlight, and went back down the road, hunting for that nozzle, After about half an hour, I found it, and lucky I did, because the batteries in the flashlight went out. When I got back, I managed to get the nozzle inserted into the other tube, and get it patched in, all in the dark. I got the tire and tube back on the wheel, and the wheel back on the car, got out the hand pump to air up the tire, but it was old and the leathers on the inside were dried up, and it did not work! I took the pump apart and found a paper cup in the car, drained some water out of the radiator, soaked the leathers in the water for about an hour, put the pump back together, and started pumping up the tire. About a third of the way up, the pump gave out again. I put everything away, got in the car, started it up, and headed for Delavan doing about three or four miles an hour. Finally, I got into town about six in the morning, pulled into the filling station, and sat there for an hour waiting for them to open up, so I could finally get the tire pumped up where it should be. It only took me nine hours to go those thirty miles!

When I returned my friend's car, I pulled into a filling station in Hebron, Illinois. I was going to stop at the gas station to fill the tank up with gas for him. I fell asleep just as I was pulling up to the gas pump, and had my first accident. I hit the gas pump and knocked it over. The owner came out, mad as a wet hen. He took the car and chained it to a tree behind the station. He said, "That's where it stays until you pay for the damages you caused!" In those days, we did not know what insurance was! It took three weeks to get the parts and get the pump back into action, and the actual cost of the damage was only fifty dollars, but back then, fifty dollars was a small fortune! I did not have it, and could not raise it, and neither could my friend, who was working on a farm for ten dollars a month and his board and room. I did the only thing I could possibly do! There was not work to be had, so I joined the CCC Camp. They paid thirty dollars a month, board, room, clothing, everything furnished, same as in the army. When I signed up, I hoped to get sent to a camp out West, as I had never been across the Mississippi River before. So where did they send me? Into Milwaukee, Wisconsin, sixty miles from home! There the camp had several projects going. One was reforestation, the replanting of trees. I got a little taste of that. Then they put me on a rock crusher, crushing rocks up to make gravel. The third project was building a dam across the Milwaukee River. As I did not like the rock crusher too well, I managed to get transferred to the dam project, where I was assigned as a carpenter's helper.

At that time, they had the dam pretty well underway, with scaffold over it solid, so a ten-ton truck could be driven over the center of it. I was allergic to heights! I could not stand to get more than two foot off of the ground. Here I was working sixty-foot up in the air. I could hardly stand to walk down the center of the scaffolding, even though a ten-ton truck could drive on it safely. I thought to myself, "Spencer, old boy if you are going to do this kind of work, you have got to get over your fear of heights." So I got on the outside of the scaffolding, and hung there with one foot and one hand, over the sixty-foot drop to concrete. It only took me about fifteen minutes, and a couple of times, I thought it would be the kill solution, but after a while, everything cleared up, and I was fine.

I was never bothered by heights after that. It only took me three months to get the fifty dollars together to pay off the filling station so my friend could get his car back.

When I first went into the CCC, everybody warned me not volunteer for anything. There was a job that came along and they asked for volunteers. They wanted to sand and refinish all the floors in all of the buildings. I volunteered for that. I suckered a friend into volunteering with me. At first he was really mad about the volunteering, but I convinced him that we really had a snap of a job there, which we did have. We spent three months sanding and refinishing floors during the day. We really enjoyed that, because there was no supervisor. We went to work when we felt like it and quit when we felt like it. It took us about three months to do the job. As we were winding up the floor in the last building, the captain came by and said, "I have another project if you boys are interested." I said, "What's that?" We have to re-roof all of the buildings in camp with roll roofing. He said, "You have done a good job here, so if you want to take on the roofing project, it is yours." I said, "Fine, I would love it." For the next four months we learned the roofing business. There were five of us, as they gave us three other fellows to help out. We re-roofed about fifteen buildings.

I had a few sidelines going besides the work projects for the camp. One was ironing khaki trousers and shirts for the boys; I made pretty fair money doing it. Another one was painting locker tops. I would sketch and paint their names, nicknames, or whatever they wanted on top of the footlockers. I was pretty good at mechanical drawing, and could do a real nice job of lettering. Another one was when some of the boys had KP duty for the weekend, but wanted the weekend off, "I would take over KP duties for them, for the big sum of five dollars. In the eighteen months that I stayed in the CCC camps, I paid off $300.00 that I owed on the outside, and had enough left over to buy myself a complete new wardrobe when I got out. The CCC Camps turned out to be a pretty good deal for me. Another odd job that I had was in the winter, when the ground was frozen solid, when they wanted to put up a new building. We had to sink about thirty posts into the ground for the foundation of the building. There was only one way that we could do it at that time. We had to dig those thirty holes and sink them down five foot in that frozen ground. At that time, we did not have any air hammers, and we had to do it all by hand. What we did was to build a fire where we wanted to dig a hole, keep it burning for about a half hour, then move the fire off to another hole and dig out the inch or inch and a half of ground that the fire had thawed out, then move the fire back into it while we went to the second hole and dug it out, shifting it back and forth. I went to the captain and told him about the difficulties we were having. "At the rate we are going, it is going to take us three months to get those holes dug unless you give us some more men to help us out." We had to have the building up by the first of April, so he gave me fourteen more fellows, and we worked in pairs, two together, moving the fire back and forth, and managed to get the holes dug in one week. They got the building up by the first of April! One day while working inside the building, my hands were practically frozen and I managed to hit my thumb with a good whack with the hammer. You talk about hurt! I didn't do any more work the rest of that day!

While I was in the camp, I had bad teeth. My teeth had started going bad when I was about fifteen. I had lost my four upper front teeth, and had a partial plate put in when I was fifteen. The teeth that the plate was fastened onto on both sides were going bad, and I had several other teeth with cavities in them. I thought I would not fool around with having two teeth pulled and a new plate made, and then go through the process again. I only had nine upper teeth left, so I went to a civilian dentist. I told him, "I want these nine teeth pulled out and a full upper plate made." He said, "Fine," and sat me down in the chair, shot me full of Novocaine, and pulled the nine teeth. He said, "Now I want you to go back to camp and rest for a couple of days. I want to wait three months to make that upper plate, so your gums will have a chance to heal up and harden up." I said, "Fine. I'll do that," but instead of waiting three months, I waited nine months before I went back to him. He went ahead and made the upper plate for me. He made it himself right there in his office. He did not have to send it away to a laboratory. That plate was a perfect fit! After he had sanded off two or three rough spots, I wore it for over sixty years without an ounce of trouble. He gave me his bill, and the charges were $1.00 for cleaning my lower teeth, $1.00 per tooth for pulling the nine teeth, and $25.00 for the plate, for a total of $35.00.

There for a spell, there would be twenty-five or thirty fellows who left camp at night without passes. They were not going into town. One of the lieutenants was assigned to check up and see what they were doing. He waited one night, and he saw a couple of boys headed out back toward a field, so he followed them. When he got there, there were twenty-five or thirty boys in line. He got in the line, because it was dark and they could not tell that he was an officer. He stood in line and waited his turn. Finally he got to the head of the line. There was a girl laying there, taking them all on, one at a time. He asked her, "Do you do this every night?" She said, "Yep!" He asked, "How much do you charge the boys?" She said, "I used to charge them ten cents apiece, but some of the boys left camp owing me four or five dollars, so I just quit charging them." Of course, that was the end of that'

We all hoped that we would get sent out West to fight forest fires, as they were having some bad ones out there, but although the camp was alerted a couple of times, we were never called out. While there, we had one big flood. It did not cover the dam project up completely, but we were afraid it was going to wash it out. There was one crane sitting in the bottom of the riverbed that had a forty-foot boom on it. All you could see was four or five foot of the boom sticking out of the water. The whole camp was up for two days and two nights fighting the flood! After it subsided, we all went back to camp and went to bed. After three hours of sleep, we were all rousted out to go fight a fire! One of the big garages had caught on fire. We were up for another twelve hours before we got back to bed. After the water subsided, we had to clean up the crane, and was that ever a job!

When I was in the CCC Camps, we had old pot bellied stoves for heating stoves in the barracks. There would be two stoves to a barrack. As long as we kept the fires up, they did a pretty good job of heating the barracks. We had one fellow that always made sure that he had his bunk next to a stove. He was really a slob. He never took a bath, and his body odor was something else. One day in January, there was about six inches of snow on the ground, and four of us came in about 1:00 a.m., and we had been drinking, and felt pretty good, so we walked over to his bunk and two of us took a hold of the head, and two took a hold of the foot, and we picked the cot up with him in it; we carried it outside and set it down about 20 feet from the back of the barracks. We went in and went to bed. Well, it was pretty cold that night, and when he finally woke up shivering, he reached down to get his shoes, and got a handful of snow. He had to get up and walk barefoot through the snow to get into the barracks. He had to get dressed and then go back out and get his cot, and get it back into the barracks, and set up again. You talk about somebody being mad. He started mouthing off the next morning, and four of the other fellows grabbed him, forced him down to the shower room, stripped him down and put him into the shower, and scrubbed him down with a scrub brush and lye soap. I think that taught him a lesson, because after that he kept his mouth shut, and once a week he would go take a shower.

A couple of other gags we used to pull, we would send a rookie out for a gallon of striped paint, or a left handed monkey wrench. One time, I had a new man working with me (I forget what we were doing) and sent him after a smoke screen. I told him to go up to the bathhouse for the screen, and the attendant said, "Gee, I had it here, but, about an hour ago, I took it over to the Supply Sergeant. You will have to go see him to get it." He went over to the Supply Sergeant. The Captain was there with the Sergeant. He asked the Sergeant for the smoke screen. The Captain asked him, "Who sent you after the smoke screen?" He said, "Spencer." The Captain told him, "You go back and tell Spencer that we just sent it out for repairs, and he will just have to do without it."

After eighteen months, I left the CCC Camp. I took a job of herding turkeys. The president of the Outdoor Advertising Company of Chicago had a couple of farms about four miles south of Delavan. On one of them, he raised about three hundred turkeys a year. At Thanksgiving, he gave each one of his employees a turkey. I had the job of taking care of those turkeys for a little over three months. Their wings were clipped so they could not fly. My job was to herd the turkeys from the farm where they roosted overnight down to a patch of woods about a quarter of a mile away where they fed all day, then drove them back to the turkey barn in the evening. If you have never herded turkeys, I'll tell you that it can be quite a job! Once I got the turkeys down to the woods, I would go back to the barns, where I remodeled one of the barns into a horse barn. I divided it into stalls and painted it on the inside. I thought sure that when Thanksgiving came along, he would give me one of the turkeys, but he never did.

I went to work in a canning factory, about five miles east of Delavan in Elkhorn, where I worked on the packing line, packing cans into cartons for shipment.

When the canning season ended, there was absolutely no other work to be had. I packed my suitcase and hitchhiked out to Ohio, where I stayed with a great aunt of mine. There was no work to be had out there, but there was a large grove of walnut trees. Nobody wanted the walnuts. I took a stone sledge and hooked it to a horse. I picked up walnuts, loaded them on the sledge, and pulled them to the riverbank in front of the house. I must have picked up a ton and a half of walnuts! I hulled out the whole works. When I got through, I had a pile of hulls that would fill a room. Then I cracked a bunch of them and picked out the nutmeat. When I finished, I had over eighty pounds of shelled walnuts. I had over eight hundred pounds of unshelled walnuts left, which I managed to sell. I got $1.50 a pound for the shelled walnuts and about a quarter a pound for the whole walnuts. I wound up with $120.00 profit off of the deal. It took me about six weeks, but at that time, that was pretty good wages!

My uncle had a neighbor who made a fortune as a dairy farmer. He sold out, and was supposed to have retired. He had moved out to a little town in Ohio called Chester. While he lived in Chester, he owned a farm about two miles outside of town. That summer, I went to Ohio and went to work for him. He had an overgrown son, Sonny, that they thought the sun rose and set in. They put him on the farm, and the first year, he had never even produced a crop. Then they set him up in a trucking business, and he failed in that. They set him up in an ice cream factory, and he failed in that. They set him up in a garage, but he failed in that. They set him up in the trucking business again, but he failed again. Then they set him up as a custom farmer, but he failed in that. All in all, when he got through with them, they were almost broke. The last business they set him up in was a roller skating rink. It was in a little wayside town called Tuppers Plains about twelve miles north of Chester. The building had been a big dance hall at one time, and they laid down a hard maple floor and remodeled it into a skating rink. My experience in sanding floors in the CCC Camps came in handy there, as I sanded the whole floor down and varnished it. As he was short of money, he could not finish it off on the inside, so they covered the walls and ceilings with old pasteboard boxes, which looked like the devil. Since it was the first roller-skating rink in southern Ohio, they drew good crowds, some people from as far as 150 miles away. I bought my first pair of shoe skates there. I was floor manager, skate repairman and teacher. With Sonny at the helm, in two years time, the rink was closed up.

I worked that summer and fall for Johnny. His wife, Mamie, thought she was the queen bee of the countryside around here. She lorded it over everybody. Johnny got tired of that, and decided to make a break for it. He was in his late 60s, and was having an affair with a younger widow. He took me out to work one day. When we got out to the farm, he wanted to know if I would help him, and I said, "Sure." He told me what he was going to do and said, "Now, I would like for you to work all day here at the farm, and then walk home tonight. If my wife asks about me, tell her that you don't know anything." I said, "Okay." I worked all day and walked home. I got home about 7:00 and Mamie asked, "Where is Johnny?" I said, "I don't know." Which was the truth, as I really did not know at that time. "He just "took me out to the farm at 7:00 this morning, and he told me to go ahead and work, and he would be back in a little while. That was the last I saw of him. I had to walk home from the farm tonight." Mamie must have known something was going on, because she went to the bus station, where she found them waiting to take off for Kentucky. She brought Johnny back. Again, he told Mamie that I did not know anything about his escapade. She did not believe him. She thought I had a hand in helping him get away (which was true). She ordered me out of the house, and did not want anything to do with me.

It just so happened that Mamie had been appointed head of the draft board in Promroy, Ohio. I just wanted to mention this at this point, as this will at a later date be very important.

I started hitchhiking back home, thinking, "Shucks, I'll go the long way around and see what Kentucky is like." This was about two weeks before Christmas. Outside of Frankfort, Kentucky, I got caught out in the country at night with no place to sleep. I found a pine tree that had low branches, so I crawled under the branches and slept on the ground, and just about froze. When I got home I came down with Pleurisy. I was sick for about three months. At night I would sweat so much that the sweat soaked through my pillow, sheets, mattress, and dripped onto the floor. They actually put a pan under the bed to catch the moisture. I went to a chiropractor that said he could have me straightened out in about three treatments. I took 36 treatments from him, and never got a bit better. I got tired of wasting my money on him, so I went across the street to a woman chiropractor. She did not say she could cure me, but she thought she could help me a little. After five treatments, I was back on my feet again.

I took what money I had left and bought myself an old Chevrolet sedan that was pretty much of a wreck. I think I gave $20.00 for it. I started to overhaul it. I took the motor completely out, completely overhauled the motor with new pistons, rebored the piston holes, new valves, new connecting rods, new water and oil pumps, put the motor back in, jacked the car up, pulled all four wheels off, put on new brakes on the rear wheels, new tires on all four wheels. The body was pretty well shot, too. The upholstery was gone and the seats were bad. I took all of the seats out, tore out the upholstery, went to the junk yard, found another sedan, same make and model, that had good upholstery and seats in it, took out the seats and upholstery out of it and put them in my car. The top was also shot. It was a canvas top with wooden framework. The wood was all rotted out. I tore the roof completely off, put in new wooden framework and a new canvas top, sealed the top with a weatherproofing paint. The door on the driver's side was hanging down, almost off. It had a hard maple doorpost in it that was all rotted out. I tore out the doorpost, got a piece of hard maple, and carved out a new doorpost, which was really a job! I don't want to do that one again! I put the new doorpost in and re-hung the door, and when I got done, the door opened and closed better than it did the day it came from the factory. I had my first car!

That fall, my buddy Joe Farkas and I went back to Ohio for corn harvest. We stayed with my great aunt and uncle, Johnny and Etta Spencer. We contracted with one farmer to cut and shock a two hundred-acre field of corn. We were to get ten cents a shock for a shock of one hundred hills of corn. We went through the field and picked out an area of 100 hills. The four center hills of corn were tied together to make a gallous of four stalks. We went through the field and tied all of the gallouses first, then came back and started cutting the corn. We used a three foot long corn knife to cut an armful of stalks by hand, then took that back to set it up on the gallous. We always packed a lunch and carried it with us. The farmer kept asking us to come over and have dinner with his family. We kept putting him off, as we had a pretty good idea of what his situation was at home, because he had seven kids. Finally, he cornered us and would not let us out of it, so we agreed to go have dinner with him. At noon, when we went over, he was not at home, but his wife was there expecting us. She invited us in, and when we got in the kitchen, we found a large, long kitchen with an army style table in the center where we were to sit. She said, "Sit down. We will start eating. My husband will be along shortly." We sat down and she served us. Then the fun began. The house was so full of flies that we had to shoo the flies off of the food, then take a bite quickly, hoping we did not get a mouthful of flies with it. She was a good cook! The food was good, but the flies were not! We were about half through the meal when the farmer came in. He was also a fur dealer. He had about four raw skunk pelts that he slapped down on the table beside his plate, and started eating without any thought of washing his hands first. When we were through, we offered to help wash the dishes, but she said, "Oh, no, we don't wash dishes now. We just turn them over and eat off of the bottoms for the next meal, and then we wash them." That is exactly what they did, too! When we got home that night, we both had diarrhea. I was back in pretty good shape by the next morning, but Joe was sick for a full week.

On weekends, we would go to Tuppers Plains to the roller skating rink to go skating. I met a girl there named Irma Groves. She was a pretty good skater. I started going with her. I fell in love with her and asked her to marry me. She said yes, but said, "I have a baby girl who is three months old." I said, "That's fine! I will just have a ready made family!" We set a date, and got the marriage license, which cost two dollars. We went into Promroy, going in early so she could buy a new dress to get married in. I took her to a dress shop, and I waited in the car while she and her sister went in to get the dress. We then went over to the minister's house, and paid the minister ten dollars to marry us. On our way back to Tuppers Plains, she told me that she did not have the money to pay for the dress, so she shoplifted it. She had been living with her sister and brother-in-law there in Tuppers Plains. They had an old ram shackled house that they were renting. We rented one bedroom from them, in which we lived. It had an old cast-iron cook stove set up in the bedroom, where we did all of our cooking. We got our water from a pump in the yard. The toilet facilities were in a little building set about hundred and fifty feet behind the house. They wanted to re-plaster their living room. Neither my brother-in-law John, nor I had ever done any plastering. We got some instructions on how to mix up your own plaster. Neither of us had any money to buy ready mixed plaster. We went down to a creek and found a sandy beach, dug up our sand, sifted it all, then got our plaster mixed. We had previously cleaned all of the old plaster off of the lathe. We went to work! We had an awful time trying to get the plaster to stick on the ceiling. After a week of working and cussing, we had the ceiling and sidewalls plastered with one coat. According to the instructions, we were to let the first coat dry for about two weeks and then put on a second coat of plaster. They were in a hurry to get the room finished so that they could use it again, so we papered over the one coat of plaster. When we got through, you could see every lathe in the room through the paper. That was enough to drive me batty, but they did not seem to mind it. Incidentally, that was my first and last job of plastering.

My folks sent us a wedding present. It was my mother's set of china. They packed the china in a bushel basket with no paper wrapped around it whatsoever, just put the china in a bushel basket and shipped it out to us by freight. It took about two weeks for the basket to come by slow freight. When I first saw the basket, I figured that all of the china would be broken up. We were fortunate that there was only one piece broken. That was the big serving platter.

I was still working for the farmer, as after we shocked the field, we bargained to shuck out the corn, also at ten cents a shock. We finally finished up the job, and I was out of work. One day, one of the neighbors came by and wanted to know if we would milk his cows for him. He had seven cows. My wife agreed. We were to get all of the milk and cream we needed, with enough to make butter. At that time, I had gone on WPA, so Irma took care of all of the milking. One day, I was at home, when she said, "I'm going down to do the, milking." I said, "Fine, I'll go along and help you." She started with a cow at one end and I started with a cow on the other end. I was doing fine, and had my cow about half milked when Irma came along and tapped me on the shoulder, and said, "Do you want me to finish that cow up for you?" I said, "No, go ahead and start another cow. I'm doing alright here." She said, "What do you mean, "Start another cow? I've got the other six already done!" I never said another word. I just got up and let her take over. I never again offered to help her milk the cows. What was the use!

We were sitting on the bed one day and Janet, the baby, was lying behind us playing with some paper. She got a long triangular piece in her throat with the pointed end down, and was strangling on it. Irma picked her up and tried to reach in her mouth and get the paper, but could not do it, so she did the only thing left to do! She jammed her fingers down the baby's throat to make her vomit. Instead of holding her over the floor, she held her over me, and Janet just covered me from head to toe! Oh, what a mess!

One night, a neighbor brought us a message concerning Irma's sister, since we did not have a phone. She was living in Parkersburg, West Virginia, and had a little boy about the same age as Janet. The message was that she had been seriously burned, so we went to see about her. She was in her apartment, which was heated by an open gas heater, and had just laid the baby on the bed. When she turned around, the tail of her housecoat caught in the flame of the gas heater and blazed around her. She panicked and started screaming and ran downstairs. There was an old gentleman who lived in the ground floor apartment who heard her screaming. When she got to the bottom of the stairs, he wrapped her in a blanket to extinguish the flames. He got the fire out, but she had already been badly burned. He called the ambulance and had her taken to a hospital. She recovered her senses enough to give him our neighbor's phone number and ask him to make the call to let us know. About 1:00 a.m. we got to the hospital. We went in to see her and found her still alive. How she managed to stay alive that long, I will never know, because both of her breasts were burned completely off, her back was burned to the bare bone, and the only place where she had flesh was where her shoes were, and a small area on the front of her face. There was a framework of sheets around the bed, since she was burned too badly to have a sheet over her. She was completely lucid and knew us as soon as we got there. She said she knew that she was going to die, and she asked us to take her boy and raise him. We just could not do it. We tried to tell her she would get well and she would come out of it. She said, "No, I know I'm going to die. There are three angels sitting up there on that bar waiting for me." About five minutes later, she died. The boy's father's relatives took him and raised him.

Irma had a half sister that lived in the mountains above Spencer, West Virginia, who had been asking us to come to pay her a visit. Finally, we got three carloads together and went to see her. When we got to Spencer, we had the roughest ride I think I ever had. They had cobblestone streets! There was no filling in between the stones to level out the street. We made it through Spencer and got about half way up the mountain where Irma's sister lived. We finally located the, house, but we, had to park the cars along the, roadside. There was no lane, path, or anything up to the house. We had to crawl through a barbed wire fence, walk through a pasture, and crawl through another fence to get to the house. There was not even a gateway. She was a rather large woman; I should say fat, and also a very jolly person. She had been expecting us and had a feast laid out that was fit for a king! We really enjoyed the afternoon visit, and it was about 9:00 when we started home. After we got through Spencer, we had to go up another mountain and then down it on the other side. Of the three cars, mine was the middle car. As we started down the mountainside, my brakes gave out! I started picking up speed, so I just laid on the horn and waved to the car in front of me to get out of my way! They finally realized what was wrong and took off. I jammed the gearshift from high into second, and then from second into low, and thought I would strip all of the gears in the transmission doing it. I got the car into low, and the low gear helped to slow me down some, but not nearly enough. Believe me that was the wildest ride I have ever had! Going down that mountainside at night with no brakes! Somehow, I don't know how, we made it down to the bottom of the mountain safely. I nursed the car on home.

At Christmas, we went into Parkersburg, West Virginia to visit another sister of Irma's. Her husband worked in a large silk mill there. We started home that night and a blizzard hit. We had to go through Parkersburg, I don't know just where we were in Parkersburg, but all of a sudden, there was a fellow who stepped out of the blizzard right in front of the car. I did not have any time to think, I just gave the wheel a full turn to the left to avoid hitting him. I figured I would ram into a brick wall someplace, but I didn't. Instead, we felt a lurch; the car gave a jump and dropped a couple of feet. We wound up on a railroad track, sitting crossways on the railroad. We had another of Irma's sisters, Susan, and her husband, John, in the back seat. John wanted to know what kind of a lousy driver I was. I guess he forgave me after I told him what happened. Fortunately, Irma saw the man too, and could verify my story. We got squared around on the tracks and had to drive two blocks before there was a place where we could crawl back out onto the road. We were fortunate that there were no trains coming through at that time. From there we made it home all right.

After about two months on the WPA, I heard about a furniture factory in Marietta, Ohio that was hiring. My brother in law and I went up there and both got jobs in the furniture factory. This was another scab job though, and in about two weeks, the strike ended and we were out of a job.

In the mean time, I had heard that there was a big construction job going on in Ravena, Ohio, in the northern part of the state. I packed a bag and hitchhiked up there. Sure enough, there was a large defense project going. I hired on there as a laborer. They put me to work on the railroad. They were laying about 275 miles of new track just inside of the project. When I first got there, I could not find a place to stay or sleep. Everything was filled up, because so many workers had come in the first week, I slept in a straw stack just outside of the project. Then, I managed to find a bed in a dormitory that housed about forty men. That job lasted about six months.

Irma had a brother-in-law that was a foreman for the B&O Railroad. With my recent experience with laying new track, I thought maybe I could get a job as a section hand. We went to Zanesville, Ohio and stayed with them for a couple of weeks while he tried to get me a job. While we were waiting for the results, I took a job selling vacuum cleaners (Electrolux). After ten days of not selling anything at all, I gave that up, About then my brother-in-law reported that he could not get me on, as the railroad was not hiring anyone at all. So I went up to Sandusky, Ohio where I had heard about another large defense project going on at the port city of Sandusky,

Ohio, the Plum Brook Ordinance Works. I hired on there as a carpenter's helper. The crew that I was on was given three big nitrate buildings to erect. The buildings were three stories high, thirty foot to a story. We had a good foreman. We got the buildings all put up, outside siding on, and roofs on.

There was only one carpenter besides myself that would work on the roofs, because they were so high, but we got them put on. Then we went to work on the insides of the buildings. They were lined with four by eight sheets of transite. Talk about waste in a government project! The transite was shipped in on a large flat bed truck. Instead of taking a crew and properly unloading the truck, the trucker upended the bed, let it slide off and pulled out from underneath his load. Transite is very brittle. I imagine there must have been close to four hundred sheets of transite in the load. When the trucker dumped it on the ground it came down so hard that most of the sheets were cracked or broken. Out of the load, there were about fifty sheets of transite that we could use. The contractor did not care! It was all a cost plus job. We got one building completely transited up, and the second one about half-done when the superintendent came around to see how we were doing. He said "What, you have one building finished and the second one half done? I did not think you had started on the inside yet." You are going to have to tear that transite all off."

The foreman said "Why"

The superintendent said, "These are nitrate buildings. All of the joints have to be caulked or the nitrate dust in them will build up and ignite and the whole thing will go boom."

The foreman said, "Nobody ever told me anything about caulking the joints."

We went back and tore out every other sheet, rather than all of them, as there was no saving, those sheets of transite. We caulked all of the joints and put in new sheets of transite. We later found out that the superintendent had been foreman on a WPA job before landing the job of superintendent. He could not have been a very good foreman, because he knew absolutely nothing about construction work. One day he had a brand new crane with a sixty-foot boom on it sitting at bottom of a built up roadway. He wanted it up on the roadway. The crane operator got in, started up the crane, and started back down the road. The superintendent stopped him and said, "Where do you think you are going? I want that crane up above here."

The crane, operator said, "I'm taking the crane back to the ramp so I can get up on the, roadway." The superintendent "You'll do no such thing. Take it right up that bank. It will take too long to go back to the ramp.

The crane operator said, "I can't do it." That bank is to steep. The crane will roll!

The superintendent said," Take it up that bank, or you haven't got a job!

The crane operator said," OK." He started up the bank, got half way up, and the boom doubled back over the top of the crane. The driver jumped out, and the crane came rolling back down. The crane operator came back down and told the superintendent, "There's your dammed crane, and you can have your dammed job!" He turned around and walked off the job. It only took three months to get the crane repaired and back on the job again.

There were a couple other incidents that happened. The first one was a fellow had a forty foot ladder sitting against a building. He had it sitting to straight up and down, although he did not realize it. He climbed the ladder, and when he got to the top, he leaned back a little, to look above his head, and the ladder tilted away from the building and started to come down backwards. The fellow was a fast thinker and a fast mover, he whipped around to the other side of the ladder and he climbed down the ladder as it was falling. He was standing on the ground when the ladder hit.

The other incident was when a carpenter was working on a scaffold when the planking broke. He fell down and impaled himself on a reinforcing rod that was sticking up. The rod went clear through him, and about six inches of the rod sticking through him. They had to get a welder to cut the rod off so they could take him to the hospital. This happened about nine o'clock in the morning. The doctors managed to get the rod out of him. It was sort of a miracle. The rod had gone completely through him without touching any vital organs. He was back working at three o'clock that afternoon. That was one for Ripley's believe it or not

When I first got to Sandusky, I was looking for a place to stay when I spotted a big mansion with a sign out front that said "Board and room." I went in to see if there were any rooms available, and the lady; the widow of a doctor had a big house with six bedrooms. She had never worked before, but she wanted to do something to help the war effort, so she opened up the boarding house. I was her first customer. I had a beautiful big bedroom 'with an excellent bed in it. When I got up the next morning to go to work, I went into the kitchen to get breakfast. She took me into the dining room, where she had my breakfast set out on the dining room table. I had a wonderful breakfast, and she said, "I have your lunch packed here and she gave me a large brown sack. I did not look at it, just picked it up and took off. I thought it felt a little heavy, but I did not think anything of it until dinnertime. When I sat down to eat, I opened my sack, started pulling my lunch out, and found that I had six sandwiches with three different kinds of meat in them, two of each type. I had two apples, two peaches, two pears, two bananas, two pieces of cake, and two pieces of pie. I have to laugh every time I think about that lunch. There was enough there to feed the whole crew. When I got home that night, I told her, "That was a wonderful lunch, the best lunch I ever had packed for me, but it was way to much. I could not even begin to eat-half of it. She said "Well I never packed a lunch before. I did not want you to go hungry." It took me a week to get her to cut the lunch down to what I could eat without having to throw anything away.

By this time we had a little money saved up. I managed to find a nice little three-room apartment (furnished) in Norwalk a small town about five or six miles away from the project. I rented it and moved my wife and baby up there with me.

One incident that I will never forget was after Janet started walking. Irma had left a jar of honey sitting open on the kitchen table. Janet managed to get a hold of the jar, and she up ended it over her head. Then tracked it through all three rooms, around about and over the furniture. What a time we had, not only cleaning her up, but also cleaning the whole house

After about seven or eight months, the job at the Plum Brook Ordinance works started to wind up. Our crew had three nitrate buildings that we were working on completed. The company did not want to turn us loose, as they felt they might be able to use us a little later on. The whole crew of twenty men sat for three weeks in one of the buildings, doing nothing, playing cards, taking it easy, sleeping. Finally, they let us all go.

I decided to go back to Delavan, Wisconsin. When I got home, I learned that our friend, Bob Slopa, wanted my dad to go into partnership with him in a foundry. My dad had put up a small building behind his large barn to use as a foundry. However, he needed a blast furnace. He had located a used one for $250.00, but he did not have the cash to pay for it. I told him, "For Pete's sake, go to the bank and borrow the money, and get that blast furnace. I don't know anything about foundry work, but I will stay here and help you, and you can teach me." He would not do that. He would not go into debt, but wanted to wait until he had accumulated the money. In the mean time, Bob was sitting there with several contracts and no foundry. He got tired of waiting on his dad and went elsewhere.

I went to work for a contractor over at Williams Bay, helping to build a bowling alley and a nightclub.

We were staying with my folks, and finally found a place to rent, It was a huge, old sixteen-room house, which had been divided into two eight-room apartments, one upstairs and one down. The rooms were all fully furnished with beautiful antique furniture. They wanted $35.00 a month for the upstairs apartment, and $30.00 for the downstairs apartment, but the downstairs apartment had to furnish the heat for the whole house. We took the upstairs apartment, and never moved into it. We had finished the nightclub and the contractor did not have any further work at that time.

I went down to Marion, in southern Illinois where there was supposed to be another big defense job starting up. However, I got there a little early, and the job was not going to start for about six months. I went on down to Texarkana, Texas to the Lone Star Ordinance Plant. I went to work there as a carpenter. For over six months, I worked as a carpenter, and the only tools I ever used were a hammer, a 10-inch crescent wrench, and a drift pin. We were building ammunition storage depots and all we were doing was setting steel forms. Texarkana was just a small city, and there were about twenty thousand workers who came into the town to work on the job. Living space was almost impossible to find. I managed to get a room in a big, old house.

I was partnered up with an older man. He and his wife managed to rent an old filling station that had been divided into two, two-room apartments. He took one apartment and rented me the other one. I managed to get Irma and our daughter down to Texarkana with me. We hired an old colored lady to come in and cook and keep house for us, as Irma was about seven months pregnant at that time. The colored lady would fix our dinner and after we were finished eating, she would eat. We told her there no point in that! She should sit down and eat with us. She said, "Oh, no! That is not proper! It is just not right for a colored person to sit down and eat with a white person!" We finally persuaded her to eat with us.

We ate more bananas there than I had ever eaten in my life before. They were cheap: five cents a pound. I would buy a whole stalk of them at a time.

The ordinance works was located about twenty miles from town. There would be three lanes of traffic going out to the job, bumper to bumper, and two lanes of traffic coming back into town off of the night shift. All of that on a two lane highway! We would get up at 4:00 in the morning, and leave at 4:30 in order to get out to the job at 7:00. We were working ten, twelve, and sometimes fourteen hours a day. There were over six months that I never saw my wife or baby in the daylight. There was one time when we were working in one of the igloos, which were, 40 by 100 feet, putting in the final row of forms in the center of the ceiling. The scaffolding ran the full length of the building on either side with cross sections of scaffolding running across the building every eight feet. I was working in the center of one section of scaffolding, and needed to get over into the next section. I thought I would be smart and instead of going back to the scaffolding running lengthwise, over to the next section, and coming out to the center again, I would play Tarzan. I grabbed hold of a section of scaffolding and started to swing across to the other section. I felt my hands slipping and knew that I was not going to make it! I just let go and dropped about 25 feet to the concrete floor! When I hit, I lit on my toes and just acted like a spring, folded up, turned three summersaults and stood up. There were two other fellows working up there, and they saw me fall, and they had to go back 10 foot to the outer scaffolding, come back almost 75 foot to a ladder, climb down it, and come back out 75 foot to where I was. When I got stood up, they were standing there by me. How they ever got there that fast, I will never know, and they won't either! They really had to be moving! They were sure that I would have a couple of broken legs and be laid up in the hospital, but other than a good jar and a few scratches, there was not a thing wrong with me, and we just went on back to work. Other than that, nothing very exciting happened on that job.

Just about the time the job was ending, the baby came. I took Irma over to a hospital on the Texas side of the line, as I did not want the baby to be an Arkie. When she starting having contractions, I said, "I'll go next door and call a taxi." She said, "No, you won't! We will just take the bus down." There was a bus that went right past the house. We took the bus. We got downtown and got off of the bus about two blocks from the hospital. I started for the hospital, realized that she was not with me, looked around and there she was going the opposite direction! I caught up with her, and she said she wanted to go do some window-shopping. So we went window-shopping! After about an hour, I managed to get her to go to the hospital. Irma was in labor for about 20 hours. The baby finally came! It was a boy, and he was just as yellow as he could be! The doctors and nurses all thought he had yellow jaundice, but after a week, the yellowness all disappeared. We had picked a name for a girl, but none for a boy. We could not agree on a name for a boy! I was reading a detective story about Ellery Queen. I threw the magazine over to her, and said, "Let's name him after this guy!" Well, we did: Ellery Raymond. Raymond was after my Dad.

While in Texarkana, I received my first questionnaire for the army draft. I had registered in Promroy, Ohio. There was a schoolteacher there by the name of Ralph Spencer. He was a single person. I received not only my questionnaire, but also his. I filled mine out, and sent his back in blank with a letter of explanation.

I went from Texarkana to Little Rock, Arkansas, where there was another defense project going. I was working on the night crew. I stayed two weeks on that job, and it rained every day and night, continually. One time, the foreman sent me to the lumber pile to get a

twelve foot 2 x 4. I got the board and came around behind the building, and as I walked along, all of a sudden
I dropped straight down. I had hit a sinkhole! If it had
not been for that 2 x 4, which was long enough that it
caught on each side of the sinkhole, I would have just
disappeared! I sank right up to my shoulders, but I managed to pull myself onto the 2 x 4 and crawl up onto
solid ground. When I got back around to the crew, the
foreman looked at me and said, "What in the world happened to you?" I was covered from head to foot with
mud! He said, "You better get yourself cleaned up! Go
home and clean up and take the rest of the night off!"
Which, I did.

With all of the rain and the dampness, my sinuses
were raising cane with me! I got to the point where I
was blowing my nose more than I was working! I decided to quit and get out of there! I took a bus back to
Texarkana. When we got to the Red River, it was full
and up to the bottom of the bridge. The bus driver stopped
and said, "I wonder if it is safe to go across?" I said,
"Let's walk over it and see!" So we did. We walked across
the bridge and back and decided that it was still safe
enough to cross with the bus. We got back in the bus and
went on over. We crossed over okay and went on to
Texarkana, where we learned that the bridge went out
about two hours after we crossed it.

Then, I decided to go to El Paso, where there was a
big defense job going on at Biggs Field. I started hitchhiking. I got about half way between Dallas and Fort
Worth at about one in the morning when some soldiers
in a Model-A with a rumble seat stopped and picked me
up. I got into the rumble seat, where there was another
soldier. It was a dark night, no moon, and we could not
even see each other. We got to talking, and I asked him,
"Where are you from?" He said, "I'm from up in Wisconsin." I said, "What part of Wisconsin?" He said, "The
southern part." I asked what town. He said, "A little old
town you probably never heard of." I asked the name of

the town. He said, "Delavan." I said, "You know something? I'm from Delavan, too, What the heck is your name?" 1 forget his name now, but he was one of my schoolmates! Talk about a small world!

After I got through Fort Worth, I decided it was going to take too long to hitchhike all the way across Texas, so at a small town west of Fort Worth, I managed to catch a freight train going into El Paso. It took about two days on the freight train to get to El Paso. I was a heck of a hobo, wearing a suit and a tie!

I got a job as a carpenter out at Biggs Field. There were about five hundred hutments that the soldiers were quartered in. These hutments consisted of a floor and four sides with a canvas roof over them. We were converting them, building up the sides and putting a regular roof on them. After two weeks, I called Texarkana, and told my friend that we were living with, to come on to El Paso to get a job with me, which he did. We managed to get partnered up again. There was a crew that went ahead of us and put up the rafters. We came along and put the plywood on. We had four Mexicans as helpers to us. They would pass the plywood up to us, and we would position it and nail it down. We put all of the plywood in place first, with a couple of nails to hold it in position, then, we would go back and nail the boards all down. We would use up a keg of nails a day. My partner asked me one day, "Can you do this?" He took an eight penny nail and with one blow of the hammer, drove the nail completely in. I said, "I don't know. I never tried it. But I will give it a go!" It took me several times and a couple of mashed fingers, but I got to where I could drive the eight penny nail up with just one blow of the hammer! If you think that is easy, just try it!

The airstrip there was solid dirt, as there were no paved airstrips at that time. The planes were lined up and parked on either side of the airstrip for about 500 feet. The airstrip itself was about 100 foot wide. We were standing beside one of the planes when we felt the wind come up and start blowing dust. As we looked, there was a tornado coming in off of the desert. It started out small, about six inches off of the ground, and spread out to where the top was probably about 200 foot high and 300 foot wide. It just came right straight down the center of the airstrip, and on out into the desert on the other side! If it had been fifty foot on either side, it would have torn up several million dollars worth of planes. As it was, it passed right through without doing any damage whatsoever.

I got my second questionnaire from the draft board while I was in El Paso. I also received a second questionnaire for the other Ralph Spencer in Promroy. I filled out mine and sent his in again with a letter of explanation, stating that the form was for him instead of me. By this time, I realized what was going on! Mamie Hoffman was playing tricks with me! As it proved out later, when I received notice go in for my physical, I also received his notice. This other Ralph Spencer was a single person and he never did go into the army. Mamie was getting even with me for trying to help Johnny leave her.

One day when I was working out at Fort Bliss, I was nailing a stud to the floor when I jarred a small piece of 2 x 4 off of the top plate. It came down, and the pointed edge caught me right in the small of the back. It just floored me! I lay there for a few seconds, then got up and went back to work. This was at about ten o'clock in the morning. By 2:00 in the afternoon, my back was hurting me so badly that I just could not do anything! I went to the medics and they sent me in to El Paso to the hospital. I was sent in an army ambulance. It was the old style van with two back doors that opened up. There were two wooden seats along either side of the van. A person either sat on one of the seats or stretched out on the floor. I was sitting on one of the seats and the ambulance driver was a real car jockey. He was going to get me to the hospital just as fast as he could! When we got into El Paso, he cut a corner too sharp, and hit a high curb, and it just threw me from one side of the van to the other, which did not do me any good! When I got into the doctor's office, he looked at me and said, "Well, that is a pretty nasty cut you have there!" I said, "What cut? I haven't got any cut!"

He said, "Oh, yes you have. Your shirt is torn, and there is a cut about a foot and a half long across your back!" Evidently, when the ambulance driver hit the curb, and threw me back and forth across the van, I must have hit the end of a bolt that cut me. I did not realize that I had been cut! As it turned out, the cut was nothing more than a long scratch, and did not amount to anything. I told the doctor about the pointed end of the piece of board hitting me in the back. He took some x-rays, but could not see anything wrong. He taped my back up solid, from my shoulders down to my buttocks. He just left the tape there on me, and finally, after a week, I had Irma pull the tape off of me. My back was just raw! The local doctor could not find anything wrong with me, and I was just getting worse, so he called in a bone specialist from San Antonio, about 800 miles away, and he took more x-rays. All in all, they took 35 x-rays, and still could not find anything wrong with me. This went on for almost three months. I was to the point where I could not even get out of bed by myself. If I was sitting down, I could not stand up. If I was standing up, I could not sit down. I told my wife, "To heck with these company doctors! They not doing me any good! I'm going to a chiropractor!"

There was a large chiropractic clinic about two blocks from where we were living run by a man and his wife who were both chiropractors. I went down to see the chiropractor, told him what had happened to me. He examined my back and my neck and said, "I am going to have to take some x-rays." I said, I've already had 35 made. I will just go down and get those for you." He said, "They took all of those x-rays of your back, from your shoulders down, didn't they?" I said, "Yes." He asked, "Did they take any of your neck, from your shoulders up?" I said, "No." He said, "That is what I need, x-rays of your neck." I told him, "Okay, go ahead and take them." He took three x-rays of my neck, studied them for a few minutes, then stretched me out onto his table and placed his fist on the back of my neck. He came down with his other hand and hit his fist just as hard as he could. Talk about hurt! I thought he had broken my neck! He said, "Now I want you to just lay there quietly for about an hour." As time went on, my neck started feeling better, and at the end of the hour when he came back in, it was feeling pretty good. When he asked how I felt, I told him, "Pretty good." He told me to put my shirt on and go on home. This was on a Monday. He told me to come back in on Wednesday morning. I walked home, and when I got there, I could sit down without any problem. Wednesday, when I went back to see him, he merely ran his fingers up and down my neck, and said, "I don't see any reason why you can't go back to work tomorrow." If I had gone to him in the first place instead of company doctors, I would have only lost a day and a half of work instead of three months. This chiropractor was what they called a hole in one chiropractor. He operated only on the neck. I have adjustments about three times a week. It is kind of amazing that the three years I spent in the army, I never needed a chiropractic adjustment. But within weeks after my discharge, I was going back to the chiropractor two or three times a week again.

We were living in a boarding house on the southeast side of town. One day I decided that I was going do a little mountain climbing. I hiked out to the foot of Mount Franklin and started climbing. Mount Franklin is an easy mountain to climb, with a consistent slope and no cliffs. The only thing wrong was that I did not have sense enough to take any water with me. I managed to get to the top, and turned around and came back down. By the time I got back into town, I was just about dead with thirst I was so dehydrated. I stopped at the first grocery store that I came to and bought a gallon of grape juice. I sat there and drank the whole gallon. It is a wonder that I did not make myself sick! Later on, there were six of us from the boarding house who decided to take a holiday and go out to Mount Cornudas in New Mexico. Mount Cornudas is just a rock mountain, all rocks! Three of us men were going to climb it. We left the women at the bottom. We had come prepared, with six canteens of water. When we got about a third of the way up, we started to get thirsty, and decided we had better have a drink of water. Lo and behold, no one had the canteens! We had left them all down with the women! We had gone that far, so we went ahead. When we got to the top, at least what we thought was the top; there was another peak higher up that we had not been able to see before. One of the fellows was Roby, a little short fellow that we had to boost up most of the time because he was too short to make some of the climbs. When we got to the top of that peak, there was a third one, even higher up yet! Every once in a while, we would come across a little hollow in the rock where a fair amount of water had collected from the rain. Although it was old and had green scum on the top, we would brush the scum aside and drink. We made it to the top of the third peak, and started down. I think Roby actually slid about two-thirds of the way down, because when we got to the bottom, the whole seat of his pants was gone! After that experience, I never did any more mountain climbing.

About that time, our daughter Janice was about three years old. I came home from work one day and she was playing out in the yard. When she saw me, she came running out to meet me. I was on the other side of the street, and before I could say or do anything, she was out in the center of the street, and almost got hit by a car. I picked her up, carried her up and sat her down in the center of the yard. I gave her a good talking to and made her promise that she would never go out in the street again. I left her there and started up on the porch of the house, but before I got half way up the steps, I heard brakes screeching. I turned around and looked and there she was back out in the center of the street, and had almost been hit again. I ran out in the street and got her, took her back into the yard, turned her over my knee, and gave her a good hard paddling. Actually, I was ashamed of myself for spanking her so hard, but I guess it was the best thing that I could have done, because she never again went out into the street. She would always stop at the street corner and look both ways before she would venture into the street.

About once a week, we would go over to Juarez, Old Mexico. At that time, there was a ruling that the only American money that could be taken into Mexico was a two-dollar bill. One time, I forgot about that and was caught with $180.00 in cash that I had to change into 90 two-dollar bills. We liked to go into Jules Bar over there and just sit and watch the people. There would invariably be some tourists come in and order tequila. They would say, "That wasn't bad at all! I could drink this all night long!" They would sit there and have six or seven shots of tequila, which did not bother them at all until they stood up! When they stood up, they would fall flat on their faces. I saw that happen more than once!

The work at Biggs Field finally came to an end. Next, I went over to Deming, New Mexico, where they were building a large airport. The first partner that I had on that job hired on as a carpenter, but did not know much about carpenter work. I had to laugh at his toolbox! He had it filled up with scraps of wood with just a claw hammer, a framing square, and a saw. Those three items were all of the tools that he had and he did not know how to use any of them. I did not consider myself a full-fledged carpenter then, but at least I knew quite a bit about the trade, and I had all of the necessary tools. I tried working with the fellow, but it just would not work out. We were framing in and hanging doors, and that is all that we did. I could show him how to do something half a dozen times, and he still would not know how to do it. I finally went to the foreman and told him that I could not work with that man any more, so he gave me a new partner. It was a young Mexican boy about 18 years old. I thought, "Oh, boy, I really do draw the oddballs!" It turned out that the Mexican boy was even a better carpenter than I was, as he had worked with his father all of his life, while I had only been working in the carpenter trade about two years. We got along just fine!

While I was working at Deming, my wife and children stayed on at the boarding house in El Paso. I received notice to report for my physical, and also received the notice for the other Ralph Spencer from Promroy. I went and took the physical, and just forgot about the other letter. I had been trying to get into the Seabees. At that time, they were taking only unmarried men. As time went on, they lowered their requirements to where they were taking married men. I went down and tried to enlist a second time, but they were not taking married men with children.

We got the airbase at Deming built, and the job closed down. I was out of work again. After a week's vacation that I spent with my wife and kids in El Paso, I headed for McAllister, Oklahoma, where there was a huge defense job starting up. When I got there, the job had been going for six months, when all of a sudden, they had shut everything down, and they were doing absolutely no hiring at that time. What had happened was that they had whole plant a mile and a half off of location. You talk about boo boos! They had about one hundred foundations built and poured when they discovered their error, and did not know what to do about it.

Rather than hang around there and wait for things to get straightened out, I headed for Houston, Texas, where I figured I could get a job in the Navy yard, building ships. The Navy yards were not doing any hiring, so I took a job in a box factory. The fellow that owned the box factory had been a Buick car dealer and was forced to close his dealership down when he could not get any new cars. He had some connections in Washington D.C. He managed to get a huge contract to make ammunition boxes. He had converted his garage into a box factory. I started work there as a sawyer. I got along fine at that job. The boss was having a lot of trouble, with better than 50% reject on the boxes, and could not figure out why. I kept thinking about that, and kept watching his assemblers. The boxes had wooden sides and ends, which were glued together. They would apply the glue, put the boxes in a set of clamps, clamp them up tight for a minute, release the clamps, and pass the boxes on to the next person, who would screw on a metal bottom. The way they were put on was to fasten them on with about 15 screws that were applied with automatic screwdrivers. Then the boxes were passed on down the line to the next person, who turned them over and put on hinges and a metal lid. I kept thinking that they just did not give the glue a chance to really set up, releasing them from the clamps too soon. All of the jarring from the automatic screwdrivers was loosening them again. I talked to my boss, got switched over to the assembly line, where I was putting on the lids. When I got the lids put on, I would slap the boxes back into the clamps and reclamp them. I marked each box that I worked on. At the end of the week, I contacted the boss and told him what I had been doing. I asked him to go check the boxes and see how many rejects I had.

Well he came back with a big smile on his face, and said, "I think you have solved our problem! Not a single one of the boxes you worked on were rejected." He gave me a fifty-dollar bonus.

I heard that the Seabees lowered their restrictions; so I went down to try to enlist again. They said yes, they would take me in. I would start at sergeant's rating, but I would have to get my teeth fixed. I only had nine lower teeth left, and two or three of those had cavities. I was supposed to get the cavities filled and a partial plate made. When I got that done, they would ship me right off. After work, I went to a dentist and made an appointment to get my teeth looked after, then went on home. When I got home, I looked at my mail, and there was my draft notice for the army. I might have been able to get around the draft notice since I had enlisted in the Seabees, but I said," To heck with it" and went into the army. I figured that the army could have my teeth fixed for me when I got in. My family was still in El Paso, and had a good spot there, so I left them there. I did not get to go see them before I entered the army.

My orders told me to report to the railroad station at 6 a.m. on a Monday morning in November. When I went down to the station, there must have been two hundred of us there. Everybody but myself had their friends, relatives, folks and wives there to see them off. I was just by myself. I think that was the loneliest moment of my life.

They got us all loaded on the train and hauled us all up to San Antonio, where we spent three days getting physical equipment and orders. We were told not to bring anything but suitcase of personal items. However, I had my toolbox, and I was not about to leave it in Houston, so I took it with me. While we were at San Antonio, I had a little free time, and I managed to get a cab and went out to pay a visit to the Alamo.

From San Antonio, I was sent to Fort Benning, Georgia, and assigned to Headquarters Company of the 55th Engineers of the 10th Armored Division.

The day after I joined Headquarters Company, I went to the company dentist to see about getting my teeth fixed. I only had seven teeth left on the bottom, and some of them were bad, so he said "Well, you might as well get them all pulled and get a lower plate." I said Okay. He sat me down in a wooden chair since he did not really have any dental equipment there, shot my jaw full of Novocaine, grabbed a pair of pliers, and said, "Open up!" I said, "Wait a minute! I've had a lot of teeth pulled before, and I know that it takes at least half an hour for that Novocaine to take effect." He said, "Open up! And

84

that is a direct order." He pulled those seven teeth in less than five minutes. I just about went through the ceiling. I went back to the barracks and lay down on my bunk. About half an hour later the Novocaine started to take effect. I just don't believe that dentist ever finished dental school.

I was issued an M-1 rifle, which I did not like and did not care about, and did not take care of it. One day the battalion Colonel came through inspecting rifles. He came to mine, put his thumbnail at the end the barrel to see the reflection to see if the barrel was clean, but he could not see the reflection at all because mine was not clean. Did he ever blow his stack at me I had to get that rifle cleaned up and keep it that way! My sergeant was going to inspect it every day to make sure it was. Our platoon sergeant's name was Smith and our first sergeant's name was Ellis. In fact, I did not even know his name. One day I bumped into him. He asked me if I knew who he was, and I did not. He asked who my first sergeant was. When I replied Sergeant Smith it really burned him up, and then I caught the devil from him, too. He informed me that he was my first Sergeant, his name was Ellis, and I had better remember that.

I had checked my toolbox in with the supply sergeant, as I was not allowed to keep it in the barracks. When I did, I opened the box up, inspected all of my tools to make sure the supply sergeant got a good look at them, and then locked them up. It was not but about two days until the supply sergeant sent for me. He wanted to know if I would loan my tools to the company carpenter for a job that he had to do. I said "Sorry. Nobody uses these tools but me." I knew the company did not have any carpenter tools worth using. The job they wanted done was working over the mailroom. It wound up that I got the job. I needed an assistant, so I asked for Lloyd Huff. One day the battalion Colonel came, inspected our work and thought that we were doing a real good job. He offered to promote both of us to corporal. We turned the promotion down, since we had only been in the army about two weeks, and did not feel that we had done anything yet to earn a promotion. From then on Lloyd and I were a pair. He got assigned to the company's air compressor, which was a big LeRoy air compressor mounted on a two and one half-ton truck. It had all of the air tools on it, such as a power saw, 120 pound and 90 pound jackhammers, air hammers and several other tools. He managed to get me assigned along with him as his assistant, which was fine with me. I became the, company carpenter, and he, was my assistant whenever I had anything to do.

When I went into the army, I had a seed wart about the size of a silver dollar on my sac. I went to sick call and the doctor sent me to the hospital to have it burnt off. This was in the morning I came back to the company area, and at 1:00 p.m., they called the company out for a five-mile hike. I went to my sergeant told him what I had done. There was absolutely no way to put a bandage of any kind on it. I asked to be excused from the hike. He said he could not do anything for me. I would have to see the first sergeant. I went to see First Sergeant Ellis and he said he could not do anything. I would have to see the captain. I went to the captain, who said I would have to see the doctor. I went to see the doctor, and he would not do anything for me. He said I was trying to gold brick, and had to go ahead and make the hike. I went back and made the hike, straddle legged, and instead of five miles, it turned out to be fifteen miles. I never will forget that hike.

After about a month, Lloyd and I got our first passes into town. We went into town with another fellow, named Joe, that Lloyd had met. Joe had been in the merchant marines and loved to fight. At that time the 101st Airborne and the 10th Armored was stationed at Benning, and there was a running feud, between the 101st Airborne and the 10th Armored. As we were walking down the street, there were three paratroopers coming toward us Lloyd nudged me with his elbow, and said "Do you want to see some fun?" I said sure. Lloyd said to Joe "I'll bet you can't whip those three paratroopers!" Joe said, "By god you just watch me." As we came up to the paratroopers, Joe never said a word. He just laid into them. That was quite a fight. Joe darned near took the three of them, but three was just one to many, and they finally whipped him.

To tell you a little more about Lloyd, he came from up in Maine, where he had been a woodsman. He was only twenty years old, but he had managed to get a team of horses and had his own small logging business going. He was married and had a son. He was a very easy going and likable person. He became the best friend that I ever had.

At that time I suffered from migraine headaches. I really mean, I had them! One time when we were out in the field, I came back into camp with a bunch of other fellows to take showers and get clean clothes and came down with one of my migraines. I lay down on my bunk, and must have passed out, when I came to, I was laying in my tent out in the field. That evening, there was a black jack game going in the tent next door. I had ten cents in my pocket, and I thought, "I'll go sit in for one hand, loose the ten cents, and just be broke." So I sat in for one hand, and instead of loosing, I won. I ran that dime up to ten dollars, and I got out of the game. I believe that is the most I have ever won in any gambling game.

Whenever we knew that we were going out in the field for a week, I would buy a carton of Hershey bars and take them with me. The extra energy the chocolate gave me really kept me going. There were quit a few of the boys that did the same thing.

One time the division put on a demonstration for a lot of Brass out of Washington D.C., to show them how fast the engineers could build a bridge over a river and run a tank across it. The platoon that I was in was selected to do the job.

We went out to the location where the bridge was to be built a week ahead of time. There were eighteen of us in the platoon. We all kept busy. We built the bridge under water, about a foot under top of the water level, so it could not be seen. It was quit an undertaking, but we got it done. We went over to the woods, about a hundred yards from the river, cut and trimmed logs and had them all stacked up in a pile. We built a grandstand for the brass to sit in. It came the day for the demonstration, and we were all ready for them. There was a truck backed up to the pile of logs. When the whistle blew for the demonstration to start, we threw the logs onto the truck, backed the truck down to the bridge, which, of course, the audience did not know was there, rolled the logs off of the truck onto the bridge and had a tank across it in exactly thirteen minutes. After the demonstration, a colonel stopped me and said, "You know that is just marvelous! You start from scratch and build a bridge and run a tank across it in just thirteen minutes."

I said, "Well colonel it is all in the knowing how." There must have been 200 officers of ranks, and I think they all believed that we had actually built that from scratch in just thirteen minutes.

We had a General who came from up in Maine, whose name was Newgarden. He decided that officers should have a thousand yard firing range. A ninety-foot tower had to be built for them to fire off of. Lloyd and I were assigned to the job, because they needed our air compressor and air hammers, as the tower was to be built completely out of logs. The job went along pretty well, until we reached the thirty-foot mark. There all of the others refused to go any higher. One other fellow and I built it the rest of the way up. One day, I was just starting up the ladder with a 12 lb. sledgehammer in one hand when a officer came by and started talking to me. I was hanging there on the ladder with one hand holding on to a rung, holding the sledgehammer straight down when it slipped out of my hand. There was a fellow standing

directly underneath me, and it hit him on the head. Fortunately he had a steel helmet on. It still put a nice dent
in the helmet, and knocked him flat. He got up and pulled
his helmet off, started to rub his head, when my buddy,
who was up about thirty feet, dropped a steel tape and it
hit him on the head and knocked him flat again! He got
up, grabbed his helmet, and said, "I'm getting out of
here!" We never did see him back on the job, and I do
not blame him. We got the tower built, and I wanted to
fire off of it, but they would not let me. It was strictly
for officers.

At one time, the captain sent for me, and said, "Spencer, I am going to send you to OCS." I said. "That is
fine, sir!" The day before I was to report to the OCS
board, they made me a PFC. I guess they did not want to
send a private before the OCS board. I passed all of the
tests without any problem. They sent me back to the
company, and told me they would call me when they got
an opening. I kept thinking about that, and I thought
"Now, do I want to go to OCS and become an officer? If
I go there and make 2nd lieutenant, they will send me to
some infantry outfit, and I will get shipped overseas as a
replacement." A 2nd lieutenant in the infantry was more
likely to be killed or wounded than any other rank. I
decided that I would not like that. I enjoyed the job I
had in the engineers. I thought it would be best if I just
stayed there.

About six weeks before we started on Tennessee maneuvers, there were two new men who came into the
company. They were more or less assigned to Lloyd and
I, one to each of us. We thought it was kind of odd, but
did not think too much of it at the time. Later on, they
will become more significant in the story.

Lloyd had an uncle who was a colonel in the German
army during World War I. His uncle had immigrated to
the United States. When he learned that Lloyd was going into the army, he taught Lloyd everything he knew
about German equipment, guns, arms, etc. Lloyd passed

all of that on to me. When the schools were held to teach us about German equipment and arms, Lloyd and I knew more about that subject than our teachers did.

One night, Lloyd was picked to stand in charge of quarters, (that means he was put in charge of the company office through the night). He was sitting at the captain's desk at about midnight. No one else was there, and he had nothing to do. Out of curiosity, he pulled open the desk drawer, and here, on top of everything else, was a dossier of the two new men who had come into the company and had been paired off with us. They were both FBI men. They had been assigned to Lloyd and I to try to prove that we were German sympathizers. From that day on, we really led them a merry chase. There simply was no evidence of us being German sympathizers, as Lloyd and I were both just as loyal Americans as anybody in the army.

We were all called out once and told that we were going on a thirty mile hike, in full field uniform, which included a 55 pound backpack, hand weapons (rifle), plus cartridge belts, canteen, dinner kit, etc. The camp record for that hike was six and a half hours, and we were going to break it. We would double time for a quarter of a mile, walk for a quarter of a mile, and continue that way. Every two hours we would get a ten-minute break. We had been told that when we got to the end of the hike, there would be trucks there waiting for us to carry us back to camp. We made the hike in six hours flat. We sat down for a half-hour of rest. We all had to pull our shoes and socks off so the company doctor could give us a foot examination, to insure that our feet were in good shape. Then they told us, "Sorry, boys, we don't have any trucks. We are going to hike back to camp. We just set a new record for this hike—six hours, and we are going to beat that record going home." Lloyd had blisters the size of a silver dollar on each heel, and his shoes were full of blood. I said, "You go to the medic and show him your heels, and get yourself a ride back in the jeep."

He would not do that, as he was just as stubborn as I was. He said if we were going to hike back, he would hike back with us, and that was all there was to it. I said, "All right, if you are going to be that stubborn, give me your rifle and I will carry it for you." There was another fellow who was the biggest man in the company who was about 6'5" and weighed almost 300 pounds who grabbed Lloyd's knapsack, and slung it on top of his own, which made 110 pounds that he was carrying on his back. We made the hike and Lloyd made every step of it. That was quite a hike, sixty miles in eleven hours and 45 minutes. We broke the record again going back by 15 minutes. Lloyd's feet took almost three months to heal.

Tennessee Maneuvers

After almost a year at Sand Hill (Fort Benning), we packed up and went on Tennessee maneuvers. We were not supposed to carry any personal luggage at all, but just before we started out, I went through all of the empty barracks, and gathered up about 400 coat hangers and packed them in a big suitcase. I hid the suitcase inside the compressor. Whenever we would have inspections or have to use the compressor, I would take the suitcase out and hide it in the brush. When maneuvers were over and we moved into Camp Gordon, there was not a coat hanger to be had! I sold out my 400 coat hangers at ten cents each, and made $40.00 off of them.

While we were on maneuvers, I had somehow managed to check my rifle back in with the supply sergeant. Sergeant Ellis, our first sergeant, was rather put out that I was not carrying a rifle when I should be. He checked a rifle out from the supply sergeant, but instead of giving it to me personally, he stood it against the tree next to my tent. When I came to the tent, I found the rifle there against the tree. I knew it was meant for me, but nobody had told me that, so I took the rifle back to the supply sergeant, checked it in to him, and told him that I had found it in the woods, and did not know whom it belonged to. When we had our next inspection, there I was again without a rifle. Did Sergeant Ellis ever blow his stack at me! "Spencer, where is your rifle?" I replied, "Sergeant, I don't have a rifle." He said, "I checked one out from the supply sergeant and stood it against a tree next to your tent. Where is it?" I said, "Oh that! I found it there and did not know whose it was or what it is for, so I took it back to the supply sergeant." He yelled, "You fall out of formation and go get that rifle!" So 1 did, and I kept it from then on.

Sergeant Ellis was mad at me, so he confined me to my tent. Anytime I was not on duty, I was supposed to be in my tent. I had a friend that was a jeep driver, and was the personal driver for the chaplain. He was moaning to me that he had to drive the chaplain every night, taking him into town and bringing him back when he was finished. He never had any evenings free. I said, "Shucks, why don't I just drive for you!" He said, "Would you?" I said, "Sure! Let's go see the chaplain." The chaplain was agreeable, so we arranged it, and in the evenings, I became his driver. I would drive him into town, he would go to visit friends, telling me to pick him up in three or four hours, so I would take off. I had my evenings free in town with a jeep to use. I know Sergeant Ellis was really burned up about that! There was not anything that he could do about it since the chaplain was a captain.

We had just changed bivouac areas when the whole division was given a thorough shake down inspection. That means that everything, our clothing, personal belongings, arms, equipment, vehicles, and etc. were thoroughly searched. Nobody knew what that was all about, not even the officers. We found out later that two lieutenants had been sent back to our previous bivouac area to check and see that it was thoroughly policed up, when they noticed a couple of pigs rooting in the dirt. When they went over to see what the pigs were trying to root up, there was a man's hand. They dug up the body, and it proved to be a major that someone had shot and killed. If, during that inspection that we had, someone had been found with even one round of live ammunition, they would have been charged with the murder, and probably would have spent the rest of their life in Leavenworth. However, no live ammunition was found, and it was never found out who shot the major.

There was one time when the engineers were building a pontoon bridge across a good sized river, I believe it was the Tennessee River, when I was standing by the compressor there on the shore and saw a fellow walking toward the river. I thought he looked a little funny, so I just watched him. He walked right up to the river, never stopped, but kept, right on going into the river. I thought, "What the heck is he doing?" Then it dawned on me! That guy was sound asleep! He was sleepwalking! I went into the river after him, and caught up with him just as the water was about up to his chin. I got him turned around, and he just kept walking right up to the shore and out of the water.

The Tennessee Mountains are mostly all rock, with just two or three inches of topsoil. Lloyd and I were kept busy with the air compressor and air hammer digging garbage pits and latrines. It was practically impossible to dig a pit with a shovel. We had strict orders not to dig any slit trenches or foxholes for the officers or anyone else. We could not even dig our own slit trenches with the air hammer. We were always making some officer mad at us because we would not dig their slit trenches for them, but there was not anything they could do about it, because they knew that we were right. General Newgarden had issued orders to the whole division stating that even when we wore fatigues, we had to have the sleeves rolled down and the collars buttoned. One day, Lloyd and I were digging a garbage pit when it was about 100 degrees in the shade. We just absolutely could not stand it with our sleeves and collars buttoned, so we had the sleeves rolled up, and our fatigues unbuttoned down to our waists, and we were taking turns on the air hammer, each one taking it for about 15 minutes while the other rested. When Lloyd took over for me, I went to get a drink of water. I walked around a clump of bushes, and ran into the Colonel. He said, "Soldier, get your sleeves rolled down and your collar buttoned up!" I said, "Yes sir!" I rolled my sleeves down and buttoned my collar. I went my way and he went his. As soon as he was out of sight, I rolled my sleeves back up and unbuttoned my shirt. I got my drink and started back to the garbage pit, walked around another clump of bushes, and ran smack dab into the colonel, almost knocking him over! He stopped to look at me, and said, "I thought I told you to button your shirt up, and roll down your sleeves!" I said, "Yes sir, you did." He said, "What rank are you?' I said "I'm a PFC, sir." He said, "You are now a private!" I said, "Yes sir, thank you sir!" I went on my way. That took care of my deal with the OCS, because that put a black mark on my record, and that automatically eliminated me from OCS.

Maneuvers lasted six weeks and in all of that time, I had not had one letter from my wife. I knew that there was something radically wrong. At the end of the maneuvers, we were all granted two weeks furlough. I did not bother to write and tell her that I was coming home on furlough. When I reached El Paso, I went to the boarding house where she was living. She was not there. She was at work. I talked to the landlady, and found out that she had been living with another man for almost all of the year that I was gone. I went in and packed up his things and set them out on the front porch. I told the landlady not to let the man back in the house. I asked her to tell him that if I ever set eyes on him, he'd had it! Irma had put the children in the Salvation Army home. I went over to the home to see the children. I found out that she had only been coming to the home about once a week to visit the children. The home charged a dollar a day each for the care of the children. She had not paid the Salvation Army any money in two months, so she owed $120.00 dollars, which I paid up. I went back to the rooming house to wait for her to come home. When she came in and saw me sitting there, she just about fainted. I had already made up my mind that because of the children; I would forgive her and take her back. After she got over her shock, we got things patched up and straightened out. We decided she would quit her job and we would take the children up to Delavan, Wisconsin and leave them with my folks, then she would go back down to Augusta, Georgia with me. My furlough papers called for me to go from Augusta to El Paso, and then from El Paso directly back to Augusta. I went to the Red Cross to see if I could get an emergency routing to allow me to go to Wisconsin, and then back to Augusta, but they said, "Sorry, they could not help me out on that." I said, "We are going to go anyway." We did and fortunately, we had no trouble. We took a train from El Paso to Chicago and then a bus from Chicago out to Delavan. We had no time to stay in Delavan when we got there, but just left the children. Then we took the bus all the way back to Augusta, Georgia. It was a pretty tiresome trip, but we lived through it. When we got off of the bus in Augusta, and got our bags together, we had a porter. When I reached into my hip pocket to get my billfold to give the porter a tip, I did not have a billfold. I made a hurried trip back out to the bus, which fortunately, had not left. I went to the seats that we had occupied, and there was my wallet.

When I got my first furlough before being shipped overseas, I needed a little more money than what I had. So I went to the Red Cross and borrowed $50.00. When I came back off of the furlough, the first thing that I did was go to the Red Cross office and pay that $50.00 off. I made sure they gave me a receipt for it. Time went on and we had a payday, and I was redlined. (Being redlined meant that you didn't get paid for some reason.) I asked a Captain, "Why am I being redlined?" He said, "You owe the Red Cross $50.00 that you haven't paid, and you will have to pay that before I can pay you." I said, "Sir, I have paid that, and I showed him my receipt. "He said, "Well, I'm sorry, there isn't anything that I can do about the redline now; you will just have to wait until next month to get your pay." The next month came along, and I was redlined again for the same reason. I explained things to the Captain, and showed him my receipt again. And again, I had to wait for the next month for my pay. Payday came, and I was redlined again for the same reason. That made three months that I hadn't received any pay. Well, I didn't say anything to the Captain this time. I just took my receipt and went over to the Red Cross Headquarters, and raised hell with them. I showed them my receipt and stayed right with them until they had it all straightened out. The next month, I received four month's payment.

Camp Gordon

We rented a room in the Dixie Inn, which was located directly across the station from the bus depot. An attorney named Jones owned the Dixie Inn. We found out soon afterwards that he was the most crooked attorney in the state of Georgia. As he had nobody in charge of the inn, we dealt with him directly. He wanted to know if we would be interested in taking charge of the inn for him, and managing it. He agreed to give us our room rent-free and five dollars a week. We agreed. The five dollars a week did not amount to much, but the room rent did. The Dixie Inn was on the second floor of a building with a restaurant on the first floor, which made it handy for us to get our meals.

After renting the room, I went out to the camp and went up to the barracks for the engineers. When I got there I could not find any of my belongings. I went down to see Sgt. Ellis and asked him where my barracks bags were. He said, "Oh, you have been transferred over to A Company, the 20th Infantry. We shipped all of your stuff over there. You report to the 1st Sergeant over there." I did not say anything, but went over to the 20th Armored area and walked into the 1st Sergeant's office. I said. "Ralph Spencer reporting for duty, sergeant." The sergeant's name was Braugh. He growled at me, "Where the hell have you been?" We have been looking for you." I said, "Oh?" then turned around and started to walk out of his office. He growled, "Where the hell do you think you are going?" I said, "I'm going into town to finish my furlough. I'll see you at midnight." That is what I did. Sgt. Braugh was waiting there for me at midnight. I turned my furlough papers in to him and he processed them. When he got through, I asked him, "How do I go about getting a transfer out of here?" The infantry was the last place in the world that I wanted to be! He growled, "You are in the infantry now. This is where you will be for the rest of your life!" I had a little money on me, so I pulled a hundred dollar bill out of my pocket and laid it on his desk, then said, "Sergeant, here is a hundred dollars that says I will see the day that you call me in here and ask me if I want to transfer out. Are you going to cover it?" He did not, as he probably did not have that much money anyway.

There were six rooms in the Dixie Inn. Previous to our taking over, the place had been a whorehouse. Of course, we did not dare to continue that type of operation, as I was in the army and the MP depot was only a block away. The MPs were already keeping a sharp eye on the place. Previously, the most that had ever been received in rental off of the rooms was $35.00 a week. Our first week when we rented to legitimate customers, all soldiers, we turned over $85.00 for the first week's take. That made him very happy, but he still tried to chisel us out of our $5.00 pay. We decided that if he was going to be that type of a person, we could play the game, too. We never turned in more than $85.00 a week, most of the time less. We were getting, anywhere from $75.00 to $150.00 each week. Once we rented a room to a major's wife. We kept an eye on her, and we soon found out that she was running tricks into her room. She would bring five or six men to the room every day. I did the only thing that I could do. I went down to the MP station and reported her to the MPs. They came down to the inn and caught her with a man. She wound up spending a year in the stockade for prostitution. I always wondered what the major thought about it all.

In July of 1944, our commanding general, General Newgarten, went to a conference at Fort Knox. When he was returning back to Camp Gordon, the light plane in which he was flying crashed in the mountains of Kentucky. Both he and the pilot were killed instantly. We were given a new general, General Morris.

One day, Sgt. Braugh called me into the office and asked me for the key to my toolbox. I asked him, "What do you want the key to my toolbox for?" He said, "Jim (the company carpenter) has a job to do, and he just does not have the tools to do the job, so you can loan him yours." I said, "Whoa, wait a minute, sergeant. Just back up there! Those are my personal tools and I don't loan them out to anybody! If you don't have the tools for Jim to do the job and you want the job done, I'll do it for you, but I am not loaning my tools out to anybody for any reason." That made Sgt. Braugh mad at me, and Jim, too, but there was not anything they could do about it, since I was in the right. So it wound up that I did the job, and then I wound up being the company carpenter. I knew that there was only one way that I would ever get out of the infantry. That would be to become a foul up and be such a bad foul up that they wanted to get rid of me, I did! I just quit soldiering right then. I had read the book of army rules and regulations, and I knew just how far I could go without getting court marshaled. I really made a name for myself in the company. "Foul up Spencer."

I was still having migraine headaches so I went on sick call one day, on a Monday, and was waiting for the doctor to see me when one of the boys staggered into the clinic, as white faced as could be. Anyone looking at him could see that he was in bad trouble. He said, "Doc, I know I have a ruptured appendix." It happened on Sunday, and he could have called a doctor in from town on Sunday to take care of him, but he did not want to louse up the doctor's day, so he waited until Monday to report in on sick call. The doctor looked at him and said, "There is nothing wrong with you! Get on back to your company and quit your gold bricking!" The boy didn't say anything. He turned around and walked out. He got out on the porch and collapsed. Just as he collapsed, an ambulance driver pulled up and saw him fall. He loaded him into the ambulance without saying anything to the doctor, because he knew what the doctor was like, and took him to the hospital, and a half an hour later, they operated for ruptured appendix. I made my complaint, but the doctor would not do anything for me. He was not about to send me to the hospital. He gave me a couple of aspirin and sent me back to duty. I did not even bother to take the aspirin, because I knew that they would not do any good. I went all that week without eating, because I could not eat because my headache was so bad. I went into town on pass on Friday night. I sweated it out there in our room until Sunday. Then I told my wife, "I am not going back out to camp Monday morning. You can call the first aid station, and they can come and pick me up. That way, they will put me in the hospital." That made ten days that I had gone without eating anything. I drank quite a bit of water and liquids so I was not dehydrated. On Monday morning at about 8:30, she called the MPs and told them that her husband was sick and had not eaten in ten days, and could not move, so they would have to send an ambulance. They sent an ambulance, carried me out on a stretcher and carried me to the hospital. They gave me a drug of some kind, I never did find out what the drug was, but it put me to sleep and I had on of the best, sweetest night's sleep that I had ever had. A nurse came around and said, "We have to give you an enema." I asked, "Why? I haven't eaten a bite in over 10 days and I have had a good bowel movement every day. There can't be, anything in me." That was the doctor's orders! They had to give me the enema. It didn't work, since there was nothing in me. They could not figure that out, so they gave me a second enema, then a third. When it didn't work, they could not figure it out. I told them, "Maybe you will believe me now. I have not had a bit to eat in 10 days. There is just not anything in there." The hospital was lousy with body crabs (lice). A friend of mine was there with a broken back resulting from a motorcycle accident. He was in a body cast from his neck down to his hips. He was real hairy on his chest, with as much hair on his chest as on his head. He was just being eaten alive with the body crabs. My wife would buy a couple of bottles of Campho-Phenque and bring a couple of wire coat hangers. We would pour whole bottles full under his cast. It would kill the body crabs instantly. He would straighten out coat hangers and use the wire to scratch himself with. The nurses would take them away from him when they found them. After five days in the hospital, I was sent to see an ear-eye and nose specialist. He was a full colonel, and was supposed to be a big specialist. When I walked in, he said, "What is wrong with you?" I said, "Well, sir, I have sinus and migraine headaches something terrible!" He said, "I've examined you, and there is not a thing in the world wrong with you." I had never laid eyes on the man until three minutes before, and he was claiming to have examined me. I said, "Sir, I've paid too damned many civilian doctors too damned much money to have them tell me that I have sinus and migraine headaches, then you stand there and you have never laid eyes on me until five minutes ago, and try to tell me that there is nothing wrong with me. I don't think you even graduated from medical school." I fully expected to get a court martial over that, but he ordered me back to my ward. Ten minutes after I got back to my bed, the nurse came and told me that the commanding general of the hospital wanted to see me. I figured that he was going to tell me that he was going to court-martial me. He asked me a couple of questions, I forget what they were now and he said "There is nothing that I can do for you I will have to send you back to duty." I went back and got my things together and reported back to the company.

We had made enough money running the Dixie Inn that we were able to send money to my folks to bring Janet down to us. One day we were out swimming in the lake. Janet was on the pier in shallow water, while Irma and I were further out. We called for her to jump into the water, expecting her to jump into the shallow water, but she ran to the end of the pier and jumped into deep water. Irma and I both almost killed ourselves trying to get to her, but even though she had never swam before, she was able to keep her head above water until we got to her.

We had six rooms in the Dixie Inn, occupying one and renting five, and there was one large bathroom for all six rooms. One day, we kept hearing the stool in the bathroom being flushed, one time after another. In the meantime, Irma was looking for a roll of one-dollar bills that she had left lying on the dresser, and she could not find them. She asked me if I knew where they were, but I had not had them. About then the toilet flushed again, and we both had the same idea at the same time. We made a break and headed for the bathroom. There was Janet with the roll of one-dollar bills. She would peel one dollar off the roll, drop it in the stool, and flush it down, and then another one. We were lucky. She had only flushed down eight or nine before we caught her.

One day, seven months after I reported for duty in A Company of the 20th, my squad sergeant told me, "The first sergeant wants to see you, Spencer.

I reported to Sergeant Braugh, who said, "Spencer, do you still want that transfer out of here?" I said, "You better believe I do."

He said "go over to the engineers and get a letter from one of the officers there saying they have a place for you and that they can use you, and you are out of here."

I said "Fine" and went over to the engineers to the headquarters company, but they did not want me back. I went on to C. Co. because I knew they were short-handed, and was given a letter saying they could use me and would take me. I took the letter back to Sgt. Braugh. He said, "be down here at six tomorrow morning with your duffel bag and be ready to go.

At six the next morning, I was there at the first sergeant's office, all packed and ready to go, and there was about sixty others there too. They pulled up with three two-and-a-half-ton trucks and loaded us all onto the trucks. All of us were foul ups and they did not want any foul ups when they went overseas. The trucks took us over to another section of the camp, dropped us off in front of barracks, and were told to report inside. We reported inside, where a first sergeant had a list of all our names. He made a roll call to make sure we were all there, I asked, "What is this all about?" I was supposed to go back to the engineers."

He said, "This is a radio school. We are going to make radio operators out of you. Do any of you boys know the Morse code?" I said I did. We attended the radio school, for about six weeks. They got three radio operators out of the bunch, and I was not one of them. The radio school lasted for six weeks, and they sent us all out to different units. I wound up in F Company of the 90th Rec. The second day in F Company, one of the fellows came up to me and said, "Spencer, the first sergeant wants to see you."

I thought to myself, "what have I done now? I haven't been here long enough to foul up." I reported to the first sergeant. He said, "I've got orders to send someone over to the railhead on a special detail. You are elected "

I said, "What are we going to do over there?"

He said I've no idea. I just got orders. You just get over there."

I went over to the railhead, and there was nothing there except a big empty field with a small group of men out in the center of it. I walked over there and found a Lieutenant and five privates there. I said to the officer," I had orders to report to the railroad. Is this where I am supposed to be?" He said, "It sure is."

I asked what are we going to do?"

He replied, "We are going to crate the division up for overseas shipment." He asked, "Are any of you boys carpenters?" Up went my hand. He said,

"Good! Do any of you boys know anything about box making?" Up went my hand again, since the last job I had before I came into the army was in a box factory making ammunition boxes in Houston.

He said, "Good, I am going to put you in charge of this little detail. I don't even know a hammer from a nail and even less about making boxes."

I said, oh boy I really got myself into something here." The officer told us that we had A-one priority for anything that we needed. He said, "Tell me what to get and we will have it the next day."

I told him that the first thing we had to have was a place to work. I told him to get six really large tents then we would need a lot of tools, especially hammers probably 200 hammers. Next we would need lumber of all sizes. We would need a lot of power equipment, such as cut off saws, and jigsaws. Then we went to pick out the location, where we would set up. It needed to be near the railroad, because we would need some rail service. We went and picked out the site. The Lieutenant said, "You boys take it easy for a while, and I will go get our supplies."

I told the other fellows that we should go get some dinner as it was almost dinnertime, and to meet back here at 1:00 p.m. When we got back at 1:00, there was the lieutenant with four big truckloads of supplies. I asked him, "How in the world did you ever get this stuff so fast?"

He said, "I told you we had A-one priority for anything we want. All we have to do is ask, and we have got it." We got the trucks unloaded. By the time we got the tents set up, we had a pretty fair sized lumberyard there. We had to start by designing workbenches and building them first. I went to work on figuring out the layout for the production line.

They got the tents put up, and I had the workbenches designed and the layout for the production line figured out, so I asked the Lieutenant about help, knowing we would need a lot of men to build boxes. He gave me a letter of authority, so I could go to the various companies and get two men from each company, as we did not want to take all of the men from one company.

I started out on my recruiting, and there was not a single first sergeant that I talked to that did not give me a hard time. They were not going to send any men; they could not spare them. I would show them my letter of authority, and say" Now do you want to give me those men, or do I have to instigate court-martial proceedings against you?" after some argument, I always got my men, we had about thirty men in the unit by then, and I set them to building workbenches. Among the fellows I had recruited was one who was a pretty good carpenter and I put him in charge of building the workbenches, while I went out to do some more recruiting. By the end of the first week, we had the tents up, the benches built, and we were getting the production line set up.

In the meantime the lieutenant had a fistful of orders for boxes of various sizes. Among the orders, there was one for 5,000 boxes. I took that one, and started making the breakdowns for it. It took 42 pieces of lumber of various sizes for each box. I had to determine the exact length and widths of each piece. I knew that by the time we got the first order completed, sawyers and assemblers would be pretty well broken in. That would give me time to make the breakdowns on the other boxes.

The Lieutenant was good to his word, and was there just to keep peace in the family and see to it that we got the equipment, lumber and, men that I wanted. When we got up to full strength, I had 264 men building boxes. I had complete authority over everything. I actually had more power than a company commander did. There were only two officers in the division that could give me an order. One was the second lieutenant in charge of my setup and the other was the commanding general of the division. In three months time we turned out 85,000 waterproof boxes. We had orders for all sizes and shapes of boxes, for example - we had one that was one inch high, one inch wide, and sixteen feet long. That was a dilly to make up. Of course we had orders not to make up any personal boxes for any one. That was posted on every bulletin board in the division. Of course there were always some that try to get a box made for them. I was making a breakdown for a box, and since my sawyers were about to run out of work. Some one pushed the plans for a box in front of me and said, "Here, I want this box made up." I did not even look up, but just said, "I'm busy making this breakdown, because my sawyers are about to run out of work. You will just have to wait until I get this breakdown finished." Half an hour later, I finished up my breakdown, turned around and looked, and there stood a full colonel. I said, "Are, you the one that wanted the box made up?" (I did not even bother to say sir to him). He said, "Yes, I would like to have this by tomorrow afternoon." I said, "This is for yourself." He said, "Yes."

I said "Well, I can't make it for you. We are not allowed to make up any personal boxes. I am not allowed to even make up one for myself, and not even for you. It is posted on every bulletin board in the division that we are not to make boxes for any one, and you know it." He left in a huff, but there was not anything that he could do about it, he knew I was right.

I was issuing over night and weekend passes to the boys. I had to have them Okayed by the lieutenant, but he always Okayed them. Two of the boys came up to me and wanted to know if I could get them a two-week furlough. They had been in the army for almost three years and had never had a furlough home. I told them that I would try, but could not guarantee it. I drew up the furloughs, gave them to the lieutenant, explained the situation, and he said, "Let me talk to the two boys."

I sent them over to him, after he talked to them a little bit he signed the furloughs and they took off.

After I had been in the box factory for about six weeks, I went back to my company area to get something out of my barracks bag, I ran into First Sergeant Walker. He growled at me, "Spencer, where in the hell have you been?"

I said," Sergeant, remember that little detail you sent me on over at the railhead?"

He said. Yes."

I said I'm still on it."

After that, I made it a point to visit the company area about once a week to let sergeant see me.

All of this time, I was missing out on all of the tests, details, hikes and whatnot, such as crawling through a mud hole under barb wire with a live machine gun firing about a foot over our backs.

I missed out on all of the tank training, even though I was in a tank outfit. That was irking Sergeant Walker, but there was nothing he could do about it. I should have had at least a Master Sergeants rating for being in charge of the outfit, but as it was, I did not even get a PFC stripe out of it.

We finally completed our last order of boxes, and then we had to tear all the tents down and check all of our equipment into division supply. All the men were sent back to their outfits. I finally reported back for duty to my company. It was just one week before we were due to ship out of Camp Gordon to Camp Shanks in New York for overseas shipment.

The night before we shipped out, Mac, a buddy of mine wanted me to go up to a little town in South Carolina with him. He wanted to see his girl friend. I said, "Mac, why don't we just stay here in the company tonight?" If we go up there, we are going to get in trouble." He was insistent. He had to go. So I said, "Alright, I'll go with you." We grabbed a cab and went up to the little town, and when we got up there, Mac directed the cab driver to a house on the outer edge of town. It was set back in the woods, and when we got there, there was no one home. We had the cab driver take us on down town, and we went into the only drugstore in town, where we each had a malted milk. I kept talking to Mac, and I told him, "Lets just get a cab and go on back to camp." Finally he agreed, and we flagged down a cab, we got into the back seat, and there was a sergeant in the front seat with the cab driver. When we started out of town, the sergeant said, "Do you boys mind if I stop for a second and say good-bye to my girl?" We told him to go ahead. He told the cab driver where to go. We ended up back out at the house of Mac's girl friend. This time she was at home. Mac started cussing. I told him to stay inside the cab and don't get out.

The sergeant got out and was standing at the front of the cab talking to the girl. Mac was getting madder by the minute. I told him, "Look, you have a wife and three children at home. That girl is not worth getting in trouble over. You just stay here." He said," She has an overseas cap of mine that I want." I told him, "I have six of the things back at camp, and I will give you five of them if you will stay in the cab." We never wore them anyway. Mac would not do that. He got out and said something to the girl. She turned around and went back to the house, and I figured she was going after his cap. She came back but did not have the cap, but she started waving her arms around in front of Mac. I saw him throw his hand up in front of his face, and then he sat down on the running board of the cab, and said, "I've been cut." I wondered what he was talking about, as I had not seen any knife. I got out, bent over to look at Mac, and he had a cut in his cheek, his nose was cut in two, and he had a cut clear through the palm of his hand. I looked around as the girl came at me. She had a two edged hunting knife with a leather thong in the handle and the thong around her wrist. She was not holding the handle, but was using the thong to whip the knife back and forth with the thong. I was standing against the front fender of the cab, and there was a big oak tree about three feet away. I was not about to let that girl cut me. I did the only thing I could in the time I had. I put my hands up on the fender of the cab, and came up with both feet and kicked her in the chest, slamming her up against that tree. I could see her eyes glaze as she slumped to she ground. I grabbed Mac and hustled him into the back seat of the cab. By then we could hear sirens coming. I told the cab driver, "Let's get out of here before those MPs get here."

We took off, leaving the sergeant standing there. I don't know whatever happened to him. If he were smart, he would have disappeared into the woods before the MPs got there. When we got into town, I had the cab driver take us to the first aid station. We went in to get Mac checked by a doctor and sewed up. We had to wait our turn, as there were at least six more ahead of us. There was one sergeant in the first aid station who had 57 stab wounds. Another fellow had shot himself in the foot, hoping he would go into the hospital to keep from going overseas. The doctor just patched him up and sent him back to duty. We finally had our turn, and the doctor sewed Mac up and we started to leave, when the doctor asked, "Don't you want to get your thumb sewed up?"

I looked at my thumb, and I had not realized that she had cut me too, there was a slice out of my left thumb hanging on by a thread. The doc sewed me up and we went on back out to camp. When we got back to camp, Mac said, "Boy, I really should have listened to you in the first place."

I said. "Yeah, but we are a fine looking pair to be going overseas now.

The day before we were to ship out, my friend Lloyd Huff was transferred out of the division to a company going to the Pacific. I guess they did not trust him to go to Germany. He was the only man in the division who I could not get to work at the box factory.

I mentioned once before that the company doctor (20th Infantry) was not a doctor at all. He was transferred out of our division to a division going to the Pacific, also, but he never made it to the Pacific. The authorities finally caught up with him, and gave him a dishonorable discharge out of the army.

We took a train from Camp Gordon to Camp Shanks. The train passed through Washington D.C., and stopped there for about an hour and a half. Since I had never been there and did not know when I would ever get back, I caught a cab and had him take me on a quick tour of the city, by the white house and the Capital building, which I enjoyed very much. I got back to the train with about 15 minutes to spare.

Camp Shanks

The first thing that we were ordered to do when we got to Camp Shanks was to get a haircut. We paid fifty cents for the haircut, and those barbers were something else. By the time we got comfortable in the chair, they were yelling, "Next," We had no choice about the type of haircut, as they shaved it right down to the scalp. We were a bunch of goofy looking skinheads.

While I was at Camp Shanks, I got one 24-hour pass into New York. I had heard a lot about Coney Island, the amusement park, so I spent most of my time there.

I don't remember the exact date, but on about the 12th of September, we left Camp Shanks, to board ship. The ship that I was on was called the Sea Owl. It was a liberty ship converted to a troop ship. In the holds, they had bunks six feet high with the top bunk just two feet below the ceiling. They were all 2' x 6'. We were not only supposed to sleep in the bunks and stay in them most of the time, but we were supposed to keep our barracks bag, our back-pack, rifle, ammunition belt, canteen, and eating gear all in one bunk. You figure out where we had space to sleep.

I was the last person to enter the hold, and all of the bunks were taken. They did not know what to do with me. Finally one of the ships officers brought me a folding cot. I sat it up underneath the stairwell. I had all kinds of space. I kept my barracks bag and all of my equipment under the cot, and I even had room to hang up my clothes on the bottom of the stairs. There was only one thing wrong with that. Fifteen minutes after I got setup, the boys started up a poker game on it. That game went day and night and never stopped until we landed in Cherbourg, France, eleven days later. If I wanted to go to bed and go to sleep, I just said, "Excuse me boys," crawled into the cot, and they just went on playing on top of me. I just wished that I could have had all the money that changed hands during that game.

It took us a day to load up, and the next morning, we moved out from the piers and headed for the ocean. Before we got out of New York harbor, one of the ships went aground on a sand bar. They couldn't get it loose, so they had to bring out another ship and transfer all of the men and equipment over to the other ship. That ship was 24 hours behind the convoy, and was by itself with no escort for three days until they finally caught up with the convoy. One day it was so foggy, that I was standing up in the very prow of the ship when we got a break in the fog, which came just in time. We were so close to the ship in front of us that I think I could have jumped over onto it. Another five minutes in the fog, and we would have rammed them in the rear.

I was fortunate that I did not get sea sick, while most of the other men in the company did. Except for one time when I had been put on KP duty and was sent to the galley to help out the cook. He put me to work cleaning out a large walk in freezer that had about a ton of natural food in it that had spoiled. I had to clean it out and get rid of it. I have a strong stomach, but I did think that I was really going to be sick before I got through with it. I managed to stave it off, and I never did throw up. Once I got that done and got back out into the fresh air, I was okay again.

The washing and shower situation was not good. All of the ship's crew and all of the officers had fresh water showers and fresh water to clean up in. The enlisted men had to take saltwater showers. They issued us some salt-water soap, but that was almost worse than useless, and you just could not get clean.

One day, about the seventh day out, we heard some thumps in the distance. We learned later on that it was a German submarine that was trying to get at us, but the ships that were protecting us had scared it off. It took us ten days to cross the ocean, because we were zigzagging all the way over. We got to the English Channel and anchored about a mile off shore from the White Clifs of Dover. That was all that we got to see of England. The next day, we sailed directly into Cherbourg, France.

We disembarked, were loaded directly on to trucks, and taken about 25 or 30 kilometers down the shore to St. Lo, where we pitched camp in apple orchards. Those orchards had no fences but big huge hedgerows for fences. The plots were all well kept up with nice green grass, just like our yards at home. By the time we had been there about a month, and it had rained a lot, there was not a blade of grass to be seen for a mile around, but just about six inches of mud everywhere.

France

Since I was new in the company, and had missed all three months of training exercises, and did not know a single thing about a tank, the first sergeant did not know what to do with me, so he put me on permanent KP. That was all right with me, as we were in a war zone, I considered it about one of the best jobs I could have. I was always with the kitchen truck, I always had hot meals while the others were eating C rations or K rations or doing without.

While we were bivouacked at St. Lo, being re-equipped, we were given the job of cleaning out mine fields along the beach (which we all loved). Most of the fellows were issued flashlights, however, being on KP, my T.O. (table of operations) Rating did not call for a flashlight, so I decided to make one for myself I got a straight stick, scrounged up three batteries, taped them to the stick, got a flashlight bulb and taped it to the top of the three batteries, took a tin can, cut it up and turned it inside out to make a reflector, and taped it above the bulb. It took quite a bit of doing, but I finally got it tightly enough that all contacts were made, and I could turn the bulb a little bit to make contact with the batteries, and I had a flashlight. It was actually better than most of the GI issue flashlights, since they only had two batteries, and I had three, making my light brighter. One morning before daylight, I was making my way over to the mess truck when my platoon Lieutenant saw me and called me over. He started to give me the devil for having a flashlight, saying I was not supposed to have one, so I must take it over to the supply sergeant and check it in right now. I answered, "Sorry, Sir, I don't think the supply sergeant would accept this flashlight." Oh yes he will" the lieutenant said. I showed him the flashlight, and told him that I made it myself, and I thought I was entitled to use it. When he saw the light, he could not say much. It was a good flashlight. At night, when I laid down in my pup tent, I would tape it to the tent pole and turn it on, and it was just like having an electric bulb there in the tent.

Before leaving the States we were told we could not take any white clothing overseas with us. If we had white shorts, shirts or handkerchiefs, we had to dispose of them, or dye them brown black or another dark color. At that time I had sinus trouble, and a pretty runny nose, so I needed a lot of handkerchiefs. I had about 75 or 80 white ones, which I dyed brown, so they came out a dirty brown looking color. At least I was able to have them with me. When we got overseas, I sat up a big 55 gallon drum, filled it with water, built a fire under it to boil the water, and that was our washing machine. It was quite a job to keep firewood on hand to keep the water boiling, since there was someone there 24 hours a day washing out their dirty clothes. After about a week, we learned that the French women in the area would do our washing and ironing for us for just a pack of cigarettes or a nickel candy bar or a can of food, they would do up to a month's washing for a bar of soap, they had not seen soap for four years, since the Germans took over.

Also, we got acquainted with the French beverage, cognac, most of us thought it was a better than our whisky, and for a pack of cigarettes, we could get a quart of cognac.

One night when I was out walking down the road, I saw two girls and a boy coming toward me. The boy decided he had to take a leak, so he just stopped right there in the center of the road, with a girl on either side of him, all the while talking to them, he unbuttoned his pants, pulled out his penis and started urinating. At first, I could hardly believe it, and then I found out that the French thought nothing of it, as it was a common thing, just a bodily function.

One day a French family invited me to have dinner with them. I went over that night for Supper and they had the table all decked out with a linen tablecloth, fine china and silverware, and they must have used up at least a week's supply of ration stamps on that one meal. I really appreciated the meal, and it was very good. For dessert, they had a cherry pie made out of whole cherries with no crust on the top. It really looked delicious They served me a piece, I took my fork, cut off a bite, put it in my mouth, and started to chew down on it, and almost broke my dental plate, because all of the pits were left in the cherries. Other than that, it was very good.

At that time, I could speak no French, and they could speak no English, but by the use of sign language, which we made up as we went along, we had a pretty nice evening of conversation. Sometimes it got kind of funny, when we wanted to get a particular point across, and we could not think of a sign or a gesture or motion that would describe it

At St. Lo, located right in the center of apple country, every thing for miles around were apple orchards. They had no fences, but they used hedgerows. The hedges were all old, large and thick, usually 7 or 8 feet high and about 6 foot wide. Some of the heaviest fighting on E day and the weeks that followed took place in those apple orchards. You could be laying on one side of the hedgerow with a machine gun set up, and a German could be laying on the other side, six feet away, with his machine gun set up, and neither would know that the other was there. Before the Germans would move out and leave an area, they would mine the whole area. Again, we had the job of searching out and destroying the land mines. It took us about a month to get re-armed and re-equipped.

The last week in October 1944, we were fully equipped, so we set out for the war zone, which was up near Metz, France. Metz was an old fortress, centuries old, and it had never been captured before. I guess the Germans thought that we could not capture it either. It took us a couple of weeks, but we did.

I was still on KP, and one afternoon as we were moving out, our first cook another KP and I were in the back of the mess truck, with two field stoves set up in the back of the truck. I don't know what happened, but one of them caught on fire. The first cook grabbed the burner, yanked it out of stove and threw it out onto the road. In doing that, he sprayed gasoline all over his back. He jumped out of the truck and his back flared up in flames from his neck down to his heels. I was standing at the end of the truck, so I grabbed my field jacket and the other KP, a short, rather plump boy that was usually slow moving, had his field jacket on. We both jumped, me first with him following, and how he did it, I don't know, but when he hit the ground, he had his field jacket off, and it was just a case of perfect teamwork. I caught the cook with my jacket from his neck to his waist and the other boy caught him from his waist to his heels, and we smothered the flames out. The cook jerked around and said, "What the devil is going on?" He did not realize that he had been on fire.

When cloth has been soaked in gasoline, the gasoline will all burn out first before the cloth starts burning. We were fast enough that we caught it before the cloths started burning, so the cook did not even have one burn on his body.

Our cook was from Kentucky. I can't remember his name, but he was a good guy and he was always looking for a large woman. He kept reminding us that if we saw one that was three axe handles across the rear, she was for him. He was the first cook and everybody liked him. He had a young fellow for his assistant that we always called Baby Joe who was just about 18. We got along good with them, but the mess sergeant was hard to get along with. After five weeks, I just could not stand the mess sergeant any more. I went to the Captain and asked him to put me in a tank. I told him that if I stayed there any longer with that mess sergeant, I would kill him. He must have had a pretty good idea what the sergeant was like, because he did not say anything, just put me into a tank.

I went in as a bow gunner. Although I did not know a thing about tanks, it did not take me very long to learn. I had fired 50 and 30 caliber machine guns in training, but I had never cleaned one. In our first engagement, up near Metz, we were sitting still in the tank and firing at the Germans up ahead of us. I was doing pretty well when I felt something ping off of my helmet. Not just one but many of them. I got scared. I thought it was enemy fire coming in on us. It literally scared the daylights out of me. Until I finally realized that it was not enemy fire. There was a 50-caliber machine gun firing right over my head. It was the empty shells from that gun that were pinging on my helmet.

After that engagement, I took my 30-caliber machine gun and a 50-caliber machine gun, field stripped them, cleaned them and put them back together without instructions from anyone. When your life depends on something like that, you learn fast.

We took over a large house and moved into it for the night. We were about half a mile behind the front lines. Our jeep driver, a very nice young fellow, and I went upstairs to see what we could find. There was nothing up there that was worth bothering with. The boy said," I'm going back downstairs." I told him to go ahead, and I would be down in a minute. When he was about halfway down, a stray shell just took his head right off. That was our first casualty. It was just an odd coincidence, but he was at the right place at the wrong time. If I had gone down with him, I probably would have had my head taken off too.

From Metz we moved over a few kilometers to just outside of Luxembourg City and had three tanks sitting out in the open. We were not in a battle zone right then, but a German plane came over and strafed us. We had orders not to waste any ammunition firing on a plane, because they were too hard to hit. All three of the tanks were mad as the devil about being strafed. We opened fire with all of our machine guns on the plane. One of us got lucky, we will never know which one, and hit the plane and brought it down. We expected to get chewed out for firing at the plane, but I guess because we hit it we did not get in trouble.

I'll take a minute to mention how we handled our laundry during battle. Any time we had a break for a few hours or a day, we would hunt up some French woman and have her do our laundry. They did not have washing machines, and many of them did not even have a scrubbing board. They would take the laundry down to the stream and do it like they did in biblical days, beat it on the rocks. When it came back to us, it was not only clean, but also starched and pressed, and they always did a very good job. They would do about a month's laundry for a cake of soap, a bar of candy, a pack of cigarettes or a little bag of coffee.

Over in France the Germans had put up concrete pyramids that were five or six feet high and about five apart in several rows called Dragons Teeth. They were supposed to stop the tanks and they did, for a couple of hours. We merely called in bulldozers, had them fill in the dragon's teeth with dirt, and built a road right over the top of them.

While we were in Luxemburg, orders came down to the captain to send a squad out to blow up a railroad bridge. Nobody knew just where the bridge was, and it could not be located on the maps. They were arguing about what to do about it when in walked a 16-year-old boy. The captain said, "What are you doing here!"

The boy said, "Do you want to blow up a railroad bridge?"

The captain asked, "How did you know about it?"

The boy replied," I was walking past your tent and heard you talking. I know where that bridge is."

The captain said, "Good! I'll send out a squad, and you can lead them to it." The boy said, "No, no squad! Just give me one man! A squad will make too much noise and we would never get to the bridge. The Germans would intercept us."

The captain was set in sending a squad out to do the job, but the boy refused to take them, insisting on just one man. Finally, the captain gave him a demolition expert and the two of them went out. They blew the bridge up and got back safely. When they got back, the boy said, "Give me a rifle! I am going to fight with you people." He did just that! The fact that he spoke fluent German came in very handy at times. He was really an excellent soldier.

Belgium

It was about the 15th or the 16th of December, when we were outside of Luxemburg City and got orders to make a night march down to a little town in Belgium called Bastogne. It was about a 75-mile march, and we made it at night, and it was COLD! That winter turned out to be the coldest winter they had in 50 years.

We were loaned out to an infirmary Colonel O'Hara to help out his troops. He stationed us at a little town about five or six kilometers out of Bastogne. We had been stationed at this spot for two or three days. Our tank was parked in the front yard of a farmhouse. We were taking turns, one man at a time, going into the farmhouse to get warmed up and take an hour's rest. The Belgian farmers were there. They had no time to get out and leave, and no place to go, so they just stayed in their home. They were good people and they welcomed us in. I was in one night at about 9:00 when their young son, about six years old, was having quite an argument with his folks. Finally they told him, "Ya!" When they did, he came over and took hold of my hand and said, "Cum." He led me across the room through a doorway into another room. Lo and behold, they had a Christmas tree set up and all decorated and lighted up. That was what the argument was all about. The boy wanted to show off the Christmas tree, and the parents did not think he should, but they finally gave permission to. In the middle of the Battle of the Bulge, our tank crew enjoyed a very nice Christmas tree. That was one Christmas that I will never forget.

Three days after we reached Bastogne, the 101st Airborne was trucked in. The 101st Airborne received all the credit for the Battle of the Bulge. They got all the publicity for it. The 10th Armored was on a secrecy list and although we were in Bastogne three days ahead of the 101st, we did not get any publicity at all for it. The 101st received a Presidential Citation. We finally received our Presidential Citation fifty years later.

At this time the Germans had us completely surrounded. They sent a captain in under a white flag with a letter demanding our surrender. The man was blindfolded, and they took him into Bastogne to General Morris. When General Morris read the letter, he merely said, "Nuts." He sent the man back. The Germans never could figure out what he meant by, "Nuts." Today there is a Nuts museum in Bastogne and it is quite a show place.

The weather had been kind of nasty, clouded over and snowing most of the time, and the air force had been grounded in England. We were running short of food, short of supplies, short of ammunition, short of everything. Then one day the skies cleared up and we had a beautiful, bright, sunshiny day. The planes started coming over. We could hear them in the distance, and when they came over, it was really a sight to see. There were over 5,000 planes that came over that day. They dropped us all kinds of supplies that day. About a third of them landed in German territory, which the Germans really liked. They loved the C rations and K rations, because they were short of supplies too, and had not had a decent meal in Lord knows how long.

Many of the planes went on bombing missions into Germany, but for eight hours, the sky was literally black with planes. Two or three days later, the 4th Armored Division managed to break through the German lines and come to our rescue.

It was at this time during the Battle of the Bulge, that the Germans had taken 35 or 40 prisoners. They were told that they would be taken back to a prison camp, but instead they were taken out into the woods near a little town called Malmedy. The Germans lined them up and then massacred them. I think that made the headlines back in the States.

We were stationed out of the town, and we were on the front lines, exchanging fire with the Tiger Tanks. All we knew was what we could see, as we were not given any information about how the battle was going. We were aware that we were surrounded, but we were not worried about it. We just did our jobs and cussed the Germans. The battle lasted 29 days from the beginning until relief came, and we were being shelled much of that time. The historians tell us that more than 56,000 Americans were killed in that winter's battle, and so were a whale of a lot of Germans. The Germans used 500,000 troops, 1,000 tanks and 800 planes in the attack. There are cemeteries for both sides. The German cemetery has all flat markers that cannot be seen unless you walk out among them. The American cemetery has thousands of crosses standing in rows.

Germany

Several incidents come to mind, and some may be out of order, but I will relate them as I remember them. After the Battle of the Bulge, the rat race across Germany began.

I don't know just where we were, but we were going down a long hill, on our way to reinforce the 20th Armored Infantry who were in a big battle, when we met a long line of German prisoners running up the hill. They were about four abreast, and after being taken prisoner, they were being run up the hill to where a PW Camp was being set up. The hill was a good mile long, with a gentle slope, but definitely a hill. There were no guards on the prisoners, but special guards were not necessary, as we were in a convoy, bumper to bumper. Every one of us was their guard. Once in a while, one would try to make a break for it, and someone would fire a shot over his head. He would get back in line in a hurry. I really felt sorry for those Germans, because it was good mile that they had to run uphill. They did not just walk fast, they ran! I believe all of them made it, but I often wondered how.

One time we had stopped in a town, I do not recall the name of it, and we were to be there for two or three day's rest. None of us had had a proper bath in over a month, so when we heard about a coal mine about thirty miles away where they had showers and plenty of hot water, we took a two and a half ton truck, which had no canvas top on the back, and twenty of us piled into the back of that truck in 0 temperature weather and headed for the mine. When we got there, we found the showers, but no hot water period. Rather than waste the trip, and mainly because most of us could not stand our own body odor, we all took cold showers. We piled back into the truck and rode the thirty miles back to camp. Believe it or not, there was not a one of us that got a cold out of that.

Another time, we were camped in the edge of a woods and I was pulling KP for the day.

As far as I knew, we would be camped in that spot for a couple of days. I had a little break, and I thought I would go for a little walk in the woods. I got lost and it took me three hours to find my way out of the woods. When I did, I had no idea in the world where I was. I could not even remember the name of the place where we camped. Like in civilian life, whenever you need a cop, you can't find one. I tried to find some MPs, but it took a couple of hours just to find one. When I did I told them who I was, what my outfit was, and that I just wanted to get back to my outfit. They started making some phone calls, and after about a half hour, they hit it lucky and found out where I was supposed to be, which was about five miles from where we were then. They put me in a jeep and took me back to my camp, but when we got there, there was no sign of my outfit. They had received orders to move out immediately. The kitchen truck was just pulling out when we pulled up. I got out of the jeep and into the kitchen truck. The cook wanted to know where in the heck I had been. He said that he stayed behind to wait for me, but had given up and was about to take off. I told him that I just went for a walk but I got lost and it took me half a day to get back. But it turned out okay.

The 10th Armored received orders from Patton to move in and take the city of Trier. We rolled into Trier around ten in the morning and by six that evening, we had the city secured. There was some light fighting, but the majority of the German troops had pulled out and left the town. The next day, Patton received a telegram from Eisenhower telling him to bypass Trier, as it would take three divisions to take the city and he could not spare the troops. He planned to have some other outfit mop up the town after we bypassed it. Patten sent back this answer to Ike. "Have already taken Trier with one division. What do you want me to do? Give it back to the dammed Germans?"

We moved into Sieric (sp?), France for a three-day rest and I became aquatinted with a French family. They invited me over to have supper and spend the evening with them. I knew a few words of French by then and they spoke a little English, so we had quite a time conversing. It turned out that the man was a jeweler and had a jewelry shop before the invasion. They had the worst looking stove, refrigerator, washer and dryer that I had ever seen, just the black cast iron framework with no enclosing panels. I asked how they ever came up with that kind of equipment? He said, "When we knew the Germans were coming in and taking over, they would loot everything that looked good and ship it back to Germany, so we pulled all of the panels off and buried them. As a result, the Germans took one look at our things, and would shake their heads and go on. They did not want anything that looked that bad. The equipment worked just as well without the panels as it had with them. He said, "Tomorrow, I intend to dig up the panels and put them back on."

They had bathtub, and I had not had a bath in a couple of weeks. I asked if he minded if I took a bath? They said, "No." They had a coal burning hot water heater, so the wife went in and fired up the hot water heater, and I had a good bath.

I asked if he had a small, fine gold chain that I would be able to mail back home in a plain envelope. He said, "I'll have to go get it. Excuse me. I'll be back." About forty-five minutes later he came back with a double handful of gold chains. All of them were mixed together and entangled with each other. They appeared to be wet and I asked, "Where did you get these?" as I thought he had gone to his shop to get a chain. He said, "Before the Germans came, I took all of my stock and dumped it into the well (which was in the basement of the house), so that the Germans could not get their hands on it. I fished them up out of the well. It took the three of us about three hours to get them all untangled and straightened out. He gave me a fine gold chain, which was exactly what I wanted. When I left, they insisted that I come back the next night, and when I did, I brought them two packages of K rations and about a dozen cans of C rations, four cakes of soap, and five packs of cigarettes, which I gave to them. Cigarettes were going for about $25.00 to $30.00 a carton on the black market at that time. They had not seen a bar of soap since the Germans took over and they were really tickled to get my little cache of supplies.

Another time, we were in a small village, stopped for a couple of days rest, and I was on KP again for the day. That day right after breakfast, we received our first beer ration that we had received since coming overseas. We took off from work right after breakfast to enjoy our beer. There were four of us KPs. We drank our beer, a couple of bottles of wine, and the cognac that we had, and by that time we were feeling pretty good. One of the fellows said, "You know, that Sergeant Walgreen has a quart of very fine blackberry brandy that he has been saving and I know where it is." We told him, "What are you waiting for? Go get it." He did and we drank that up. By that time, one of the fellows had passed out, and the other two could hardly sit up, let alone walk. I was the only one still walking, but I won't say how steady that walk was. The sergeant came in (not knowing we had stolen his brandy) and saw the condition we were in. He asked, "Spencer, can you navigate?" I said, "Yep." He said, "Take the kitchen truck and go to the water point and fill all of the water cans. We need it for dinner." I loaded up all of the water cans except the one that was full, and took off. It takes 50 gallons of water to prepare a meal and clean up afterwards. I got to the water point, and there was a big long line of trucks, probably 30 trucks, waiting to load up with water. I fell into the line and after about half an hour, I realized that the line had not moved up at all, and thought that I was not going to get any water if I sat there until midnight. I pulled out of line, still feeling pretty good, and went over to the neighboring town, where there no American or German soldiers in town. When I got in there, the Burgomaster latched onto me and insisted that I be his guest for the day. He told his wife to get busy and fix up a good dinner for me and took me all around town, showed me everything and told me all about the town in his fairly good English. He introduced me to several frauleins. From then on I had a good looking one on either arm who went wherever I went. That did not make me mad. I had a good dinner, enjoyed the afternoon, and had a great supper, and finally decided that I had better get back to the company.

I was feeling pretty good, and I had had quite a bit of good schnapps during the day. I got back to the company area about 9:00 p.m. without any water. It took at least 50 gallons of water to prepare a meal and clean up afterwards. I had left just one five gallon water can with the company. The nearest water was a hand pump about a block away. The mess sergeant and the two cooks had to walk to the pump, pump the can full, and carry it back, prepare the meal, serve it, wash up afterwards, and then start to carry water again for the supper meal. I felt sorry for the two cooks, but I did not feel the least bit sorry for the mess sergeant. Nothing was ever said about that day to the officers. It was a standing order in the division that if a sergeant had any of his men foul up, the sergeant was responsible and he could be broken down to a private for it. Wallgreen was scared to death for fear of losing his stripes, and did not dare say a word. He did not even ask where I had been or why I did not have any water.

One night we were making a forced march to somewhere, and it was about 2 a.m. We were on a concrete highway. There were eight vehicles in the convoy, two

Jeeps in the lead, four tanks, and then two more jeeps at the tail end. All of a sudden the second jeep blew up! It just went sky high! All four men in it were killed. When that happened we came to a very sudden halt. We were in a minefield. It had to be a hasty minefield, as the mines were scattered on the surface of the road. We just sat there until daylight. That was all we could do. When it got light enough for us to see anything, I looked down and there was a nice big mine about six inches from the track of our tank. The lead jeep had gone completely through the minefield, and was out of it. If the second jeep that had blown up had gone 20 feet further it would have been out of the minefield too. As it was all the rest of the vehicles were still in the minefield. Fortunately, that jeep was the only one to hit a mine. We had to clear the minefield before we could move. We were on level land, so we got out and I got a rope out of the trunk of the tank, fashioned a noose in one end of it, slipped it over the mine, tightened it very carefully, extended the rope to the end, about 150 foot, and then pulled the mine off the road onto the grass, very carefully and very slowly, until it was about 200 feet away from the tank. In the meantime, the others were doing the same thing with the other mines. We got them all off the road and into the field without setting any of them off. Then, we took our machine guns and blew the mines up. After that we were able to get on down the road again.

Another time, we pulled into a town that had been taken about an hour before. As we pulled up to the town square, there was one of the goriest messes that I have ever seen in my life. There was a pile of 12 or 15 dead soldiers piled up, and a tank had turned around over the top of them (not our tank). I sure felt sorry for the graveyard detail that had to clean that up.

We pulled into a town called Rotz, a fair sized city, with two roads going into it and two going out of it on different sides. After we got to the bridge that we were to secure in the center of the town to keep the Germans from blowing it up, C Company was supposed to follow us in and reinforce us. This was at dusk. They decided that they did not want to move into the town after dark so they waited until morning to come in. We got down town with the four tanks and one jeep. One tank was posted at the bridge, one tank on the roads going east, north and south. The jeep circled among the tanks. There was a lot of German soldiers in the town, but they must have been tired of the war, because they started surrendering to us. After we had about 20 prisoners, we realized that we had no way to guard them, so we just disarmed them and sent them on their way. When others turned themselves in, we just took their weapons and told them to get.

We took over one house that had a room on the ground floor that our squad was using to sleep in. I went in and lay down, pulled my shoes off and stuck them under my head for a pillow. The sergeant asked me, "Spencer, what are you doing with your shoes off?" I said, "I'm going to get some sleep, and I hate to sleep with my shoes on."

He said, "What would you do if a German slipped in here and threw a hand grenade at us? And you without your shoes on?" I said, "Sergeant if that happened, I sure would not need my shoes, I would be dead." With that I went to sleep. When I woke up the next morning, I noticed that some of the others, including the sergeant, had pulled their shoes off to.

Along about 3:30 at night, we were awakened by machine gun fire. I could hear someone screaming. It turned out that was a woman with two children in a boat who were trying to get to the Americans. The guard in the tank on the bridge had spotted them, and not knowing who or what they were, had fired a few rounds over their heads. When he heard the woman scream, he stopped firing and called her on in. About seven thirty the next morning, C Company finally came in to reinforce us.

Another incident occurred one day while we were traveling along a highway - we could see a German soldier on a bicycle on another highway about a half mile away Our gunner on the 75 said, "Just stop the tank for a minute." Although we had orders not to waste the 75 ammunition on a single target, he lined up and fired one shot, and the soldier on the bicycle just disappeared. That boy was one of the best gunners we had.

Another time, we moved in to take a fair sized city. There were three hills surrounding the city, and we had a tank parked on each one of the hills. At that stage in the war, rather than open fire on a city immediately, we would send a jeep with four men into the city to contact the Burgomaster (mayor) to tell them that if we met no resistance we would not do any damage to the city. There was a road that led down into the city with an S curve at the edge of the city where there was a clump of trees. Our jeep with five men in it started down the road, and every thing was fine until they got in front of the clump of trees. The Germans had an anti tank gun set up in the clump of trees, which we did not know about. The jeep got into point blank range, and a shell was fired into the jeep, blowing it up and killing all five boys. Our gunner said, "I'm going to lay a shell right down the barrel of that damned gun."

Of course, once they had fired at the jeep, they had given their position away, and we could then see the gun. Our gunner lined up on the anti tank gun as they were lining up to fire at us. He fired one shot, and we could see the barrel of that gun burst apart! He had done exactly as he had said he would do, put a shell right down the barrel of that gun.

After that, we sat there on the hilltops and blasted away at the city. The town was practically leveled. There was only one large building standing when we finished. Then we moved on in and met no further resistance.

We set up our headquarters in the building that was left intact and I went exploring in the building. I opened a door into a room and went in, there was hardly room to enter as it was packed full from floor to ceiling with packages of all types. I thought, "What the devil are they storing in here?" This was at a time when it was impossible to buy a clock in the States at all, an alarm clock or any other type of clock. Clocks of all types and descriptions were packed into that room. They had looted them from other countries.

This was about 6:00 p.m. and we got orders to move out of there, and take the next town about six kilometers away. With our three tanks we moved out, and got about five kilometers up the way. We reached the foot of a large hill, and the Germans were dug in at the top of the hill, in front of the town. The Germans opened fire on us, and they had the advantage, since we were sitting at the bottom of the hill and firing up at them, and they were dug in firing down at us. There was a patch of woods off to the right and another off to the left with a couple hundred yards of meadow in between them. We had a pretty good battle going there when two deer came out of the woods on the right, headed for the woods on the left. All of us in the three tanks had the same thought - to heck with Germans, get the deer - and opened fire with three thirty and three fifty caliber machine guns on the deer. Well despite everything, the deer made it across safely. We must have fired close to a thousand rounds of ammunition and never hit them. By that time it was getting pretty dark, so we folded up and went back to the headquarters in the city we had leveled. The next morning, we went out to take the town, and we sailed right on in without any opposition. The Germans had pulled out during the night and had retreated to the next town down the line.

Once we were making a forced march to reinforce C Company, who was in a very heavy firefight, trying to take a fairly large city. There were four of our tanks, an armored car and a couple of jeeps in our convoy. It was night, close to midnight, and we were moving right along when someone opened fire on us with a rifle. One man with a rifle against four tanks and an armored car! We came to a halt and opened fire on him, but he was laying in a slit trench right by the edge of the road, and we could not depress our guns down low enough to hit him. Our tank was right opposite of him, so I grabbed a grenade, pulled the pin and tossed it at him. It did not hit him, but was close enough that it made him decide to surrender. He came out of the slit trench calling, "Don't shoot! Don't shoot!" in good English. He was a First Lieutenant in the SS Corps. We took and set him up on the front of the lead tank and told him to just sit there. We said, "If we get fired on, you will be the first one hit!" We moved on into the town and joined in the firefight. He never got hit, and we turned him over to a PW pool that C Company had set up. The Germans put up a real fight for that city, but by morning when it started to get daylight, they were, leaving the city or surrendering. The big fight was over, and we occupied the city.

Like I said before, some things will be out of sequence, and this is one of them.

About two weeks after landing at Cherbourg, we were all issued new sleeping bags. Naturally, I was the last one in the company to get mine. I got just the outside cover and no insides for it. I kept after the supply sergeant for a couple of weeks to get me insides for my sleeping bag. But, he never did. I guess he probably couldn't get one. So as we were moving up through France, I kept seeing blankets along the side of the road that someone had discarded. I gathered up three of them, and every time we stopped for a break or an overnight stay, or a day to rest, I would work on those blankets. I cut them all down to a shape that would fit into the outside cover that I had, and sewed them all together. Of course, this was all handwork. But, I had an excellent sewing kit that my stepmother had put together for me. It took a lot of doing, and I took a lot of razzing from the fellows, but I was darned if I was going to freeze to death at night. And, cold weather was coming on. Now on the new sleeping bags that had been issued to everybody, the zipper was on the outside, and once you had crawled into the bag, you had to reach outside to zip it up. When you got it zipped up, you had a heck of a time of getting your arm back inside. So, on mine, I put the zipper on the inside, and after I had crawled in, it was a simple thing to zip it up on the inside. Using the three blankets, that gave me triple thickness all the way around. There were some nights when it was ten to fifteen below zero that we had to sleep out on the ground, and I was just as warm as toast all night long. Of course it made a very bulky roll, about three times as big as the GI issue. One day, one of our first lieutenants approached me, and wanted to buy it from me. He offered me $100.00 for it. I told him that I would sell it to him, but he would have to give me his officer's sleeping bag (they are much better than those issued to the GIs). But, he said he couldn't do that, those bags were for officers. Then he raised his price. I still wouldn't sell to him. He finally went up to $250.00. I still wouldn't sell to him, because the $250.00 wouldn't do me any good, and I would be freezing my fanny off. He got pretty mad at me about that. He held a grudge against me the rest of the time that we were together. Then he ordered me to get rid of my bag, because it wasn't a government issue. It was too bulky, took up too much space and didn't have enough room to store it. I just kept the bag, and tied it on the outside of the tank, where there were all kinds of room for it, and used it all winter long.

I guess this would be a good time to say a little about life in a tank. Up in the turret floor, there is a space large enough for one man to lie down and sleep. It was a corrugated steel floor, but you would get so tired that you could go to sleep as the tank traveled along. There were no bathroom facilities, so if we had to urinate or move our bowels, we would wait until the tank came to a stop for a few minutes, then grab our little trenching shovel, jump off of the tank and into the field, dig a hole, squat over it and do our job, then fill the hole up again. It did not matter if it was daylight, and at times there were a lot of refugees walking down the road. They would holler at us and make fun of us. We carried enough beer, wine, whiskey, vodka, and cognac on our four tanks to stock an average tavern back in the states. We usually carried two or three dozen eggs in the tank so that we could fry some eggs if we had an opportunity. We would build a little fire and fry the eggs in our helmets. One time we were stopped and we knew that we would be stopped for a quite a while. One of our boys said, "I'm going to get some eggs for us."

He went up a little way to a farmhouse and knocked on the door. When the people came to the door, he asked them for some eggs, maybe a dozen, just enough to make a meal for all of us. The woman went into the kitchen, came back and handed him two eggs. He started back to the tank, and we could see him with an egg in each hand, looking back and forth at those eggs and getting madder by the minute. He was close enough that we could hear him when he said, "They can't do this to me!" He turned around and went back to the farmhouse. The people were still standing in the doorway watching. He got up to them and told them to hold their hands out. When they did, he mashed the two eggs into their hands. Then he pulled his pistol, pointed it at them, and said, "I know you have eggs in here, and I want them! If I don't get them, you are dead!" They took him into the house and about fifteen minutes later; he came back out carrying a big basket piled high with eggs. There must have been ten or twelve dozen eggs in that basket! He got back to the tank with the eggs and said, "Do you know where they had these hidden?" We could not guess, so he told us that they had taken him upstairs to their bedroom, opened the door to the clothes closet which was piled full of clothes, and started digging in the clothes to come up with this basket of eggs. He said, "I only wanted about a dozen eggs to begin with, and if they had given him the dozen, that would have been the end of it. When they gave me two eggs, that was insulting my intelligence, and I just could not let those Nazis get away with that!"

Another time, we pulled up in front of a farmhouse and stopped. There were three chickens running around. We got out and managed to catch the chickens. We snapped off their heads, took them in to the farmwoman, and told her to pluck the chickens and cook them for us. She was upset about that, as they were the last three chickens that she had. She got them plucked, and put them into the oven to cook just as we got orders to move out. She saw that we were leaving and had a big smile on her face. She thought we would leave the chickens and she would get to eat them. It did not work out that way. We put the chickens into a bag, hung them on the outside of the tank. It was in the winter, and below zero, so the chickens froze and stayed frozen. Three days later we were able to thaw out the chickens and have ourselves a chicken dinner.

If we wanted to take a bath, we would have to build a fire, fill our helmets full of water, heat the water in the helmets, strip down and take a sponge bath out of the helmets. One time, one of the fellows had just heated his water and stripped down naked when the Germans pulled a surprise counter attack. We had to take off in a hurry! Right now! He was a sight, running for his tank stark naked. It was either that or stay there and be captured by the Germans.

During the war, the Red Cross put on a big campaign stateside to gather up cigarettes for the boys overseas. The people were generous, and they managed to collect enough cartons to fill up one ship. The cigarettes had all been donated to them, but instead of giving them to the boys, they went through the hospitals and sold them for fifteen cents a pack. At that time, we could buy cigarettes for a nickel a pack through the Army Commissary.

One of the fellows in my outfit was supposed to get a nice jacket for Christmas; his mother had bought it and sent it to him. She wrote him a letter describing the jacket to him and told him, "If you will open up the lining, you will find a $20.00 bill inside right over your heart." She said that she was sending it through the Red Cross, so that he would be sure to get it. He never got the jacket. One of our Lieutenants got a five-day pass to Paris. When he came back he was wearing a new jacket. The fellow happened to see him and recognized the jacket from the description his mother had given him. He told him, "Sir, I think you are wearing my jacket." The officer said, "Oh no I'm not. I just bought this jacket in Paris." The boy said, "Who did you buy if from?" He said, "Well, I bought it from the Red Cross." The boy said, "I know that it is my jacket and I can prove it." The officer said, "How?" The boy said, "Well, if you will just open up the lining on the inside there, you will find a $20.00 bill on the inside." Well, the officer pulled the jacket off and opened up the lining, and there was the $20.00 bill.

Once when we pulled back behind the lines for a day's rest, the Red Cross truck pulled into the area and pulled up by the kitchen truck. This was 8:00 a.m. in the morning. We had just finished breakfast and everybody was fully coffeed up. The two girls turned everything over to the mess sergeant then disappeared with the officers. The mess sergeant had the KP's set up their shop, make the coffee and hand out the donuts. That was quite a deal for the KP's, as they had to do their own work in cleaning up after breakfast in order to get ready for dinner, and also make the coffee for the Red Cross girls, which nobody wanted right at that time. They had had all of the coffee that they could have for breakfast. We never did see the girls until they were ready to leave in the afternoon. Then people wonder now days why I don't have any use for the Red Cross.

I had always been clean-shaven, but I decided to grow a beard and mustache once. I went for six weeks without shaving. My face could hardly be seen. It got to itching so badly that I could not stand it, so I shaved it all off again, and that was quite a chore! I felt a lot better without the beard and mustache. I have never been tempted to grow one again!

We had orders to move out and take a big mining city. When we got to the city, there was not any real opposition, so we moved right on into the city. Along the main street, the people would watch out of the windows and in two or three places, there were American flags flying out of a window. From the next window, there might be someone sniping at us. We would stop at the house and go in to clean it out, and we usually found that the sniper was a 12 or 14 year old boy who belonged to the Hitler Youth. That was the only opposition that we had in that town. A large river, flowing down the center of it, divided the town. We were moving into the center of the town to take the bridge before the Germans destroyed it. As we pulled into the center of the town, in sight of the bridge, we could see a huge mob on the other side of the river. As we pulled in, they broke loose and came across the bridge. There must have been about 5,000 of them. They were slave laborers that the Germans had working in the coal mine. They were waiting there for us to appear. When we showed up, they knew that they were free! They flooded in around us, stopping the tanks because they were packed around us so tightly. They clamored over the tanks, and one big filthy, smelly Polack just reached down and grabbed me under the armpits and hauled me out of the tank, wrapped his arms around me and gave me a big bear hug and started kissing me. I did not like it, but I had to take it, because I could not do anything else. We were all being treated that way! After things quieted down a little bit, one of the first questions they asked was, "What kind of a president will Truman make?" We responded that we did not know, as Truman was the vice president, and Roosevelt was the president. They said, "Oh no, Roosevelt died last night! Truman is president now!" That is how we found out about Roosevelt's death. Those slave laborers knew about it because they had hidden radios that they were listening to. No word had come down to us, yet. In fact, it was about three days before we got official notice of Roosevelt's death. Later that afternoon I had some free time and knowing that we would not be moving out for a couple of days, I decided to explore the city. I was about a mile from downtown, walking down the center of a wide street with no other Americans within a half-mile of me, when I heard the tramp of feet behind me. I turned around and looked, and there was a whole company of German soldiers, about 250 of them. The captain was in front with his side arms. I thought, "Oh boy, I've had it now!" I got off of the street onto the sidewalk, and they just went right on past me. I don't think a one of them even looked at me. We had a seventeen-year-old boy from Luxemburg who had joined up and had been fighting with us since Luxemburg. Here he was at the tail end of the company, with a little carbine slung under his arm. They were all his prisoners! He spoke good German, and he talked to the burgomaster who told him that there was a company of Germans in the woods waiting to surrender. He went out by himself and brought them in. I had not had decent gloves and my hands were always about half frozen. The captain had a big pair of aviator gloves, which I helped myself to. Man, were they ever nice and warm! After that, I did not have cold hands anymore.

Another time, we pulled into a little group of farmhouses along about dusk, and we stopped in front of a house where we could hear the phone ringing. One of the boys who spoke excellent German went in and answered the phone. It was a German colonel in the next town down the line who was calling to find out if the Americans had reached that point. The speaker told him, "No, no sign of the Americans at all. Since it is getting dark, they probably won't show up until tomorrow!"

Unlike in America where every farm had its own farmhouses in Germany they did not live on the farms but either in town or as in this case, in a group of a half dozen farmhouses grouped together, and went out from there to work their land. This was the only time during the war that we dug a foxhole. We only had three tanks at that time, so they were out posted, one on the east, one on the west, and one on the south, with nothing to the north. We went in behind a farmhouse on the north side and dug a foxhole. It was about 10:00 p.m. when we got the foxhole dug. I was the lucky person to draw sentry duty in it! I was to stay until 2:00 a.m. when I would be relieved. There was an expanse of land to the north, and we knew if the Germans came, that was the direction they would come from. I don't know how long I had been out there. I had a wristwatch but it was too dark to tell the time. It may have been a half-hour, or it could have been two or three hours. I had been concentrating on the field to the north when I caught out of the side of my eye, a man coming toward me. It scared me, and I just froze! And I mean froze! Seeing this man coming toward me, I could not say a word, not even move my eyeballs. I was straining to see him out of the side of my eye, and he kept getting closer and closer. Finally, I said to myself, "Spencer, old boy, you have to do something. He is going to be heaving a hand grenade in on you!" I finally managed to shake my head, and when I did, I could turn my head and look to where the fellow was. Lo and behold, there was no man there! What I had seen was a little group of trees way off to the right. One tree stood out separate from the others. That is what I had seen. My imagination had done the rest of it. I don't think I have ever been as scared as I was at that time!

After Trier, we fought our way up to Worms, taking several cities and villages in route, and two or three thousand German prisoners. Worms was a fairly large city, and we were told that we would have a couple of day's rest there. Our company took over a large old house, and after we were moved in, I went exploring a little bit. In a closet across the hall from the kitchen, I found three huge gunnysacks that stood about six feet high and were about three feet in diameter. I was curious about what was in them, because when I felt of the sacks, I felt hard packages with sharp corners on them. I opened one of them up and they were full of American cigarettes, carton after carton of Lucky Strikes, Camels, Chesterfields, Marlboros and a few other brands. This was at a time when we were short of cigarettes in the company, and there were enough cigarettes there to supply the whole company for a month. I guess what had happened was that our planes had bombed a red cross train by mistake, and the people had looted the cigarettes out of the train.

The first cook was trying to prepare dinner for us in the kitchen. He kept stepping on a board that squeaked and felt loose. Being curious, he wondered why only one board was squeaking. He bent down and took hold of the board, which was completely loose, pulled it up, and there, under the floorboards, were 800 pounds of sugar. We were also short of sugar, but from then on, we had all of the sugar we needed for the rest of the war. We got about 16 hours of rest there, and then received orders to move on down the way at about 10:30 at night.

We moved out and started down the road and were about three miles along the way when we came onto a long convoy that was pulled off of the side of the road, just sitting there. We pulled off of the road, at the tail of the convoy, and had just stopped when we got orders over the radio for the three light tanks that had just stopped at the end of the convoy, to bypass the convoy and come to the front. We did not know what was up, but we knew that it meant trouble for us. We bypassed all three miles of that convoy, and when we got to the front, there was a large river and the engineers of my old outfit, the 55th Engineers, and they had thrown up a pontoon bridge across the river. The Germans had a field gun on the other side of the river and had managed to hit the bridge and set fire to it. That whole bridge was blazing, and had things lit up like daylight! The engineers were right beside it, throwing up another bridge. Colonel Sheffield, was in charge of the crossing and told us, "As soon as that bridge is completed, you get those tanks across there and knock out that field gun!" All we could do was say, "Yes sir!" although we did not like the idea very much. A twenty ton tank crossing a pontoon bridge has to travel at a rate of about two or three miles per hour. It was not too long until the engineers had the bridge finished, and we started across. We were looking every second for the Germans to hit us or hit the bridge and knock it out, dropping us into the river. But we made it across safely. We went on up the hill and knocked out the German field gun, and then we went on our merry way. There will be more about this bridge later on in the story.

After the river crossing, we were moving fast, covering twenty, thirty, and sometimes forty miles a day. The whole division wound up at Crailshiem. Being a reconnaissance outfit, we were the first ones in to Crailshiem. We pulled up to the railroad depot in the center of town, and just as we did, a troop train pulled in and stopped. About 200 German officer cadets got off of the train to spend the night in town. They were not armed and walked right into our hands. Instead of a night on the town, they spent the night in the PW camp that we set up. We moved on out of Crailshiem about 12 miles to a little town called Illshoven, where we took over a house and set up our headquarters. Each tank got one room in the house for a bedroom. There was a large apple orchard in front of the house. We were assigned the task of running a road patrol between Illshoven and Crailshiem. The way it was set up, one jeep and one tank were sent out every two hours. We had our tank parked under a large apple tree and we were standing out by the tank talking to the company doctor. He was new, having joined the company two or three days before. The German planes came over and strafed us. My buddy and I dove under the tank, and the doctor tried to make it, but could not. After the planes were gone, we got out and were standing there, and the doctor told us, "You boys show me how to get under that tank. If they come back again, I want to get under there!" I told him, "Well, Doc, if they come back again, you will not need anybody to show you how to get under that tank!" Right then, another group of planes came over, strafing us again. You had better believe that the doctor beat us under the tank!

At 10:00 p.m., our tank drew the road patrol. We started out with the jeep in the lead. Just outside of Illshoven about a mile, we sideswiped a truck, and upset it into the ditch. We never stopped, but just kept going. We did not know whether the truck that we sideswiped was American or German. As we got close to Crailshiem, we could see that the sky was lit up, almost like daylight. There was a large airport on the outside of Crailshiem, where the air force was flying in gas, food supplies and ammunition to us. Just before dark, the Germans had come in and strafed the airport, and had set fire to a big B-47 transport plane. It was burning, lighting up the sky. We went on into Illshoven. We turned around and headed back, and just as we got past the airport, just beyond the light and in the dark again, we got hit by a German infantry patrol with panzer Faust. They had infiltrated in and were lying in the ditch at the roadside. They fired one panzer Faust, and the burst was so bright that it blinded me. I absolutely could not see anything. I felt the tank lift almost straight up into the air! I figured that it was from the panzer Faust blast that had gone off underneath us. Then the tank dropped back down and we started rolling. We got about 150 yards into the field when the tank engines conked out. I heard the tank commander yell, "Fire! Everybody out!" I still could not see anything but believe me, I was out of that tank and onto the ground with my Tommy gun. We knew that a good many of the panzer Fausts had been fired at us, but after about five minutes with no further activity, the tank commander told the driver to get back in and see if he could restart the engines. The engines started right up, so we all got back into the tank. By that time, my sight was beginning to come back. We started out across country in a wide circle, figuring to make a half circle in the field and come back onto the road beyond the ambush. What we did not know was that there was a small dirt road coming in at an angle with a bank about four feet high on either side of it. We hit that, doing about 12 miles per hour. I was standing up in the cockpit, the tank commander was standing on top of the tank, and that little side road was almost a perfect tank trap! We nosed down into it at such an angle that we buried the nose of that 75 into it on the other side. I happened to look up and saw the tank commander flying over my head, going headfirst like he was shot out of a gun. I did not have a chance to think! I just threw my arms up, wrapped them around the tank commander and pulled him back down. He grabbed the muzzle of the 75 for support. I really saved his life there, because if I had not grabbed him, he would have hit head first on the other side of the road and with the speed he was going, it probably would have broken his neck and killed him. The tank driver started the engines up, put it in reverse, and managed to back up out of the roadway. He squared the tank around so that he could ease it down one bank and up the other. We went on our way. We got back into Illshoven, and as we got out of the tank, the tank driver asked," Spencer, did you see that that tree we hit?" I said, "No, I was blinded." He asked, "Didn't you feel the front rise up in the air?" I said, "Yes, I felt it but thought it was from the Panther Faust." He said, "No, we hit a tree that was so big that you could not wrap your arms around it. We uprooted it and kept right on going." Believe me that was the night we really learned to love those tanks.

The next morning about 8 a.m. we went out to see about the truck that we had sideswiped It was an American truck and was lying on its side in the ditch. The driver was sitting by the truck, waiting for someone to come along. Thankfully, he was not hurt at all. We hooked onto the truck and set it up on its wheels. I ran a cable from the back of our tank and hooked onto the front of his truck and we started to pull him out of the ditch. I was standing about half way between the tank and the truck and about 15 feet from the tank. I heard something rattle off the pavement and looked down to see bullets hitting the pavement about six inches from me. I never gave it a thought! I just went up into the air, made an about face, and made a beautiful swan dive under the tank. I figured that I would lose about half the skin off my face and arms. I slid under the tank, slick as a whistle. I never had so much as a scratch.

The Germans had a new jet plane with no motor on it. It could not be heard until it was past you. One of them had come over and done the strafing. That, incidentally, was the last day that the Germans had a plane in the air.

After he had gone, we managed to pull the truck out of the ditch, and we sent the driver on his way. We went on up the road to check out the ambush sight. When we got there, sure enough, there was a tree. I got out and tried to wrap my arms around it, but I could not do it. On the other side of the road, there was a stack of Panzer Faust shells stacked up very neatly. There were thirteen of them. They had fired 13 shells at us at point blank range, and had never hit us. It must have been some Hitler youths who had no training.

We had been moving so fast that we were way ahead of our orders. We were fifty miles beyond where we were supposed to be. I guess we were supposed to go the other direction, and not gone into Crailshiem at all. We got orders to withdraw from the Crailshiem area and go back fifty miles to rejoin the rest of the army. Our unit packed up and left, except for our tank, which drew the job of rear guard.

We were parked on the south side of Illshoven with a view across the meadow for about five miles. There was a big hedgerow, about eight-foot high, running parallel north and south, so we could not see off to right at all, just straight ahead. The tank commander said, "Here, Spencer, take these binoculars, go around the hedgerow and pick out a spot and stand guard there, if you see anything coming, let us know. Otherwise, if we want you, we will sound the siren. If you hear the siren, come running."

I went around the hedgerow and found a slit trench that some one had dug where I could stay. The whole division had pulled out and forgot about us sitting out there as rear guard. I stayed out there in my position for six hours, from 10 a.m. to 4 p.m. in the afternoon, and that was really a lonely vigil. Finally, I heard the siren. I took off at a run and got back to the tank and was climbing up the outside to get into the tank when I heard the tank commander say, "Don't fire until Spencer gets in." I thought, "Where in the world did the Germans come from?" I had a clear view of five miles for six hours and had only seen one person about three miles away.

I was just about to climb in the tank when the 75 was fired. All hell broke loose! I went in headfirst and was trying to claw my way through the steel floor to get out of it. The other three men were just laughing their heads off at me. What had happened was that there was a wagonload of German ammunition about 150 yards out in front of the tank. I had forgotten all about it. One 75 shell was fired into the wagon and you talk about 4th of July fire works, we had it. After I calmed down and found out what had really happened, I had a good laugh about it to, but at the time, I think I was even more scared than I had been in the foxhole.

Some one finally remembered that we had been left behind as rear guard and radioed back to tell us to come on and join up. There we were, one tank and four men deep in German territory without another American within fifty miles of us. Not a very good feeling. We started out and after about three hours, we finally crossed over the American line.

We were passing through a small town, which had only been taken about an hour before. The citizens had all been warned to stay inside and off the streets. The town had cobblestone streets and it was raining, which made it very slippery for the steel tracks of our tanks. The streets were so narrow that we only had about 18-inches clearance on either side of our tanks. We were passing through a section of town that had a 10-foot concrete wall on the right-hand side.

There was a woman running alongside this wall. As we came up even with her, the tank skidded and the front of the tank brushed against the wall, catching the woman and pulled her underneath the tread of our tank. We had run halfway over her by the time the driver got the tank stopped.

I had to get out in front of the tank and direct the driver as he backed off of her. The tank treads had caught her from her hips down to her feet. She was mashed out to about an inch thick and was stretched out almost 6-feet from her hips to her feet.

There was a doorway in the wall about 10-feet from us and a woman came out of it and the two of us managed to pick the injured woman up and carry her into the courtyard. When I got back to the tank the driver was standing in front of it. He said, "Spencer, you're going to have to drive. I just can't do it anymore." That's how I became a tank driver.

I forget the exact location of this incident, but we were traveling a highway and we could see in the distance, planes zooming down, evidently strafing something. We could tell that they were on our side, because by then the Germans did not have a plane in the air. Finally, the planes must have run out of ammunition or gas, because they gave it up and headed home. About an hour later, we reached the spot where they had been strafing It was a German convoy, a huge one ten miles long. They had completely devastated the entire convoy! The convoy was made up mostly of horse drawn vehicles but there were also a lot of motorized vehicles, including three or four tanks. They had killed everything in that convoy. There were dead horses and men all over the place. Even a few cows that had been used as horses were dead. The devastation was so horrible that I really can't begin to explain it. It was so bad that Eisenhower, Bradley and Patton all made a special trip up there to see it. I believe it took us about 5 hours to traverse the length of the convoy, because we had to get out and remove dead bodies, dead horses, burned out jeeps, half-tracks, and three tanks and other trash off the road. After Crailshiem, we moved into Bavaria and our last mission of the war was to take a bridge across a large gorge before the Germans could blow it up, which we did. The Germans had the bridge fully mined but never had a chance to blow it up.

Along the way, we passed through a fair sized city, and for some reason we were stopped. We looked across the street and saw a bank with the front of it blown off. We could see the vaults inside, but the vault door was locked. The little gunner on the 75 said, "No problem. I'll open it up." He turned the 75 around, took aim and let off one shot. He was right the vault was opened up wide. We went in and helped ourselves to over a million dollars worth of German marks. It was good money, and we divided it between every one in the company. We did not know that we could spend it in the stores ourselves, so we were handing out big handfuls of marks to all the refugees that were on the road. That made them happy, and we knew that they could use it. When we learned that we could spend it in the German stores ourselves, we only had about $1,500.00 worth of marks left, which we turned into the company fund.

At one time after the war, one German woman gave me a big cardboard carton full of German marks. This was inflationary money remaining from WWI. I think a mark is worth about a dollar today. In that box, I found one 2,000,000-mark note, and at the time it was printed, it was probably worth about ten cents. She told me that back then, if you wanted to buy a loaf of bread, you had to have a wheelbarrow full of paper marks in order to buy one loaf of bread.

The War Ends

I was not in on this incident but Company C of the 55th Engineers, following up information received from German prisoners and using metal detectors, found a cache of gold near Walchensee that included 728 bars of gold, each worth about $15,000.00, and about $400,000.00 dollars in American money. There were other smaller but similar caches found by the Allies throughout the country, including art masterpieces in a salt mine.

We moved into a small town called Pieting, where we settled down, as the war was over. Our company took over about 20 houses along one street. We just moved the people right out and took over. Along the street there was a park where we parked our tanks. Since I was a carpenter, the captain called me in and told me to make up 500 coat hangers. I said, "Well, Sir, I am going to need some equipment. Some power saws, band saws, sanders..."

He said, I think I saw a carpenter shop a couple of blocks down the way. Go check it out They should have equipment like that." I found the shop and the owner was in there, busy working. I told him what I wanted and he said, "No way he was to busy and could not be bothered with me. I said. "Let's look at it this way. You have a job to do (he was building a new house) and I've got a job to do. We both want to get those jobs done. I'll let you go ahead and do your work and I'll do mine. If that is not satisfactory, I'll call the MPs and have them lock you up. I'll go ahead and do my job, and you will be in jail and not be able to do anything.

He did not like that, but he had to go along with it. He had a nice supply of lumber so I used his lumber and his tools and cut out the 500 coat hangers. When they were sanded and varnished, I was stuck without anything to make the wire hooks from. I went scouting around town, and in the window of a hardware store, I spotted a big spool of heavy wire. I went in and took a look at it, and it was ideal for the coat hangers. I went back to the captain and got written orders to buy the wire. I took the spool back to the shop and finished up the hangers, told the owner, "Thanks a lot" and went back to the company with the coat hangers.

The house that we were billeted in was a two-story house. Half way up the stairway between the two floors was the bathroom. It was just like one of our outside toilets at home, except it was inside the house. One day, we came to the house, and there was the worst stench in the yard and the house, it almost turned your stomach. The woman who owned the house was mad because she had been put out of it and we had taken over, so she came by that morning and cleaned the toilet and dumped it in the front yard for fertilizer. She had done it on purpose to get back at us, because the toilet had not really needed to be cleaned out. There was little that we could do, except put up with it. It did take about two weeks for the stench to disappear and the air to get back to normal.

About two days after I finished the hangers, my first lieutenant told me, "I'm going to send you to carpenter school. Maybe you can learn something."

I said, "Fine. That sounds good to me the school was in Garmish, and Garmish was one of the twin cities. The other was Partinkirkshen. They were big resort cities. In fact the 1936 Olympics had been held there. They were right in the heart of the Barvarian Alps, some of the most beautiful scenery I had ever seen. I found the school located in an old hotel, which was small, quite old, three stories high, but beautifully kept up. They had one ballroom on the third floor for the school. I had a beautiful bedroom on the second floor for my living quarters.

When I reported up to the ballroom for the class,

they're about 12 men there, but no instructor. The major in charge of the school learned that I was a carpenter, so he put me in as the head instructor. I was in charge of it all. Later when I was back in the company area, I ran into the first lieutenant. He said, "Dam it, Spencer, I sent you there to school to learn something, and they made you the head instructor."

I said, "Well, sir is there anything wrong with that?" He just turned around and clumped away.

That assignment lasted for about three months. I managed to get a couple sets of carpenter tools various saws, rip saws, hammers, squares, couple of power saws, and other tools. I think I did a pretty fair job of teaching there, since the others had no knowledge of carpentry, but when they left, they all knew a little something about carpentry.

During that time, they decided to celebrate the division's third anniversary by holding a big fair. They wanted it to be something like a state fair. I got orders to take my whole class out to the grounds to build all of the booths. They wanted an archway built across the entranceway. That archway took a little doing, because we had no steel beams and it had to be fabricated completely from wood. We got a good supply of ten-foot 2 x 12s, and by nailing them together in six layers, we made a 40-ft. beam twelve inches thick and twelve inches high. We fabricated the two end posts the same way. When the end posts were planted and in position, I went to the motor pool and got them to send out a huge wrecker used for pulling in tanks. That wrecker was used to lift the crossbeam and set it on the two posts. Then one of the fellows, who was a good artist, took a piece of half-inch plywood, drew the outline of a tiger on it and we used the bandsaw at school to cut it out. There was also an art class there, so one of the artists painted the tiger on both sides of the plywood. It was hoisted up onto the archway to complete it.

Patton came in for the celebration, and when he saw

the archway with the tiger on top of it, he thought it was a pretty good piece of engineering, and asked to meet the man who built it. So I got to meet Patton and shake his hand.

There were all kinds of booths there at the fair, several serving food, hot dogs, hamburgers, cheeseburgers, ice cream and cotton candy. About 15 game booths were set up, and somewhere, they had found a circus, so there was a three-ring circus. It was really a blowout. It lasted for three days.

We had a ten o'clock curfew in the city. One day when I had been out exploring, I was at the far side of the city having forgotten all about the curfew. When I looked at my watch and saw that it was 10 o'clock I figured, "I'm in for it now." The MPs were pretty strict about picking up curfew violators. I headed back for the hotel, which was about a mile away, and I was slinking along in the shadows, taking cover wherever I could when the MPs spotted me. I saw them as they saw me, and I knew that they had spotted me, so took off at a run, cutting through yards and over fences. They had to leave their jeep to chase me on foot. At one point, I came up to a big house with a high fence that I knew I could not get over, so I tried the front door, which was unlocked, and went in. I went up the stairs to the second floor into a bedroom where a man and a woman were in bed. I said, "Guten tag!" to them, then went right on out of their bedroom window, onto the porch roof, and dropped down to the ground. I don't know what those people thought when the MPs came through their bedroom, too. I went around the house, around to the back, where there was a porch with a low flat roof I got onto the roof and laid down flat. It was not long until the MPs came around. Thank the Lord, they never thought to look up on the roof. When they could not see me any place, they gave up and went back to their jeep. I lay there for about 45 minutes until I was sure the MPs were long gone. Then I dropped down to the ground and made my way back to the hotel, and got back to my room safely without getting caught. Fun and games!

Partinkirkshen sat right at the base of the Zugspitz Mountains. There was a big ski resort on top of the mountain. There were two ways to reach the top: one was a cable car lift that went up the side of the mountain. It started about a quarter of the way up the mountain and went up to the top. At one point, the cable car is about 600 feet above the ground. It is quite a thrill to ride the cable car up. The other way is a cog railroad. It started at bottom of the mountain, and about half way up, went into a tunnel that zigzagged back and forth. When the train comes out of the tunnel, it is on the other side of the mountain at the top. I went skiing there, the only time in my life that I have ever skied. It was in the middle of July and I stayed on gentle slopes and flat land.

During the war, infection was never heard of. A person could be wounded and lay in mud and filth for a day or two before receiving medical attention, and never have infection. Immediately after the end of the war, the hospitals were flooded with infection cases. I had a little scratch on the back of my left hand that did not even draw blood, but infection set in and it took me six weeks to get it cleared up. I had an ingrown eyebrow hair over my right eye while I was at the carpenter school in Garmish, and infection set in, and there was ball of pus that just kept growing. I had to go to the doctors in Garmish and they would not help me, they said I had to go to my company doctor. I went back to my company to see the doctor, and he told me that since I was on special duty he could not treat me. He sent me back to the doctors in Garmish. They also refused to help me, sending me back to my company doctor again. By that time the ball of pus had grown so big that it had completely closed my right eye. The company doctor tried to send me back to the doctors in Garmish again, but I told him, nothing doing. I want this thing lanced, and I want it lanced right now. If you won't do it, I'll go back to my room and take a jackknife and do it myself.

I guess I convinced him that I meant what I said, because he got out a scalpel and lanced it for me. It did not take him five minutes to do it. He took out a ball of pus half the size of a golf ball and gave me some Epson salts to soak it with. I did that for two days and it just kept draining. I went back to him and he sent me to the hospital in Garmish. They gave me penicillin shots every three hours, day and night for nine days before it started to heal up. I was in the hospital for almost three weeks as the result of an ingrown eyebrow. While I was in the hospital, I ran across a Red Cross girl who was in the hospital, too. I asked her what she in for and she said, "I got a dose of the clap." I replied, "That will teach you to stay away from these GIs."

She said," It was not a GI who gave it to me, it was a German civilian."

After I got out of the hospital, I was sort of at loose ends. The company thought I was still on special duty, but the carpenter school had been closed down and they thought I was back on duty with my company. As luck had it, I met a couple of fellows when I was trying to hitch a ride back to the company area. In talking to them, I learned that their company had gone off on maneuvers for a couple of months and had left them behind to guard the company area. They had a jeep and all the gas they wanted. They were just out seeing something of Germany. Instead of going back to my company area, I joined up with them. For the next two weeks, we went sightseeing all over Bavaria. We tried to get into Austria, but we needed a special pass from the commanding general to get across the border. Anyway, we really enjoyed our two weeks of cruising around Bavaria. They decided that they had better get back to their company area and make sure things were okay, and I figured I had better get back to my company. When I got back, I just reported in, and that was it. Nobody had missed me.

The town where we were stationed was called Pieting

was near Oberamergau where the famous passion play is held annually. It was kind of odd, but one pattern was repeated throughout Germany. There would be three towns. The first one you came to would be Unteramergau, then came Amergau, then Oberamergau. They had not had the Passion Play for several years during the war, but they were getting ready to have it again that winter. I was hoping to be able to go to it. However, they shipped us home before the play was scheduled to start.

From the website, Bavaria.com, here is a description of one of the opulent castles visited two or three times after the war, and a couple of times since. Especially impressive were the solid gold statues.

Linderhof

Probably King Ludwig's preferred castle, a true rococo jewel case. It resembles the "petit Trianon" (Versailles) and is the only one of the three castles that was actually completed. Located close to Neuschwanstein, the King often retired to Linderhof to indulge in his "loneliness." Italian, French and English style gardens extend to the front; in the middle a fountain emits a 100-foot high jet bathing the golden statue of Flore. But it's the castle itself that holds the boldest of Ludwig's fairy tale realizations: the Venus grotto made entirely of cement with artificial lighting, rainbows, wave machines (and heating) to recreate what is described in Wagner's Tan Hauser. You can also find a bronze statue of the much admired Sun King and an elevator-table which disappears below the floor into the kitchen to be filled with succulent foods only to reappear completely set.

I was able to visit the dining room described and watched the table function. There was a teahouse there that had originally been built by India for the 1890 Worlds Fair in France. King Ludwig saw it and fell in love with it, so after the fair, he bought it and had it moved to Bavaria. In this teahouse, there is a glass peacock, which I believe is the most beautiful thing that I have ever seen in my life! The rooms were all very ornate! They were decorated in 24-carat gold. King Ludwig was a very large man, and in his bedroom was a very small bed, only ten-foot long and ten-foot wide! After building that castle, King Ludwig started another castle, planning sixty rooms for it, which was to be more ornate than the Linderhof castle. He got it about half-finished when he ran out of money. He became so despondent because he had started something that he could not finish that he walked out into the lake and drowned himself. More information on King Ludwig's life and his three magnificent castles can be found on the web site, Bavaria.com.

I was not back in the company but two or three days when I was given another special assignment. I was sent to another town outside of Garmish where they had a huge German PW camp. I reported in there and was assigned two busloads of German prisoners, about 40 to a bus, and told to escort them back to a point near their hometowns. That was to keep them off of the highways, clogging them up. We were given three days to make the round trip. The busses were old German busses, and naturally, parts could not be found anywhere. We had only gone about 20 miles when the second bus broke down. The rear axle was broken, and it would have taken weeks to get it repaired. We pulled it off to the side of the road and told the forty Germans, plus the driver and his assistant that they were on their own to get home any way they could! I went on with the first busload of prisoners. It is kind of odd, but the driver was named Fritz, the assistant was named Hans, and they were a couple of good people who had been in the Wermacht, the German regular army. I had my Walther automatic that I had taken off of a German captain in a shoulder holster and an M-1 rifle. I never did like the rifle! It was just too heavy!

The second day out, I gave the rifle to Hans and told him to take care of it for me, which he did. He did a beautiful job of caring for it. On the way, we pulled into an army gas depot to refuel. Hans told me, "When we get in there, get the attendant and take him behind the building somewhere so that he cannot see what is going on." I did, and while I was talking to the attendant and keeping him occupied, some Germans got off of the bus and hijacked about 70 gallons of gas, which they loaded on the bus. I signed a receipt for 25 gallons of gas, and we went on our way. We were supposed to make the trip in three days, a day and a half up and a day and a half back, but we made the trip up in one day and started back home. We did not go directly home, but made a wide swing through Germany. It took us three weeks to get back. Hans and Fritz had made the trip before, and they knew where to go. They picked up refugees along the way and charged them fares. We always had a full bus. We passed through Wiesbaden, which was Hans' hometown in the center of the wine country. While we were there, we picked up 48 bottles of prime champagne, 3 five-gallon jugs of white wine, and one five-gallon jug of red wine. From then on, we stayed drunk for the rest of the trip. For our meals, we would stop at an American depot and I would go in and have my meal. I would inveigle the cooks to put up a couple of meals for Hans and Fritz. Some of the cooks would give me an argument - they were not putting up meals for Germans, but I always managed to convince them to do it. At night, we would pull off to some little Hamlet off of the beaten path, and Hans would get in touch with the burgomaster and have him find me a room for the night. It had to the best one in town! They really took good care of me that way!

All of the time I was on special duty at the carpenter school and escorting German prisoners home, everyone in the company was receiving furloughs to England, which I missed out on because I was not in the company area. They also received a week at the Tigers Lair, which is in a large hotel on the Eibsee, a lake about half way up the Zugspitz Mountain. I also missed out on those. One day shortly after I rejoined the company, after my tour of Germany with the German prisoners, the captain called me into the office and told me to pack up my things and be ready to leave, as he was transferring me to another outfit that was being shipped home, as I was high point man in the company at that time with 82 points. That afternoon, the first sergeant called me into his office and wanted to know if I wanted a furlough to England. I told him, "Sergeant, I want a furlough to England, but two hours ago, the captain told me that he was sorry, and the furlough went to a replacement, who had just joined the company the day before.

Everybody was on a point system, so many points for each month of service, combat, special assignments and so on. Anyone with 85 points at the end of the war was flown home within a week's time. I had a Purple Heart, received for a very minor wound, and the doctors gave it to me and said that they would send the paperwork down to the company, but they never did, or the papers got lost en route, and the Purple Heart was never entered on my service record. It was worth five points. If I had received that five points, I would have had 87 points at the end of the war, and could have flown home the first week with the others. But I did not, so I sat there with my 82 points.

"*Terrify* and *Destroy*

10

TIGER
TRACKS

These are the "TRACKS" of the Tiger Division in its preparation as a fighting unit

TIGER TRACKS

WE of the 10th Armored Division have chosen to call ourselves "Tigers" because of the tiger's many soldierly characteristics. Tenth Armored "Tigers" should be able to describe to their friends, as well as be able to impress their enemies, with these tiger qualities. The "Tiger" is primarily a field soldier. He is at home in the field, jungles, or woods. His motto is to "Terrify and Destroy." He is able to carry out his motto because of his marvelous muscular development, smooth coordination, his ability to maneuver and surprise his prey; and when he hits, he hits hard, and shoots straight at the mark with devastating accuracy. No one ever saw a fat "Tiger"—he keeps himself in perfect condition—not to mention his coat, which is always clean and neat. The "Tiger" has one weak spot—he hates water, but he can be taught to swim.

The "Tiger's" favorite attack is made in the dark—he has such a good sense of direction, and he has worked so much in the dark, that he never gets lost. The "Tiger" never quits. He is the most ferocious fighter in the animal kingdom. We have 12,000 "Tigers" that will never be licked!

Major General Paul W. Newgarden.

The Wig Wag Flag was used for signaling before being replaced with Morse Code.

10th Division's shoulder patch

Ralph Spencer's medals and other insignia

ENLISTED RECORD AND REPORT OF SEPARATION
HONORABLE DISCHARGE

1. LAST NAME - FIRST NAME - MIDDLE INITIAL	2. ARMY SERIAL NO.	3. GRADE	4. ARM OR SERVICE	5. COMPONENT
SPENCER FAZELL R	38 247 622	PFC	CAV	AUS

6. ORGANIZATION	7. DATE OF SEPARATION	8. PLACE OF SEPARATION
CPT 90 CAV RCN SQ	28 Oct 45	SEPARATION CENTER FORT SHERIDAN ILLINOIS

9. PERMANENT ADDRESS FOR MAILING PURPOSES	10. DATE OF BIRTH	11. PLACE OF BIRTH
532 2nd St Delavan Wisconsin	26 Sep 1918	Kenosha Wisconsin

12. ADDRESS FROM WHICH EMPLOYMENT WILL BE SOUGHT	13. COLOR EYES	14. COLOR HAIR	15. HEIGHT	16. WEIGHT	17. NO.
See 9	Brown	Brown	5-10 3/4	165 lbs.	3

18. RACE	19. MARITAL STATUS	20. U.S. CITIZEN	21. CIVILIAN OCCUPATION AND NO.
WHITE X NEGRO OTHER (specify)	SINGLE MARRIED X OTHER (specify)	YES X NO	Carpenter General

MILITARY HISTORY

22. DATE OF INDUCTION	23. DATE OF ENLISTMENT	24. DATE OF ENTRY INTO ACTIVE SERVICE	25. PLACE OF ENTRY INTO SERVICE
23 Nov 42		23 Nov 42	Houston Texas

SELECTIVE SERVICE DATA	26. REGISTERED	27. LOCAL S.S. BOARD NO.	28. COUNTY AND STATE	29. HOME ADDRESS AT TIME OF ENTRY INTO SERVICE
	YES X NO	2	Houston Texas	913 Lee St El Paso Texas

30. MILITARY OCCUPATIONAL SPECIALTY AND NO.		31. MILITARY QUALIFICATION AND DATE (i.e., Infantry, aviation and marksmanship badges, etc.)
Carpenter	050	None

32. BATTLES AND CAMPAIGNS

Ardennes Rhineland Central Europe

33. DECORATIONS AND CITATIONS American Theater Ribbon European African Middle Eastern Theater Ribbon w/3 Bronze Battle Stars 2 Overseas Service Bars Good Conduct Medal GO 10 HQ 90 REC 1945 Bronze Star Medal GO 207 HQ 16th AD 1945

34. WOUNDS RECEIVED IN ACTION

None

35. LATEST IMMUNIZATION DATES				36. SERVICE OUTSIDE CONTINENTAL U. S. AND RETURN		
SMALLPOX	TYPHOID	TETANUS	OTHER (specify)	DATE OF DEPARTURE	DESTINATION	DATE OF ARRIVAL
In Aug 44	St Sep 45	St Aus 44		12 Sep 44	ETO	23 Sep 44

37. TOTAL LENGTH OF SERVICE						38. HIGHEST GRADE HELD			
CONTINENTAL SERVICE			FOREIGN SERVICE				3 Oct 45	USA	13 Oct 45
YEARS	MONTHS	DAYS	YEARS	MONTHS	DAYS	PFC			
1	10	4	1	1	2				

39. PRIOR SERVICE

None

40. REASON AND AUTHORITY FOR SEPARATION

Convn Of Govt RR 1-1 Demobilization AR 615-365 15 Dec 44

41. SERVICE SCHOOLS ATTENDED	42. EDUCATION (Years)
None	Grammar 8 High School 4

PAY DATA VO 13224

43. LONGEVITY FOR PAY PURPOSES	44. MUSTERING OUT PAY	45. SOLDIER DEPOSIT	46. TRAVEL PAY	47. TOTAL AMOUNT, NAME OF DISBURSING OFFICER
YEARS 2 MONTHS 11 DAYS 66	TOTAL 300 THIS PAYMENT 100		56.25	204.01 LELAND E RICE CAIT FD

INSURANCE NOTICE

IMPORTANT IF PREMIUM IS NOT PAID WHEN DUE OR WITHIN THIRTY-ONE DAYS THEREAFTER, INSURANCE WILL LAPSE. MAKE CHECKS OR MONEY ORDERS PAYABLE TO THE TREASURER OF THE U. S. AND FORWARD TO COLLECTIONS SUBDIVISION, VETERANS ADMINISTRATION, WASHINGTON 25, D. C.

48. KIND OF INSURANCE			49. HOW PAID		50. Effective Date of Allotment Discontinuance	51. Date of Next Premium Due (One month after 50)	52. PREMIUM DUE EACH MONTH	53. INTENTION OF VETERAN	
Nat. Serv. X	U.S. Govt.	None	Allotment X	Direct to V. A.	October 45	November 45	6.70	Continue X	Continue Only Discontinue

54.	55. REMARKS (This space for completion of above items or entry of other items specified in W. D. Directives)
RIGHT THUMB PRINT	Lapel Button Issued
	ASR Score (2 Sep 45) 90

56. SIGNATURE OF PERSON BEING SEPARATED	57. PERSONNEL OFFICER (Type name, grade and organization - signature)
Fazell R Spencer	L A GRINGER 2nd LT INF

WD AGO Form 53-55
1 November 1944
This form supersedes all previous editions of WD AGO Forms 53 and 55 for enlisted persons entitled to an Honorable Discharge, which will not be used after receipt of this revision.

2. FINAL INDORSEMENT COPY (Affixed to final indorsement page of Service Record)

Ralph Spencer's discharge papers

Certificate of Appreciation from France

RÉPUBLIQUE FRANÇAISE

CONSULAT GÉNÉRAL DE FRANCE À HOUSTON

Mr Fazell R; Spencer
1108 West Ave
Wellington, TX 79095

Houston, December 1, 2001

Dear Sir,

Please find enclosed the "Thank-You-America ! " certificate which France has issued for soldiers like you who contributed to the liberation of France during World War II.

This Certificate is meant to express the gratitude of the French people. Even though this gratitude cannot be limited to such a gesture, it also recognises your courage and devotion in France's time of need. Indeed, even after such a long time, it is important that nevertheless these qualities be remembered and honoured.

With this diploma, we extend our heartfelt thanks for your service to France.

Respectfully yours,

Denis Simonneau
Consul General of France

RÉPUBLIQUE FRANÇAISE

MINISTÈRE DE LA DÉFENSE

SECRÉTARIAT D'ÉTAT À LA DÉFENSE, CHARGÉ DES ANCIENS COMBATTANTS

CONSEIL RÉGIONAL DE BASSE-NORMANDIE

DIPLÔME

de reconnaissance de la France envers les soldats des armées alliées, engagés dans les combats du débarquement en Normandie et de la Libération 1944-1945

à M **Fazell R. Spencer**

1944   1945

Consul Général de France à Houston

Denis SIMONNEAU

Jean Pierre MASSERET

Le 1er Novembre 2001

167

50

BATTLE OF THE BULGE
1944
1994

Certificate of Appreciation
awarded to
SPENCER, Ralph
for his contribution to the Liberation
of Luxembourg in 1944 - 1945

Camille KOHN
President

Token of gratitude from Luxembourg

James Fuller, uncle, and Ralph Spencer, 1943

ɔh Spencer in Bagtogne, at the ɔ Anniversary of the Battle of the ɡe.

Pontoon bridge built by the 55th Engineers, over the Rhine River. "I was in the second vehicle (tank) to cross this bridge."

Going Home

We were part of the army of occupation for about six months. About the 12th of September 1945, we received notice to turn in all of our tanks, jeeps, trucks and equipment to the division quartermaster, because we were on our way home. We embarked for Marseilles, France. We were loaded on board an old freight train in boxcars that were called 40 and 8, because they would hold 40 horses and eight caretakers. There were probably 50 or 60 people to a boxcar. We set out across Germany for France. Somewhere in Germany, I forget the town, the train halted and we all got off and lined up for dinner. They had a kitchen there that served over 5,000 meals a day. Believe it or not, the food was really quite, good! While we were in line, I ran into an old buddy of mine that I had not seen in several months. He was on his way back to Germany. He had been transferred into an outfit, which had been headed for the Philippines to take part in the war in the Pacific. They were about half way across the Atlantic when the war with Japan ended, so instead of going on to the States, where they could have landed in another five days, they turned the ship around and sailed back to France, then loaded the soldiers on trains bound for Germany to join up with an outfit that was being shipped home!

We pulled into Rhiems, France where we unloaded and stayed for about five days while we were being processed for shipment home. We were in a large, modern railway station and I had to use the bathroom. I thought at least that nice station would have American style bathrooms. Was I ever fooled! I got into the bathroom and there were no stools, only a pipe about six inches in diameter set flush with the floor. One had to squat over the pipe, and hope to hit it! Oh, well, such is life! There at Rhiems, I got a 24-hour pass into Paris. We loaded up on trucks. Our pass started when we left for Paris and ended when we got back to Rhiems. It was a six-hour trip by truck to Paris, which left just 12 hours to see Paris. When we got into Paris, the first thing I did was to hunt up a black market dealer and sold them 20 cartons of cigarettes that I had saved up for $20.00 per carton, which came to $400.00. I imagine that he doubled his money on them. The Red Cross had taken over a very large hotel in Paris, which catered strictly to American soldiers. I had heard a lot about it, so I went in to see it. I had an excellent meal there. I needed to go to the bathroom again. The hotel was more up to date than the train station. They did have stools, urinals and washbasins, but what threw me for a loss was that they had two beautiful young ladies who were the bathroom attendants. It was a pay toilet, so they sat right outside the door and collected the money, and the door was kept wide open all of the time so they could see everything going on inside. I had heard a lot about the Paris subway, so I decided to take a ride on it. I had never been on a subway before, but that one was simply marvelous! I don't know how to describe it. If you really want to know, take a trip to Paris and take a ride on their subway. It is worth it! They had maps all over the place, and it was almost impossible to get lost. I had also heard about Pig Allee. That was the Red Light district for Paris. I got to Pig Allee and took a walk down the street for about six blocks, then turned around and came back. During that short walk, I must have been approached by 25 or 30 ladies of the night. All of them were very beautiful, and all wore dresses temptingly. I was married and had a wife and two children at home, so I really did not want any part of them. But the experience is one to be remembered. I also went to the Paris Follies that night. That was quite an experience! When the chorus line came out, they had on tights and braziers, which were fine, but the braziers all had a large hole in the center of the cup. They might have just as well left the brazier off. I only got to see about half of the show, as it was 11:00 p.m. and I had to catch my truck back at midnight. We got back to Rhiems completely worn out, so we went to bed and slept most of the day. At Rhiems we were loaded onto trucks for Marseilles. Just outside of the city of Marseilles' we passed a meadow that was about 5 miles square, and in the meadow there was a line of medium tanks that stretched as far as the eye could see. It was all brand new equipment. Then there was a line of two and a half ton trucks. Next, there was a line of light tanks. All stretched as far as the eye could see. Then, there was a row of self-propelled 75mm guns; next, a line of antiaircraft guns; then a line of jeeps; then a line of half-tracks. Next, a line of large trailers, then a line of small trailers, plus, more lines of other types of equipment. We never did find out what happened to all of that new equipment. I'm sure it was not shipped back home. My guess is that it was donated to the French government.

We stayed at Marseilles for two days, where we were billeted in tents. On the third day, we were lined up and marched to the piers to board ships for home. When I came over, I came on a liberty ship called the *Sea Owl*. As we marched down the docks, past several ships, there sat the Sea Owl. I thought, "Don't tell me we are going to be shipped back on the ship we came over on!" We were not. We marched passed it to the next ship in line. Later, there will be more about the *Sea Owl*. We made the trip over in ten days, in convoy and zigzagging, but it only took seven days to return home, since we were by ourselves, going in a straight line. Going back, I was not as fortunate in my bunk as I was coming over. I had a top bunk, five bunks high. To get to it, I had to climb up the other bunks, one foot on one side of the aisle and the other foot on the bunk on the other side of the aisle, and then when I got to the top, do a handstand to flip myself into the bunk. Coming over, we had to take salt-water showers while the ship's crew and officers had fresh water showers. On that ship we knew that there was plenty of water for everybody to have fresh water showers every day. Again, we were told that we were to have salt-water showers. Everybody was complaining about that! Two of the fellows with us who had worked as plumbers on the Liberty ships when they were being built, and knew the plumbing systems inside and out. They told us, "You wait and see. Tomorrow or the next day, we will have fresh water showers." I asked, "How do you know that?" They said, "Well, we were plumbers on the Liberty ships, and if we don't get fresh water showers, nobody will get them. There will be no fresh water to be had! They won't be able to get it! Not even any fresh water to cook with!" They disappeared for a couple of hours that evening after supper. The next day, there was an announcement over the ship phone that there would be a delay in breakfast because there was no fresh water. Time went on, noon rolled by, and another announcement was made that the cooks would serve cold sandwiches because there was still no fresh water. Same thing happened at suppertime. The next morning, it was announced over the ship's phones that as soon as they got the fresh water going again, we would have regular meals and everybody would have fresh water showers. The two plumbers disappeared again for a while, and it was announced over the ship's phones that the problem with the fresh water had been solved, and regular meals and fresh water showers would resume. We enjoyed our fresh water showers all of the way home.

On the 13th of October we arrived at Camp Patrick Henry in Newport News, Virginia. The Red Cross girls with coffee and donuts met us at the docks, but they did a pretty poor business, as most of the fellows were fed up with the Red Cross by that time, and just passed them by. The first thing we all did was to get on a telephone to call home. After three hours of waiting, I finally got a phone, and like all of the rest, I talked and talked and talked. That phone call only cost me $51.00.

I had been inducted down at Houston, Texas and that was where they wanted to send me back to. I told them, "Are you crazy? I come from Wisconsin! I need to go to the Great Lakes!" I finally convinced them to send me to Fort Sheridan by the naval academy. When I got to Great Lakes, I asked, "I don't know why they sent me here, I should have gone to Houston! That was where I was inducted." They told me I would just have to take my discharge here. I asked how I would get back to Houston, since I was broke! They agreed to give me extra $85.00 travel pay. I took my discharge, started to walk away from the table, and there was a major set up at a card table, and as I went past him, he flipped a paper around and said, "Sign here!" I said, "What am I signing?" He said, "Don't be a smart ass! Just do as you are ordered! Sign here!" I said, "Wait a minute," shaking my discharge in front of him. "I'm a civilian now. You cannot give me orders! I am not signing anything unless I know what it is!" He growled, "It is your enlistment into the reserves." I said, "No, it is not! I don't want any part of the reserves!" I stayed there for about an hour telling every man that came through, what it was that they were being asked to sign. Only two or three signed when they found out what the papers were for. Was that major ever mad! I figured that I had better get out of there before he had the MPs come and drag me away. I walked outside the gates of Fort Sheridan and started hitchhiking. In an hour and a half I was home!

It was about 5:00 in the afternoon when I got into town, and I was uptown and had about 3/4 of a mile to go, with a heavy duffel bag, so I called my folks to come and pick me up. When they picked me up, I asked my dad if I could drive the car home? He said, "No I'm afraid you don't know enough about driving." I said, "Look Dad I have been driving a car for about eight years. I drove a jeep, and a 2-1/2 ton truck through Tennessee maneuvers. I drove jeeps, trucks and tanks half way across Europe, and most of that was black out driving at night. And, you think I can't handle this old Chevy?" But no, he wasn't convinced he could trust me, and I didn't argue with him any more.

Housing was tight at that time, and we were forced to move in with my folks. I had my old room back. The room was about 8 by 12 with a single bed in it. For the six months at home, that's where my wife and I were cooped up. I went to work for a local contractor, who was building an apartment house. After about three months I was out of a job. I took a job in a local factory (Borg Warner Corporation). At first I was running a knitting machine, knitting nylon hosiery. I got along well enough on the machine when they transferred me to a department upstairs where I was steaming and stretching sweaters, and pressing them on a steam mangle. During those six months, nobody from the church, or for that matter, from the city, ever called and welcomed me home. Then I had a bit of luck. There was an old couple who owned a big old two-story house at the east end of town and they wanted to do something for a GI. They were living in another home that they had in Williams Bay and they put this house on the market, at an extremely low price of $5,000.00. All they wanted was a $100.00 down payment on the house, and I was lucky enough to be the first one to contact them. They sold me the house for $100.00 down and a low monthly payment of $100.00. Well, that was a seven-room house, with a big bathroom upstairs and a small room with a stool in it downstairs in the kitchen. We went head over heels in debt to get furniture and moved in. Two days after we moved in, about 8 o'clock at night, the doorbell rang. I went to the door and answered it. It was one of my old school mates and the Methodist minister. I invited them in, took them into the living room and cleared off the davenport, so they would have a place to sit down. Then, I said, "What can I do for you gentlemen?" The minister said, "We are here to get your donation to the new building fund." Well my mouth kind of fell open. In six months neither of them had ever called on me, or even asked about me. I had not even been asked to come to church again. He was a new minister and I had never been introduced to him. I had no idea of what his name was, and they were dunning me for money. If I had been introduced to the minister and they had sat down and chatted to me for five or ten minutes, asked how I was doing, or about my time in the army, I would have got out a ten dollar bill and given it to them and pledged a couple of hundred dollars for future payment. It just made me mad, and I pointed to the doorway and told the minister, you see that doorway you just came through? He said, "Yes," I said, "Well get your fanny back out of it just as fast as you can get." Both of their mouths fell open, and they never moved. I said, "Dammit, I meant what I said, "Get." This time they got and I never heard from either one of them again. But, for every three months, for the next five years, I would get a dun from the Methodist Church, wanting me to pay up my pledge to the new building fund. Which of course, I never paid, because I had never made a pledge.

About this time I was getting tired of factory work. My dad had a large barn on his property at the southwest edge of town. He had a smaller building behind the big barn that he had built just before the war, with the idea of opening up a foundry in it, but he never did. So the building was standing empty. The build was 20 x 30 foot and one side was all windows. I had been thinking about that building, that it would make a beautiful shop for me. I rented it from my Dad for ten dollars a month and opened up my own business. I managed to get a large cut-off saw, and a few other pieces of power equipment. I went to work, and built myself a couple of workbenches then opened up a small box factory. I contracted with one local factory that manufactured pumps to build crates for them to ship their pumps in. I gave them a good sturdy crate and they were using about 100 crates a week. I was doing pretty well with them for about four months until they finally contracted with another company who would make a much cheaper crate. Not only cheap, but it was flimsy. I could not see how they could chance shipping their pumps in such flimsy a crate. Well, that practically put me out of business, and I had to do something in a hurry. I got the bright idea, that there were a lot of mink ranchers in that area. I started contacting them, and almost every one I contacted, gave me orders for mink cages and nesting boxes. I was back in business in a big way. I think I must have built over thirty five hundred mink cages and nesting boxes. I put six men to work at a dollar an hour. After about a month my sister came down from Whitewater one night. I was out in the shop at midnight, working by myself. She came out and said," How many men do you have working for you?" I said, "Six." She started jumping up and down, yelling, "My brothers going to be a millionaire! My brothers going to be a millionaire!" I thought to myself, yeah, I am going to be a millionaire, all right. I'm going to be a million in debt. As I was running about $200.00 a day in debt at that time.

One day an old buddy of mine stopped by the shop and said, "I hear tell, that there is some good money to be made in spray painting." I said, "If there is good money to be made in it, then let's get into it." Neither of us knew boo about painting, let alone spray painting. We went to some of the farmers that we knew, and darn if we didn't manage to sell three big paint jobs. One of them was to a big dairy farmer. He had a red barn with the old red barn paint that would burn through anything. He wanted to change it over to white. I had accidentally heard some place that in order to seal in that old red paint, you had to cover it with a coat of aluminum, which was the only thing that would seal it in. So we sold him a three-coat job: one coat of aluminum, to cover up the red and two coats of white to cover up the aluminum. Here we sat with three nice big painting contracts and not even a paintbrush to work with. I was convinced that we could make money at the work, but how in the dickens were we going to get the jobs done? We were both flat broke. I was subscribing to the *Milwaukee Journal*. That night, as I was going through the paper, I happened upon a fair sized ad saying some outfit in Milwaukee was selling air compressors and spray painting equipment.

My buddy's name was Joe Farkas. Right after graduating from high school, Joe went out to Los Angeles, California, I guess with the idea of becoming a movie star. But that didn't work out for him, and while he was out there he changed his name to Terrance De Wolf. He was Hungarian and Farkas in Hungarian meant wolf. Anyway the next day we hit the banks in town to try to get some money to get some equipment with. But, naturally they wouldn't have anything to do with us. I had another friend in town whom I knew had a little money saved up. So, I went and talked to him, and he agreed to lend us $500.00 dollars. We took the $500.00 and went into Milwaukee and located the company that had run that ad. It turned out to be a Jewish outfit and they were building air compressors out of Model A engines, with two cylinders firing and two cylinders compressing air, and they had all the other equipment necessary, so we bought a compressor, two 100 foot lengths of air hose, two 100 foot lengths of paint hose and two spray guns. We gave them $385.00 as a down payment, and that left us $115.00 to buy paint with. We went back home and went to work, and managed to get those three paint jobs done. That taught us a little something about spray painting to boot. By the time we got those three paint jobs done, we were beginning to have a little trouble with the air compressor. We had contracted to do a hotel roof in Elkhorn, Wis. The hotel was four stories high with a very steep-pitched roof. There was a businessman named

Smith that had his business just one block away from the hotel. We had been in his store talking to him one day about paints, and he had put us onto this hotel roof job. He had an asphalt based aluminum paint that he claimed would cover the rust and seal it in, just the way it was, without having to scrape and sand the rust off. We got it and started on it. That day, we had more troubles than you could shake a stick at. Our guns were acting up (We had found out that they were bastard guns and that we couldn't get parts for them.) The paint hoses were going rotten and were, blowing holes here and there, the air compressor got where it took one man on the ground just to keep it running, while the other man was up on the roof trying to paint. Not only that, our pressure pot which had been guaranteed to hold ninety pounds of pressure, blew its gasket. So, we shut down. We couldn't work that way. We were sitting there by the compressor, moaning about our bad luck, and about what the heck we were going to do, when Mr. Smith came along. He said, "What's the matter boys?" We told him what was the matter. He said, "Well, that's simple, just go and get your self some new equipment." I said, "That's fine. New equipment costs money, and we haven't got any. We are both flat broke. "Well" he said can you boys raise any money at all?" I said, "Yes, but, we know now what kind of equipment we should have, and what we can raise won't pay for half of it." He said, "How much money do you think you can raise?" "Well." I said I think we can raise about $1,500.00. But, I know we need about $3,000.00 to $4,000.00 to be able to get the right kind of equipment." Mr. Smith said. "Well, why don't you boys go back to Delavan and see just how much money you can raise, and then come back and see me. So we went back to Delavan, and went to the State Bank, and since we already had done three big paint jobs for well known farmers that were customers of theirs, knew that we were onto a business that could grow, they agreed to loan us

$1,500.00. So we signed the papers, and got the check for $1,500.00. We went back to Elkhorn, went into Smittys store and he was in his office working on his books. We went back into the office, and he looked up and said, "Well, how did you boys make out?" I tossed the check for $1,500.00 down on his desk, but I said, "I don't know how that is going to do us any good, because we need at least twice that much." He picked the check up, looked at it, and handed it back to me, and said, "Why don't you boys go and get your equipment?" I was just ready to smart off, when I felt the check slide between my fingers. I looked down, and there was his check for $1,500.00. We let out a big breath and said, "We're on our way to Milwaukee." But first, we went back and cleaned up our equipment, loaded it all up on the truck, and hooked the compressor up to the truck. Two hours later we were in Milwaukee. We went to this Jewish outfit that we had bought the equipment from, and wanted to turn it back into them, and told them they could keep the $385.00 that we had paid them, that all we wanted was a clean bill of health. But, no they had to be difficult. They had a contract that we had both signed. We had to keep the equipment and pay them the rest of the money that we owed them. I got to thinking, there was a big criminal lawyer there in Milwaukee who was Jewish. He had a mink ranch just three miles east of Delavan, and I had made up about 1500 mink cages and nesting boxes for him. So I told Joe, "Let's get out of here." We went across the street and got on a phone. I called this attorney named Swidler and he said, "What can I do for you?" I told him what our problem was and he said, "Those bastards. I just got through keeping them in business. The city was going to put them out of business for violating the blue law." He said, "What is your phone number there?" I gave it to him, and he said, "You just stay by that phone, and I'll call you back in about fifteen minutes." So we hung up and waited, and, sure enough, fifteen minutes later, the phone rang and it was Swidler. He said, "You boys go on back across the street there, and I think they will give you just about anything you want." We went back over, and sure enough, they were very happy to see us.

They took us up into their big private office, broke out a couple bottles of whiskey and fixed us both drinks. They said, "Now what can we do for you boys?" "Well" I told him, "We just want to turn the equipment back to you, and you keep the $385.00 that we already paid you and you just give us a clean bill of health." He said, "No problem, no problem." So, they fixed the papers up and we left there and went down to another company that dealt with air compressors. We bought another small air compressor from them, but it was a good one. That cost us $1,700.00 and left us $1,300.00 to play with. We dropped down to Racine and went to a Binks store. We had studied up on equipment and knew Binks was the best to buy. There we bought three guns. Two were regular paint spray guns and one was a special gun for spraying the asphalt based aluminum paint with. We also knew that we needed a lot more hose, so bought two new sets of paint hose, 250 feet long each; two new air hoses, 250 feet long; a new ten gallon pressure pot; three fifty foot lengths of 3/4 inch air hose plus a bunch of spare parts for the guns and paint pot. Then we headed for home and got back in time to get in a couple of hours of work that day. Needless to say we paid Smitty back every penny, and he never charged us one penny of interest. As a result, we did a very large business of coating roofs, and over the years, we probably bought over 1,000 gallons of roof coating from him. Well our partnership lasted about six months. Joe was the type guy that had to have everything his own way and things were just not working out. Because I had started the original business and been responsible for getting both loans to get us going in the painting business, I told him that we would have to split up with him going his way and me going my way. Well he sat down and did a little figuring, and said, "Okay you pay me $1,500.00 for my half, and that's it." I said, "Well, now Joe, let's kind of refigure this financial deal here." "We've got some loans out, that you are half responsible for. One of them is $800.00 for Smitty, yet, and my other friend about $300.00, and I forget what the others were." It wound up with him walking away without a penny, which is only right. Because, I had been furnishing a truck, and all the hand tools. Joe had a wife and five children and most of the time he didn't have any food in the house for them to eat. I know because at Christmas time my wife and I had put up a big meal and took it out them, and if it hadn't been for that, all of them would have went hungry on Christmas day. At the time I went into the CCC Camps. Joe had enlisted into the Marines. When the war came along, his outfit took part in the invasion of Peleliu Island. After they had taken the island, they were assigned occupational duty there on the island for the rest of the war. That was the only action that he was really involved in. But when he came home from the Marines, he had married a farm girl out in southern Ohio. She was from a very well to do family. His first year at home, her brother, who lived in Columbus, Ohio, offered him a job for the summer, driving an ice cream wagon, selling ice cream bars and cones and other frozen treats. He did real well with that, and wound up with $5,000.00, which he promptly turned around and bought a brand new, large Buick, which he was driving around and couldn't afford the gas for it. Half the time his family was going hungry. I don't know how he managed to do it, but two weeks later he had two big air compressors. They were four times the size of my little compressor and he was back running competition to me, which was all right, because there was plenty of work for both of us. We were the only ones painting barns. For almost six years during the war, there had been no painting done because the farmers could not get paint or anyone to apply it. There was a large girls camp located on the Island out in Delavan Lake. It was owned and operated by a little red-headed Jewish schoolteacher in Chicago. There was a huge 36-room mansion in the camp, and a large two-story caretaker's house. There were six large cabins for the girls, two fairly good sized machine sheds, a wooden water tower, and a big two-story boathouse. I managed to get in with her (I forget what her name was) and I painted for her every year that I was in the painting business. I had no competition there; she would never even talk to another painter. She had three six weeks terms during the summer season. She handpicked every one of her girls and got $200.00 apiece for each girl for the six weeks period. She had about one hundred fifty girls per period. And while all of her expenses were high, she still managed to coin money out of that girls' camp. When I was painting out there in the summertime, I would get out there at about 7:00 a.m. to start working, and that was just when the girls were getting up. They had a communal bathroom, for all of the girls. And it was nothing to see ten or twelve of the girls running naked between the cabins and the bathroom every morning. She was a really good customer. The only thing she ever told me was what she wanted painted. She never asked for an estimate or price, I would just go do the work, give her the bill, and she would never question it. She would just pay it. But, for that reason, I never took advantage of her, I always gave her a first class job, and never overcharged her for any thing. I had another customer like her, except this one was a farmer, who was farming about three thousand acres at that time. He must have had eight different farms there, all with different barns, machine sheds, hog barns, corn-cribs, plus a lot of other specialized buildings. That was called the Hughs farms. Mr. Hughs was in his fifties, and he had actually had a doctor's degree in agriculture. He had spent the war years in Washington D.C. as FDR's farm advisor. He was the same way, he would just take me to one farm, and tell me, "I want this painted, I want that painted, I want the house painted, etc." Then we would go to the next farm, where he would do the same thing. I did anywhere from $3,000.00 to $5,000.00 of work per year, but never less than $3,000.00. And after my second year of painting for them, he never asked me for a price either, because he knew I would give him a first class job and not overcharge him for it. In the mean time, I kept my little wood working shop going. I designed a set of lawn furniture, all made out of wood, four chairs, a table, and a footstool, all made out of wood. While it was not a real big item, I did manage to sell several sets of them. This I would do in the wintertime. One time, I was talking to a friend of mine, and she said, "You know, I have a friend whose company is sending him to Germany. He needs somebody to pack his furniture, dishes, China, glassware, and ship them over there for him." I said, "Well, I can do that for him." So she took me over and introduced me to the party, and I made a deal with them. I picked up all of his furniture and belongings and trucked them over to my shop. I packed all of his woodwork and crated it up. I took an old fifty-five gallon wood barrel and packed all of his China, dishes, and glassware in that. First, I wrapped everything good in paper, and I had a very large supply of sawdust. I would put a layer of sawdust in the bottom of the barrel, put a plate in, covered it up with sawdust, put in another plate, and cover it up with sawdust. I told them when they got over to Germany and got their stuff to please write back and tell me how it arrived. So one day, about four months later, I got a letter from them, telling me that they were really pleased. There was not so much as one scratch on any of their furniture, and not so much as one dish or single glass broken. So, I started running an ad in a local paper, saying that, I would crate furniture, China, glassware, etc., for overseas shipment. I was really amazed at the response that I got from that ad. Because Delavan was just a small country town, but, over a period of about four years, I packed and shipped furniture and glassware to:

1. Russia	16. Mexico City
2. Germany	17. Hawaii
3. France	18. Panama Canal Zone
4. Belgium	19. Guatemala
5. England	20. Puerto Rico
6. Spain	21. Chile
7. Switzerland	22. Johannesburg, Africa
8. Australia	23. New York
9. Malaysia	24. Boston
10. Philippines	25. Miami
11. Japan	26. Los Angeles
12. China	27. San Francisco
13. Rio De Janeiro, SA	28. Portland, OR
14. Alaska	29. Denver, CO
15. Canada	30. Phoenix

Of course, I didn't get all of those jobs locally. Once I'd handled three or four jobs, I started advertising in the *Milwaukee Journal, Chicago Tribune,* the Madison, Wisconsin paper, and Rockford paper.

When I was packing and shipping dishes and furniture overseas, I had scrounged up all of the fifty-five gallon wooden barrels in the county, and I went into Milwaukee to a barrel factory, and bought up a truck load of barrels (24 of them). Another time after I had scrounged all of the rags in the neighborhood, and still was running out of them, I went into a large junkyard in Milwaukee and bought 250 lbs. of rags from them. Well, that was enough to last me for several years.

The Delavan Lake and Lake Geneva areas were great fishing areas. I kept seeing fishermen lugging their outboard motors from their cars, down to their boats, and I kept thinking that there ought to be an easier way of transporting those outboard motors to their boats, and from the boats back to their cars. I thought to myself, there ought to be a cart that they could push them on or roll them on. I designed a cart for outboard motors, and at the same time, the idea struck me that the cart could be modified for golfers to haul their golf bags on. I had no knowledge of manufacturing processes, and I made one bad mistake, in making my carts. I made them out of steel rods, where as later, I found out that they should have been made out of pipe, because after a while, the weight of the outboard motors would make the steel rods bend. I was also ignorant about patent rights. So, I made up about fifty carts, and scattered them around the county at the various fishing resorts and bait shops, I put them out on a consignment basis. I figured that well, if they sold, and I saw that they were going to sell, then I would go ahead and get a patent on the deal. They sold all right, but, there was some outfit in Chicago who bought a couple of them and, after checking for a patent on them and finding none, they redesigned them to be made out of pipe and went ahead and took out a patent on them. On the land right next door to my Dad's property, there had been a big, old, milk factory that was about three stories high. It belonged to the Nestle Company and had been closed down for several years. This company, Rollo King, came out and bought that property, tore the old factory down and built a new modern factory there, just to manufacture their golf carts and outboard motor carts. Talk about rubbing salt in an open wound. They made millions off of those carts, and I didn't make one red dime.

Along about that time, I got to thinking about toys. They were always the big selling item, especially during the holidays. I had the idea for three different toys. One of them was an old fashioned sleigh. I had three sizes, a real small one, a little larger one for toys, and a real large one, large enough to hold a one-year-old baby in. One was a wooden frame about 3 feet high, with narrow troughs in it that angled back and forth, down to the bottom of it. Its function was really simple. You drop about ten marbles at the top of the trough, and then they would roll back and forth down to the bottom. We tested it out on all of the kids, and the neighbor's kids, and they all seemed to be fascinated with it. Even my wife and I would play with it ourselves. I forget what the third toy was. I thought I would play it smart this time. Every year they have a national toy show in Chicago. I figured I would go in there and rent a space to display my toys. If I were fortunate, I would get some large orders for the toys, because there would be buyers from all over the world there. Some of those big distributors, if they like the item, they could order a hundred thousand or better at that time. Well, I went in there and I needed six square feet of space, to display my toys in. They only wanted $3,000.00 for rental for that size of space. Well, that knocked that in the head because, I didn't have $3,000.00 and could not raise $3,000.00.

About six years later, I came across one of my marble toys in a dime store. It was made out of metal and some outfit out in Pennsylvania had made it and manufactured it. They did not steal my idea, they evidently had the same idea abut the same time and had the knowledge and money to develop it and put it on the market.

About twenty years later, I was sitting in my truck outside of a small paint factory, in Woodstock, Illinois, where I had bought most of my paints, when one of the managers came out, carrying one of my wooden marble games that I had made. I could hardly believe my eyes when I saw it. I got out of the truck, went over to him, and asked him, "Where did you get that?" He said, "Well, I picked it up at a yard sale up at Delavan. It looked pretty shabby, so I brought it up here and had some of the workers to repaint it for me."

One day in August of '47, a friend of mine who worked with the telephone company, poked his head in my shop door and wanted to know just how busy I was. I said, "Well, I've got work, but I'll always take on some more." He said, "Well, the telephone company is going to put some cables underground up on main street, and they need somebody to take up the brick paving, so they can dig a trench to put their cable, in. There isn't anyone in town that we can find to do the job. You are always doing a lot of odd jobs, and I thought you already have an air compressor, so maybe you could rent an air hammer someplace." I said, "Well, when do they want this job done?" He said, "Tomorrow." I said, "Okay, I'll take it. You just get the heck out of here, so I can get in my car and head for Milwaukee." He said, "What have you got to go to Milwaukee for?" I said, "That's where my air hammer is." He said, "I didn't know you had an air hammer." I said, "Well, I don't, but, I will have by this time tomorrow." So, by 10:00 a.m., I was on my way to Milwaukee. By this time, I had accumulated a little operating capital. I had about $1,000.00 to play with and I knew I could get the air hammer, along with the points and fittings that I needed for about $750.00. Well, I was in Milwaukee by noon and stopped at a restaurant and had some dinner. I went on to the heavy equipment dealer that I knew handled air hammers, picked out a nice ninety pound hammer, and got about fifteen points of various types for it and headed home. The whole kit and caboodle run me about $725.00. The next afternoon, I was out tearing up the street. Well, all the businessmen in town there said I was nuts for spending that kind of money for an air hammer, for just a half a day's job. I didn't tell them, but I knew where I could get several more day's work for that air hammer, and I knew as time went on, I would get more jobs. As it turned out, I now had the only air hammer for hire in three counties, and, I did get quite a bit of work for it. That year, winter set in early. The ground was frozen up hard by the middle of October and there was a good snow coverage. It was extremely cold all winter long and usually the frost went down about six foot in the ground, but this winter, it was so cold, the frost went down as much as seven or eight foot. All the farmers had their water lines frozen up. From the first of November through to the last of February, I was going practically twenty-four hours a day, just digging up frozen water lines for the farmers. It was more than one night that I had finished digging up one farmer's line at about 2:00 a.m. in the morning, and there were other farmers around arguing about who was going to get me to do theirs next. It was so cold, that my air hose would freeze up solid. Then, of course, I had to shut everything down, and take a blowtorch and work an hour or two, to get the air hose thawed out, and then go back to work. I even became a gravedigger that winter. Usually, when the ground was frozen solid that way, the undertakers would just store bodies until the spring, then they would have the funerals and bury them in the spring. However, there were five people that insisted on having their funerals immediately, and again, I had the only equipment that could break through that frost. But it would take me three ten-hour days to dig just one grave. The ground was just so hard, that it would just flake off in little flakes at a time. In those four months, I took in somewhere between $5,000.00 and $6,000.00 with that air hammer. After that winter, I didn't care if the air hammer sat in the shop again and never went out. But for almost three years after I bought the air hammer, I had a monopoly on the air hammer work in all three counties. And, finally, other contractors began to get wise and bought their own air hammers.

I got an air hammer job in Rockford, IL. It was about sixty miles from Delavan. I started out for Rockford, and was pulling my compressor. I was moving along at a pretty good speed, and was going up an overhead bridge, and about half way up, I felt my air compressor jerk loose. I looked back and the damn thing was chasing me. I had to step on the gas and get out of its way. I was afraid that it would come to a stop and start rolling back. There was another car about a quarter of a mile behind us. I got up to the top of the bridge and came to a stop in the center of it, and the air compressor followed me up and came to a stop, too, about ten foot from me. I backed up to it, got out, hooked it up, and went on my way.

A cousin of mine came in from Fargo, ND. He was looking for work and I needed help, so I gave him a job. Right about that time, the state health authorities were clamping down on the dairy farmers. A lot of them had just absolutely filthy barns, and they were making them clean and paint them up on the inside. So, naturally, I was the only one around there that was doing that kind of work. I was called in by three of them to clean up the inside of their dairy barns and paint them. Most of them had low ceilings about seven feet high and they were completely covered with manure. We had to go in there with hot water and scrub brushes and scrub those ceilings down, so that they were clean. You talk about a stinky and filthy job, that was it. All of that filthy water was dropping down on us all of the time. And, when we got through at the day's end, I think we could be smelled a block away. When I got home, I would go around to the back door. And pull all of my clothes off outside, then go inside and take a good bath. I went through a lot of work clothes on those jobs, because, we would just throw the filthy work clothes away. We would wear them one day and throw them away. My wife was not about to let me put them in the washing machine. Later on, I invested in a steam cleaner and used that to clean the barns down with. It was a little better, but not much. We still had filthy water dripping down on us all of the time. But, at least, we didn't have to do all of the hard scrubbing.

One day, I read an ad in the paper where the Armstrong Company was putting on a five-day school for carpet layers and floor tiling. I thought well, it wouldn't hurt me to know something about both of those deals. So, I took five days off, went to Milwaukee and took in the school, where I learned how to lay wall-to-wall carpeting, and how to tile a floor or wall. They also had a class on laying linoleum, which I took. In the years to come, I did quite a bit of carpet laying and tiling.

My wife had been cheating on me all along. I know the townspeople all wondered how Spencer could be so dumb, not to know what was going on. Well, I wasn't dumb. I knew what was going on, but I also knew that anything that I done or said wouldn't stop it. I couldn't afford a divorce then. So I just kept my mouth shut and put up with it.

Another time, I was coming back from Williams Bay, and I was in behind an old fellow who was poking along. I swung out in the left lane to pass him, and honked my horn that I was passing, and the dam fool pulled over to the left lane in front of me to make a right hand turn into a driveway, never gave any turn signals at all. I had to slam on my brakes, and swerve over to the side of the road to keep from hitting him. When I did that, I felt the air compressor come loose, and I looked back to see and here it was rolling over and over out in the field. I was so mad, I never stopped. I knew if I ever went in and said anything to the old fellow, I would lose my temper and beat him up. So I just kept on going into town and stopped at the Ford agency. I told them what had happened and where and for them to take their wrecker and go out and pick up the air compressor, bring it in and fix it up, which they did.

There was one farmer that called me who had bought a farm about three miles east of town at the Inlet of Delavan Lake. It had been a dairy farm and he was re-modeling the barn so that he could raise horses. He said, "I've got a cement floor that I want broken up and hauled away." I said, "Fine, I'll be out there tomorrow morning." The barn was 40 x 100 foot and it took me two days. It took one day to break the concrete all up and the next day to load the rubble up and haul it away. Well, I went home that night and I was worn out. I went to bed and got a good night's sleep. At 6:00 a.m. the next morning, the phone rings, and it's the farmer again. He said, "Bring that damn hammer back out here again, I've got another floor." There had been a layer of gravel there, and when he cleaned the gravel off, there was another cement floor down there. It had been remodeled previously. So I spent another two days, knocking that floor out and hauling it away. Went back home, had supper, and went to bed, and promised myself that I would sleep until noon. But, that wasn't to be. At 6:00 a.m. the next morning, the phone rang. It's the farmer again, mad as all get out, and says, "Bring that damn hammer out here again, there is a third floor down here." So, I went back out for another two days and, finally, had him straightened out. But, that barn had been remodeled three times before he bought it, and each time, they would just pour a layer of gravel over the old floor and pour a new floor on top of the gravel.

The next spring, I had just started a really large farm job, (painting), about twenty miles west of town, over near Janesville, when a party I knew from Elkhorn, called me up and said, "I got a little job for your air hammer." I asked, "Well, just how little is it?" He said, "Well, it is just a little patch of concrete about fifteen foot square." I told him, "Well, I would like to do the job for you, but I just started a huge paint job near Janesville yesterday morning and the farmer is going to holler like the devil if I pull the compressor off to do that. Why don't you get a couple of sledgehammers and give them to your men, and get your men to knock that little amount out by hand? They can do it for you cheaper than what I could pull my compressor and knock it out for you." He said, "You know, I had not even thought about that, but, you are right, I think that I'll just do that." So as time went on, and I didn't hear any more from him, I figured he had got that little patch of concrete knocked out okay. About six months later, I bumped into him in town and he told me, "You remember last spring, I called you and wanted you to knock out a little patch of concrete for me, and you told me to give my men a couple of sledge hammers and knock it out by hand?" I said, "Yeah, I remember." He said, "Well, you know I done that, they knocked out that whole patch of concrete by hand, and underneath it was a huge old foundation that no one knew anything about, and that had to come out. I went into Milwaukee and rented a compressor and air hammer, and you know it cost me over $6,000.00 to get that old foundation knocked out. It was the hardest concrete I've ever seen in my life. I bought over two hundred-fifty points for the air hammer before we got it all knocked out." I said, "Two hundred-fifty points?" He said, "Yeah, we would use a point and a half an hour later, we would have to use another point, because the other one would break." I said, "I wish you had called me back. For that kind of a job, I could have just bought another air compressor. But, how come you had to buy so many points? I could understand you buying two or three dozen, but, not two hundred fifty." He said, "Well, they kept breaking on me." I said, "Well, did you ever take any of them to a blacksmith and have them sharpened up?" He said, "No, I didn't know you could have them sharpened." I said, "Yeah, any blacksmith would sharpen them up for you for twenty-five cents apiece." Well, I bought three-dozen points from him for fifty cents apiece. They cost $2.50 new. I took them down and had them all sharpened up. I had enough points to last me for the rest of the time I had the air hammer.

There was a car dealer in Whitewater, which was another town, just twenty miles northwest of Delavan. He called me up and told me he had a job for my air hammer. I said, "Okay, what is it?" He said, "Well, I just bought a big, old mansion out on Whitewater Lake and there is a boathouse out on the lake, and it has a concrete seawall running out from the outer edge of it. It extends about three-foot above the water level. He said, "I want it knocked down to the water level, and I don't want any rubble down in the bottom of the lake." I said, "Are you in any hurry for that?" He said, "No." I said, "Because, I'm pretty well tied up for a month or so, but

I'll think about this." I did think about it for about two weeks. How in the world was I going to knock that sea-wall down to water level, without getting any rubble down into the bottom of the lake?

To the readers, you think about this, how would you do that? I'll give you my solution a little later on. I have posed that question to many people over the years, and that includes some very well known engineers and contractors, and none of them have been able to come up with the right solution. Now that you've had time to think about it, I'll give you the solution. I merely waited until January, when the lake was completely frozen solid. I went in and knocked it down to the level of the ice, which was the water level, and took a wheelbarrow and hauled all the rubble off of the ice.

One day, early in January, a fellow called me about 1:00 p.m. and told me that he had a job for my air hammer the next day. I asked him what it was and when he explained it to me, I knew that I was going to need a special point for the hammer to do the job, which I didn't have. I said, "Okay." I called Milwaukee, but they didn't have the point that I needed, but they gave me the name and phone number of an outfit in Madison, Wisconsin, and said that they would have it. So, I called Madison, and they said, "Yes, we have a couple of them." So I said, "I'll be in for it this afternoon." They said, "Well, we close at 6:00 sharp." I said, "I'll be there before that." I told my wife that I had to run into Madison to pick up a special point for the air hammer, and she said, "Just a minute, and I'll go with you." So, we left at 2:00 p.m. for Madison, which was ninety miles northwest of us. Ordinarily, it would be just an hour and a half drive, but, we had a sleet and ice storm and the highways were all icy. And, I do mean, it was ice, all ninety miles of it. So we didn't make too good of time. By a quarter after five, we were still about twelve miles out of Madison and I was in behind a big semi-truck. He was just crawling along. I knew if I stayed behind him, I would never make it into Madison by 6:00, So, I started to ease out into the left lane to pass him, and my wife said, "Don't pass." Well, I was so used to her back seat driving, that I didn't pay any attention to her. I didn't realize that she could see around the right hand side of that semi and there was another semi coming towards us. If she had said that there was another truck coming, I would have listened to her, but she merely said don't pass, so I eased out into the left lane and here was this semi coming towards us. I knew it was going to be a head on crash. There was a five-foot ditch on the left side of the road, and I thought to myself, if I hit him head-on, we are both dead. So, I'll just take my chances with the ditch. I yanked the steering wheel as far to the left as it would go and hit the brakes at the same time. We made three complete turns on the highway, wound up in our own lane, heading towards Madison, and missed everything. Talk about someone having his heart up in his throat that's where mine was. Well, we made it into the warehouse at about ten minutes till six. We picked up our point, headed home, and got there at about 9:00 p.m.

Another time, a boat company in Williams Bay (small town on Lake Geneva) called me up and said that they needed my air hammer. They were building a new boat factory there, and the architects had made a mistake on one room. They were going to knock the floor out and lower it. When I got over there, they showed me the room. It was a small room, about 8 x 10, with a 4-1/2 foot ceiling, no windows, just one door way leading into it. Well, I started to work in there, with that low ceiling, I had to stay on my knees and hold the jackhammer out at arm's length, and then I was almost cracking my knuckles on the ceiling. Well, after I had five minutes of that, there was so much dust in there; I had to get outside. Luckily, I had a painting mask, which I never used while I was painting because it was too hot. But, it was made of clear plastic, and it covered my whole head, and I had an air line coming into the back of the mask, so I had a stream of fresh air coming around my head at all times. But to make matters worse, every six inches, there were reinforcing rods, and when I hit one of those, I'd have to chisel out around it, then take a hack saw and cut the rod, which really slowed the job down. Well, that floor was a foot and a half thick, with three layers of reinforcing rods. It took me three weeks to knock that floor out. But they paid the bill and never said a word. It would have been much cheaper to knock the building down, used the floor and put a new building on top of it. I swore then, that I would never take another job like that.

Once I had my truck backed up to the shop door to load it. When a couple of planes came over and buzzed the town. They passed directly over my head about 200 feet up. That scared the daylights out of me, and I hit the ground digging with my hands. There was an old fellow living in a little house trailer parked about 50 feet away from the shop. He was standing in the doorway watching me. After the planes had passed over and I had gotten up, he said, "What in the heck were you trying to do?" I said, "Boy I was digging a slit trench. I thought those planes were strafing me." Another time, I was out cultivating corn for my uncle when a plane passed over my head about 200 foot up. And again, I thought that I was being strafed. I just barely stopped myself before I jumped off of the tractor to dig myself another slit trench.

My oldest sister Vinetta, a schoolteacher, had married a childhood friend of ours, and his name was Arthur Houghton. He was a farmer. About this time, they were working for Hershey Dairy Farm near Libertyville. They wanted to go farming for themselves and had heard about and old farmer up near Whitewater, Wisconsin who had several farms. He had set each one of his sons up on a farm, with provisions that they keep the farms up and in good shape, and pay him $40.00 a month until he died. I never would have done it, but they had the gall to go to that farmer and ask him if he wouldn't put them on a farm the same as he had done his sons. It so happened he had one son who was worthless and wasn't working the farm, and was letting the buildings go down. He was wanting to get them off that farm, so he kicked them out and put my sister and her husband on it in their place. They stayed on the farm four years, and paid him the $40.00 a month until he died. After four years the farmer died, and they had the ninety-acre farm free and clear. And, it had cost them less than $2,000.00. My sister came to me one day and wanted to know if I would go over to Elkhorn with her. She had an appointment with the county agent. She was trying to get a loan, so they could buy a herd of dairy cattle, and thought that I had just went through the business of buying a house and getting a loan on it I might be able to give her some good advice. So I said, "Okay." We went to Elkhorn and saw the gentleman, and he asked her," How can I help you?" She started talking, and talked and talked and talked. All the time complaining about how nobody would help a poor person to get started for themselves. The man told her, "If you will be quiet for a while and let me talk, maybe, we can work something out." She said, "Okay." He started to talk, and I don't think he got five words out his mouth when she was off and running again. Well, the second time, he told her, "Would you Please be quite and let me talk?" She said, "Oh sure." But once again before he could get one sentence completed, she cut him off and started talking and talking and talking. Finally, the man said, "I've got another appointment in five minutes." He got up and ushered us to the door. As she went out the door, he motioned for me to come back. I went back in and shut the door. He asked me, "What in the hell is wrong with your sister? I actually told her to shut up three times and let me talk and she just would not do it." I said, "Well, I don't know how familiar you are with school teachers, but, she is a school teacher and they all think alike. They think they know it all, and no one else knows anything. He said, "Well can you come back tomorrow by yourself?" I said. "Sure, what time do you want me to be here?" He said, "1:30 will be fine." So the next day at 1:30 p.m., I was back there. He invited me in and sat me down. He said, "Now, I'll tell you what I couldn't tell your sister, that I'm going to give them the loan that she wants. But you will have to tell her that when she comes back here she will have to keep her mouth shut if she wants the loan." I said, "Okay, I'll give her the message." Well, she went back to see the county agent, but I didn't go with her this time She must have kept her mouth shut, because they got the loan.

The next year, my brother-in-law, Art, wanted to put up a couple of silos, and there were two old silo foundations there where he wanted to put his silos up. They had to be broken up and taken out of there before he could put in new foundations. So they wanted to know if I would bring up my air hammer and knock them out for them. I said, "Okay." So, the next day, I hooked onto my air compressor, loaded the truck up and drove the thirty-five miles to their farm. I knocked out the two old silo foundations and it took me from 8 a.m. to 5 p.m. to do that. I didn't bother with the rubble. I figured he could handle that himself. I got every thing loaded ready to head for home. I saw Art coming out from the house, Fumbling with his hip pocket, he somehow just couldn't seem to get his billfold out. I told him, "I will make it easy on you. You have chickens and they lay eggs; we eat eggs, so give me a couple dozen eggs now, and when you go back to Delavan to visit the folks, bring a couple more dozen with you and leave them with the folks for me. You can do that every time you come to Delavan until you have brought me ten dozen." Eggs at that time were going for about 35 cents a dozen. Ten dozen eggs would be $3.50. That made him real happy. He went in and got me two dozen eggs I said, "Don't forget when you come down, to bring a couple dozen more with you. The next time they came down, he brought down one dozen and left it with the folks for me. I never saw another egg after that. So, for $1.50 I hauled my air compressor seventy miles, ran it for eight hours, burned up 15 gallons of gas in the air compressor alone not counting the truck, and my labor which was worth $5.00 an hour at that time, if I had billed him like I should have. I should have had $85.00 for that day's work. As it was I got $1.50 out of it.

We'll get away from the painting and air hammer work for awhile.

For three years I'd worked with a crew putting in piers and docks in the lake. Up there you can't leave the piers in over winter you pull them out in the fall, and then put them back in the spring. It was kind of interesting work. Of course you had to work out of boats all the time. We had two rowboats and a fairly good-sized flat bottom scow. One day we were working on the south side of Lake Geneva, it was about 1 p.m., and we could see that there was a storm coming up. Those storms could last quite awhile some times and we didn't want to be stranded on the south side of the lake without any shelter. So we wrapped things up and headed for the north shore. It was about a mile across the lake there at that point. When we got about halfway across, that storm hit us. Well, there for a while, we thought we were not going to make it across. The storm was blowing up three and four foot waves, and we had one-foot sides on the scow. There were four of us, and two of us rowed, and the other two bailed like the devil. It took us almost an hour to get back to the north shore, but we made it, and boy, were we glad to get our feet back on land again.

In 1946, my friend Joe (whose family owned a home and several acres of land just a block and a half away from my shop) decided to put in a drive-in. The building was set one hundred and fifty foot back off the highway. He had to dig a ditch for a sewer line from the building to the street. The ditch had to be seven-foot deep in order to get the pipe below the frost line. It had to be three feet wide in order for us to be able to work in it. He and

I dug that ditch by hand. Fortunately, it was kind of sandy soil, so the digging wasn't too bad, but there was some gravel in it. It took us one week to get that ditch dug. They opened the drive-in up. But they didn't do to good with it. Actually, they lost money on it. So the next year, they wanted to rent it out. My wife, who was an excellent waitress, thought that she would like to take it over. She had another friend that was interested, too. So the two of them went into it together. We erected three big billboards eight-foot wide and twelve feet high, with three of them on either side of the building. I knew a local fellow that was crippled, but he was an excellent artist, and had him to paint a girl on each one of them. Two of them were in shorts and a halter, two in swimsuits and two of them were in evening gowns. One was blond-headed, one black-headed, one white-headed, one with auburn hair, one redheaded, and one was a brunette. I put up the money for my wife's share to get them started. The girls did pretty well that summer. They didn't get rich off of it. But, they did make a fair profit off of it.

As we had a couple of extra bedrooms in the house, we had my grandmother living with us to baby-sit the children while we worked. We didn't expect her to do any work whatsoever, just be there with the children. But of course she did do part of the housework. Things worked out pretty good, until one day after I finished breakfast I didn't have anything to do until 10 o'clock I slipped back into our bedroom and laid down on the bed to catch a little sleep. We didn't have real expensive furniture, but we did have good furniture. We were always particular about not letting the children jump up and down on the davenports or beds, and would punish them if we caught them doing it. I was lying there on my bed, and my grandmother had evidently thought I had gone to work. She came into the living room with my boy and I heard her tell him, "Well, Ellery, your dad has gone to work now, so you can get up and jump on the davenport now if you want to." I didn't say anything, I just kept quiet until they went back into the kitchen. I slipped out and went to work. When I came home that night, I waited until the kids were put to bed, then, I asked my grand-mother, "Why did you tell Ellery that since I was gone to work, he could jump on the davenport?" She said, "Oh, I never said any such thing." I told her, "you didn't know it, but I was lying there on my bed resting a little bit, and I heard you tell Ellery to do exactly that. We had it out kind of hot and heavy, and as a result, I told her that she was going to have to get out, because we couldn't have her countermanding all of our rules and regulations for the children. Well, we had to have a housekeeper and baby sitter then. So we hired a young girl who was married and her husband was in the army. She had a baby about six months old. She was a fair cook and did a fair job of housekeeping. At the end of the season, my wife and her partner closed up the drive-in. Then my wife took all of her profits and took a vacation trip and went out to Ohio to visit her folks. She never paid me back a penny of the money I had advanced her to start up on, and I could have really used it. Although I had pretty steady work during the summer seasons and made pretty fair wages, it had taken everything that I had made to make our house payments, make payments on the money I had borrowed and to keep food on the table. I had paid very little attention to myself, and at this particular time, I realized that as for clothing I was down to just what I had on my back. So I decided that if my wife was going to blow all of her money on a vaca-tion, that I was going to take the profits off the job I was just winding up, and get myself a new wardrobe. I had about $750.00 profit off the job. I took and blew the whole works on a new wardrobe. I got two suits off the rack (good ones), six dress shirts, three pairs of slacks, two pairs of dress shoes, a new pair of work shoes, six pairs of work pants, six work shirts, a dozen pair of shorts and under-shirts, a good overcoat, a new hat, a pair of driving gloves and a half dozen ties.

Our new housekeeper's husband would call her collect and talk for hours at a time. I didn't know this until I got my phone bill and found out that it was over $120.00. One day he came to visit his wife and just moved in and took over the whole house as if he owned it. He was trying to tell me what I could do and what I couldn't do. That didn't go over too good with me. I ordered him out of the house. He refused to go and said that he would go when he got good and ready in a couple of weeks. He was a large person, larger than me, and a roughneck. I went to the police station and told our chief of police what the situation was. I wanted him to come and put the guy out. He said, "Well you will have to swear out a warrant for him." I said, "Anything, just get him out of the house." I swore out the warrant and the chief, who was a big guy himself at about six foot seven or eight and about 300 pounds, came down and collard the fellow. By comparison, he made the guy look small. The guy started to give him a rough time. He didn't argue. It took about two minutes to handcuff his hands behind his back. He took him out, put him in the squad car and took him to the jail. He then called the MPs and told them that they had him in jail there. The MPs said, "Good, we are looking for him ourselves. He is AWOL and we'll be out to pick him up." Which is what happened. I never heard anything more from or about him after that. He couldn't phone his wife So I had no trouble with the phone bill after that. On the other hand, she couldn't phone him either.

When I eliminated my partner Joe Farkas, I called one of my stepmother's brothers, with whom I had been very close buddies before the war, and asked him to buy in with me as a partner. He had been in the army and had been stationed in Hawaii, and he had come home on furlough. While he was on furlough his outfit had been shipped out for the South Pacific. He returned to Hawaii where he was assigned to permanent duty and spent the rest of war there. He and his wife were living in

Maywood a suburb of Chicago. He was working for a large company that was operating several gravel pits. He agreed to come out and work with me. I took my truck, which was a large flatbed truck, and made three trips into Maywood and back to move him out to Delavan, where he had rented a nice apartment, and he went to work. He didn't know anything about the painting business, but he was a willing worker and learned quickly. The first year we got along very well. Starting in the second year though, he seemed to think that it was more his business than mine. We could be working on a job, say thirty miles east of Delavan, and when we were finishing up the job at five p.m. and only had two more hours of work left to complete the job, I wanted to stay and complete the job, so that in the morning we could start another job west of Delavan. He said, "No, my wife will have dinner ready for me at six p.m. and I have to be there." So, we went home, and he had his dinner. The next morning we had to go back out and finish up two hours work. That killed the entire morning for us. Then he took a two weeks vacation, which he should have taken during the winter, and of course I was working all that time and splitting 50/50 with him on what I made. When he came back from vacation he worked one day and then took off and went down to his brother's farm near Hebron, IL. He worked the farm for two weeks while his brother went on vacation and when he came back, he brought his brother's big farm truck with him and spent the next week building a nice rack on it for his brother. I told Ray that I couldn't go on like that any more. I would just buy him out of the business. By that time I was fed up with partners, so I went it alone.

I hired a young fellow who was a very nice person and a good worker. He was having a lot of trouble at home with his folks and we had a spare bedroom so let him have it. We gave him his board and room and fifty cents an hour wages. I usually paid $1.00 an hour at that time, but with giving him his board and room, he was actually making about $1.50. Also, he made a pretty good baby sitter when we wanted to go out for an evening. One Sunday we took off and went down to Hebron to visit my aunt and uncle and were going to be gone for the whole day. He agreed to baby-sit the children for the whole day. When we got back home at about 10 p.m. Sunday night, he was waiting up for us. He had the kids in bed and told us, "...about 5 p.m. this afternoon, they got mad and decided they were going to run away. I helped them pack a suitcase, and they packed one blanket and most of their toys. When they were ready to go, I put them in the truck and drove them out to the edge of town, set them out on the edge of the highway, and went on down the highway for about a mile, turned around and came back. When I got back to them, they had opened up the suitcase and got the blanket out and were wrapped up in it. She had her doll and he had his teddy bear and they were ready to come home. I brought them home, fed them some supper and put them to bed." I guess that taught them a lesson and they never wanted to run away again.

We wanted a dog and some friends of mine had some relations living in a large apartment house in Milwaukee who had a pure bred, pure white Collie (which was rare) that they had raised from a puppy. The management of the apartment house had told them that they had to get rid of the dog or move. They had been in the apartment for about three years, and other apartments were hard to find at that time. They were looking for a good home for the dog. So, we agreed to take the dog and the people brought him out to us. His name was Rex and he was perfectly housebroken. He had his own bowls to eat and drink out of, and if you would put food out on a piece of paper for him he wouldn't touch it, it had to be in his bowl. At that time, we didn't have wall-to-wall carpeting; we had carpet down where there would be about a foot of floor space around the carpet. He would never step on the carpet he would walk on the floor around the edges of the carpet, without getting, on the carpet, and he never got up on a piece of furniture. Once, I threw his ball up on the davenport and he wanted to go and get the ball, but he wouldn't get up on the davenport. I kept urging him to go get it, finally he did jump up on the davenport and get the ball. But, when he realized where he was, he was just scared to death. He loved to ride in the car or truck. At night he knew about when I would get into the shop, which was about a mile across town from where we lived. I'd find him sitting there waiting for me so he could ride home with me.

He would get up every morning and walk the kids to school, which was nine blocks away. He would stop on the sidewalk across the street from the school and sit there and watch the kids until they entered the school. I know because I watched him a couple of times. The children got out of school at 3:30 p.m. in the afternoon and unfailingly at 3:15 p.m., he would go to the door and want out. He would go meet the kids and walk them home. He was a perfect house dog and perfect with the kids. We had him for about five years. He was a fairly old dog when we got him, and when he started to get sick and would throw up in the house (he just couldn't help it), we were discussing the idea of having him put away. We decided it was the best thing to do, because he was just to sick and the vet couldn't do anything for him. We decided we would call the police and have them come pick him up and take care of him. The wife picked up the phone and called the police department, it rang several times but she got no answer. As she hung the phone up, she said, "Well Rex, I guess you get a reprieve." He looked at her and then he looked at me with kind of sad eyes, turned around and went to the door and wanted out. We let him out and that was the last time we ever saw him. When he didn't return I started asking around town about him, but nobody remembered seeing him and they all knew him. Then out of curiosity, I made big circle around town, stopping at every farm asking about him, nobody had seen him. He went away to die by himself, and that was it.

One day Janet brought home a note from her teacher, telling us to teach her arithmetic at home. We believed in helping the kids and would help them with their homework, but they did have to do it themselves. For some reason I kept that note and laid it aside. The next week she brought home another note telling us to teach her geography at home, then the third week she came home with a third note telling us to teach her history at home. I put that note with the other two, and the next week she brought home a fourth note telling us to teach her reading at home. So I put that note with the other three and the next week she brought home a fifth note, from the teacher telling us to teach her spelling at home. Well, about that time, I told my wife, "What the devil are we sending her to school for if we have to teach her everything at home?" She said, "I was beginning to wonder that myself." The next morning as I was going to work, I had on my old work cloths and they were really filthy. When I did a paint job, I would wear the same paint cloths all the way through the job and then throw them away. I had a hat that must have had twenty five layers of paint on it. But I went to the school anyway, and walked into the principal's office, the secretary took one look at me and didn't know what to think. I asked for the principal and she said, "Well, he is not in right now." I said, "Fine, I'll just wait for him in his office." She said, "Oh you can't go in there." I just kept going and said, "Who is going to stop me?" I went in and sat down in his office, and it wasn't five minutes until she had him back there. He said, "Well, Mr. Spencer, what can I do for you?" I said, "For the last five weeks, we have been getting notes from Janet's teacher telling us to teach her English, history, mathematics and geography at home. We are thinking about pulling the girl out of school if we have to teach her everything at home. There is no point in sending her to school," He said, "Do you have those notes?" I said, "I sure do." He said, "May I see them?" I said, "You sure can." I handed them over to him. He looked them over and said, "You just wait right here and I'll be back shortly." I sat there and it was about ten minutes before he came back and handed me the notes. He said. "I'll guarantee you, you will never receive any notes like that again." He didn't say, but I know that teacher got a good going over from him.

In 1956, a paint store in town put on a program for painters. They had a paint chemist From Milwaukee come out and give us a lecture on paints, and he told us how paints were made and how to properly apply them. This was in the evening from 8 p.m. to 10 p.m. After the meeting, I was standing outside talking to the chemist and some how the conversation drifted around to the war, and the chemist said, "Well, you know there was a night that I will never forget." I said, "Tell me about it." He said, "It was the night that we crossed the Rhine River, about five miles below Worms. The engineers had thrown up a pontoon bridge across the river, and there was a German field piece on the other side of the river that had managed to hit the bridge and set fire to it. It was blazing and had the place lit up like daylight. They were out there throwing up another pontoon bridge right beside the one that was burning. Our convoy must have been backed for two or three miles, waiting for them to get the bridge finished so we could cross it, when three light tanks came out of nowhere, just as the engineers got the bridge finished. They went across the bridge and knocked out the field piece, and we made a safe crossing of the Rhine River." I'm standing there with my mouth wide open and told him, "You want to know something? I was in the second tank to go across that bridge." That was when I learned it was the Rhine River that we went across; all we ever knew was that it was a large river that we crossed.

We had an old colored garbage man, and everybody in town kind of looked down on him. If we were at home when he came to collect the garbage, we would always invite him in to have a cup of coffee with us and chat for a few minutes. He had me paint his house one time. As we were finishing up the job, he was out there with his checkbook wanting to pay us, which, was more than I could say for a lot of the white tradesmen that I had painted for in town. He and his wife invited us over for dinner once, and when we went there, their house was spic and span and as clean as it could be. She put on a marvelous meal for us and we really enjoyed it. Finally, the old gentleman died and did the townspeople ever get the shock of their lives when his estate was settled up. He was president of an extremely large colored organization in the southern part of the state. They found out that he owned one complete block of apartment houses in Detroit, Michigan. He was a multi-millionaire.

One time I came home from work and my wife was sitting there having coffee with a stranger, and as I came in she said, "I want you to meet Mr. Hackbarth. He wants to show us some cookware that he is selling." I said, "Well, there is no point in that, we just absolutely cannot afford it, I'll make a deal with him though, if he will go out and sell me a good paint job, I'll buy a set from him." She said, "That's just exactly what I told him you would say." "Well," he said, "Do you have any spare time?" I said, "Sure every day after dark." He said, "Well would you be allergic to earning some money in your spare time?" I said, "No, I'm always willing to earn money." He said, "Well I need a representative out here, and I would come out and train you." I said, "Tell me about it." It turned out that he was working with a crew out of an office in Racine, WI. They were selling Wearever Waterless cookware. He said, "I'll go out and get my samples, and I'll show you what it is like. Since it's supper time, I'll even cook supper here for you." Which he did. I have to say that the food was some of the best that I had ever eaten. I agreed to give it a try. He said, "Fine, you go get yourself cleaned up and we will go out right now. I have a couple of leads here in town," I took a bath, shaved, put on a suit and tie, and we started out. When we got about six blocks from the house he pulled over to the curb and stopped. He said, "Before we start in, we are going to have a little talk. There is one thing I want you to promise me that you will do." I said Okay. What is it?" He said, I want you to go out and put on ten displays." I said, "Well, I guess that I can do that alright." He said, "If at the end of ten displays you haven't sold anything, there is just one more thing that I want you to do," I figured he was going to say get the heck out of the business. But I said, "Okay, what is that?" He said, "I want you to go out and put on ten more displays." I said, "Well, I guess I can do that alright," then that will make twenty displays, and if after twenty displays you haven't sold anything, there is just one more thing I want you to do." I said." Yes, what is that?" He said, "Go out and put on twenty more displays. That will make forty displays, and if at the end of forty displays you haven't sold anything, there is just one more thing that I want you to do." I said, "Yes.' He said, "Get out of the business, you will never make a salesman." I promised him faithfully that I would put on the forty displays. We went on to his first appointment, and I sat there and watched him sell a seventeen-year-old girl a $360.00 set of cookware, out of which he made a ninety dollar commission. Then we went on to his next appointment, and he repeated the performance. That made him $180.00 in commission for two hours of work. It took me a week of hard work to make $180.00. I thought for that kind of money I'm getting into this business. We went home and I signed papers with them. He said, "We have a weekly sales meeting in Racine every Friday night which we would like for you to attend." I said, "Well, I guess I can do that." Racine was just sixty miles away. He said. "Fine, I'll bring a sample kit out to you next Monday, and work with you some more. I'll show you how to get leads and make appointments." Which he did, he worked with me all of that week, until I felt fairly confident that I could go it on my own. I started out and put on my first ten displays and never sold a thing. We'll, I thought I promised him I would put on ten more displays so I put on ten more. Never sold a thing. Well I thought that's twenty, and I had promised him I would put on twenty more, so here goes. Well, I put on seventeen more and on my thirty-seventh demonstration, I had an appointment with a young girl over in Walworth, a small town about twelve miles away. This was in December and it was cold. I put the demonstration on for Joyce (that was her name), and she was interested. I knew that she would like to have the set. It was the small set that I was trying to sell her for $85.00, but I simply couldn't get her to sign. She said that she couldn't sign without her boy friend being there. I gave a sigh and packed up my samples, put my coat and hat on, and went to the door. I had a hold of the doorknob and was saying good-bye to Joyce when I felt the knob turn and the door pushed in, almost knocking me down. In stomped her boy friend and he said, "What in hell is going on here?" I said, "I was just showing Joyce a set of cookware." He said, "Lets see the dammed stuff." I thought Oh boy here I go! I took my coat and hat off and went through the whole display for him. When I got through, I asked him "Well what do you think of it?" He never said a word. Just got up and stomped out of the house. I thought that's it. I packed up my samples again, put my coat and hat on again and was standing there by the door saying good-bye to Joyce a second time, when the door slammed open almost knocking me down again. In stomped her boy friend and he threw $85.00 down on then the table and said, "Give her the dammed set." I got out my order book and wrote her up. I went home for the night all pepped up. I went out the next night and sold another set and went out the next night and sold a third set. Three sets in a row. I went to the weekly meeting in Racine and turned in my orders for the three sets.

I figured I really had a grasp on the situation now and was going to town. Well I went for six weeks without another sale. Then I made another sale, just one. Then for a while I would make one sale a week, then, occasionally, I would come in with two sets a week.

Once in a great while I might have three sets. If anybody learned to sell cookware the hard way, it was me. I knew that I wasn't going to make any fortune out of it, but it was a good supplementary job.

Occasionally in the wintertime a group of six of us would get together and go to a town that we had never worked before, such as Waukegan, IL. We would separate and work in pairs. One pair would take one section of town, and the others would take another section of town. We would go to a grocery store and buy enough food to feed eight people, then we would pick out a likely looking house where we knew the woman was at home and, although we were complete strangers, we would go up to the door, each one of us with a sack of groceries in his arms. When the woman would come to the door, we would tell her, "Ma'am, my name is Hackbarth and this is Mr. Spencer here. We work for the Wearever Aluminum Company and had an appointment with one of your neighbors down the street to put on a dinner for her and her husband and some of their friends. We bought all of this food here, which we showed her, and when we got to their house nobody was home. They must have forgot all about our appointment. We were just wondering if you would let us come in and cook supper for you and your husband tonight? We'll furnish all of the food; we have it right here. She would think for a few minutes and say, "Sure, come right in." We would go into the kitchen and start unpacking our cooking utensils, and were separating the food and setting it out, Hackbarth would say, "Gee, we've got enough food for seven or eight people, why don't you get on the phone and invite some of your friends over." We would end up putting on a supper for six to eight people and, of course, we had her to watch us so she would see that we didn't use any water of any kind, even boiling an egg without water. Then, after the meal we would put on our demonstration, and, if we were lucky, we would sell about three sets there, which we would more often than not.

I made an appointment once with a farm girl. I had told her that I would cook her a cake on top of the stove. When I got to her house about 5 p.m., she met me at the door and took me in to introduce me to her mother, and her mother said, "Did you tell Dorothy that you could bake on top of the stove?" I said, "Yes, Ma'am." She said, "Well, come into the kitchen, if you can bake on top of the stove, I'll buy a set, too." I went into the kitchen, and she had an old wood cook stove there, which she had all fired up. Well, I hadn't ever cooked anything on a wood or coal stove I had always used gas or electric and I didn't know whether I could bake on that stove or not. But I thought, I'll give it the old college try. I mixed up the batter, put the cake on top of the front burner, and when the pan got hot enough, I moved it to the back burner where there is less heat. The cake came out perfect. After the demonstration, her mother was good for her word and bought a $360.00 dollar set, and when she, did, the girl bought one, too.

There were two girls in Lake Geneva, who shared an apartment. I had been trying to get a hold of them for over a month, but never found them at home. One night I came through Lake Geneva about 12:00 p.m., and I noticed the lights were on in their apartment. I stopped and thought, was this too late to go up and see them? I had been trying to get them, and could never find them at home. But, they're home now, so I'll just go up, they can't any more than say no. I went up and knocked on their door, and they came to their door in their pajamas. I told them who I was and what I wanted. I caught them at just the right time. They were ready for bed and weren't sleepy and had nothing else to do. I went back down and got my sample kit and put on a display. At 1 a.m. in the morning I wrote up orders for two sets.

Whenever we sold a set, we would always ask for referrals and get three or four, or sometimes a half a dozen of some of their friends, who were engaged or wanted to fill their hope chest. That was always a good source of good leads. We would always watch the daily paper, to see who had just gotten engaged. Or, we would get a hold of a high school annual, and just pick a bunch of names out of the senior class, and start calling them, and usually we would manage to make two or three appointments that way.

Finally, the Wearever Company came out with a set of knives and kitchen cutlery, which were absolutely the finest knives ever made. They were guaranteed for a lifetime and I have a set in my kitchen now that I have had for forty years, and they are still as sharp as they were when I got them, and they have never been sharpened. Well, we would be real sneaky. After we would sell a girl a set of Wearever, we would pack up and get ready to go, and then, one of us would say, "Oh golly, I almost forgot, the company has come out with a beautiful set of knives, would you like to see them?" We'll, they were all pepped up in the buying mood, and they would say, "Yes." Usually, we would walk out with a double order, one for the cookware, and one for the knives.

When we first bought our house, I had over estimated my earning power. We had gone heavily in debt for furniture. We had picked up a used dining room set, for $900.00. It was a beautiful set, with table, six chairs with upholstered backs on them. And also, for a stove, refrigerator, washing machine, living room furniture, davenport, two overstuffed chairs, and two bedroom sets with all of our cooking equipment. And, a month after we had moved in, a salesman came along, selling blown in insulation for attics, and I let him sell me a job, our attic really needed it, but, I couldn't afford it at the time, because it was another $350.00. We had a coal furnace in the basement that we had to buy a winter's supply of coal for, which wasn't exactly cheap, plus all of our living expenses. Also, I was buying power equipment and tools, in order to set up my shop. It got to the point that we couldn't make our house payments. So, after three years, we had to sell the house. We did get enough out of the house to make a down payment on another smaller house. I had been juggling loans between the two banks in town, to keep things going. But, eventually, that caught up with me, too. The banks were calling my notes in. So, we had to sell that house.

About a month before we sold the house, I had hired an auctioneer to auction off my shop equipment. When the day came for the auction, there were only three people that showed up for it. He had never even advertised it at all. I called the auction off and hired another auction firm to auction our household stuff off, and they were supposed to advertise it in our daily paper and the daily paper of several neighboring towns for about a month in advance. They were supposed to put out flyers in the stores. They didn't do any of this. Three days before the auction, they ran a little, small ad in the local paper, and as a result, there were only a dozen people there for our auction. And, they were there mainly to see what we had, and not to buy. The auctioneer put a piece up on the block and called for bids, and one person would make an opening bid for $5.00 or $10.00, and nobody else would bid against them, so the auctioneers would sell it for that price. When it came to our dining room set, that we had paid $900.00 for, somebody made an opening aid of $7.00, and nobody would bid against them. I told my uncle that was there to start bidding on that and run the bid up. He did, and we ran the bid up to $55.00, then dropped the bid and let the other person have it for $55.00. It was a widow woman that was a friend of ours. Well, anyway we realized a total of $150.00 off all of our six rooms of furniture. We should have had at least $1,500.00. We were then without a home, so we moved in with my aunt and uncle on their farm, down near Hebron, IL. I still had my painting equipment, so I kept painting, until it got too cold in the fall. Eddie Hackbarth had been promoted to superintendent, and was given southern Michigan as his territory. He wanted me to come out and work with him. I had an old clunker that I was driving, so after talking it over with my wife, I decided to go out and join Eddie. I had a $1,000.00 profit that I had made off of my last paint job that I could take with me. I figured that would last me quite a while, and I could bank most of my commissions. I headed for Michigan on the first of November and got just east of Gary, IN, when the tie rod broke on my car. The car went out of control, left the road, and rolled over three times into a field. Fortunately, I was not hurt. I was shook up a little, but that was okay. I hitched a ride back into Gary, bought another car, an old Chevrolet sedan. That car dealer knew a sucker when he saw one. The car he sold me had been a taxi and must have had at least 100,000 miles on it, and it gave me nothing but trouble. I managed to keep it going. I had to because I was just about broke after buying it. But anyway, I got out to Kalamazoo, and I figured I would be working there with Eddie, but he said, "No," that he wanted me out at a little town about twenty miles outside of Kalamazoo. So, I went out there and rented a room. I was doing pretty good, coming in with three or four sets a week. At that time, Michigan still had all of their one-room school houses throughout the countryside, and I would go out and hit one of the school houses at noon, and put on a demonstration for the teacher, and sell her and go on down a few more miles to the next little school, and get the teacher right after school was out, just before she left. This worked out pretty good for me until I started running out of schools. One day I sold a girl, named Alice, a large set of Wearever and asked her for referrals. She gave me the names of two of her friends. I went and called on the first one, and she let me put on the

215

demonstration for her, then she bought a set, too. I asked her for referrals, and she gave me one name, then she said, "I suppose Alice gave you her sister's name." I said, "No, she never even mentioned that she had a sister." She said, "Oh yeah, she has a sister. She works in Kalamazoo and shares an apartment with five other girls there." I said, "Give me her name and address, and you will get full credit for any business that I do off of her." The girl's name was Mary - I can't think of her last name now. Anyway, I headed for Kalamazoo and got over to the apartment shortly after the girls had got home from work. I knocked on the door and when one of the girls answered, I asked for Mary. Mary came to the door and I told her who I was and what I wanted, and that her sister bought a set, and her friend bought a set, and had referred me to her, and that I would like to put on a demonstration for her and the other girls. She said, "No, I'm not interested." She shut the door in my face. I started down the steps, and I thought to myself, Spencer old boy, there are six girls in that apartment, and you've got to get in there somehow. So I turned around and went back. I didn't knock; I just opened the door and said, "Hey Mary." She turned around again. I said, "How would you like it if I came in Friday and cooked supper for you girls? I'd furnish all of the food, do all of the cooking and work, and all of the cleanup work afterwards. They wouldn't have to do a thing, just watch." Well, that kind of hit a chord with her and the other girls; they heard that, too. She came back to the door and I made arrangements to come over Friday afternoon and put on the dinner for them. One of the other girls volunteered to quit work early that afternoon and be there at the apartment at 3:00 p.m. to let me in.

I knew that this was going to be too big a deal to handle by myself. So, I went to see Eddie, and told him what I had lined up. I said that I needed his help. He said, "Fine. Let's just sit down right now and figure out what we are going to need in the line of food." Well,

Friday morning, we went shopping at the supermarket and picked up enough food for ten people. At 3:00 p.m. that afternoon, we were at the apartment, and the girl that had volunteered to come home early, was there and let us in. We went in the kitchen, unpacked our food and set to work. We had the girl stay right with us all of the time, so she could see what all we were doing and could vouch to the other girls that we hadn't used any water to cook with. We even hard-boiled an egg without water. So, when the girls got home at 5:00 p.m., we had the meal all cooked and the table all set. They pulled their coats and hats off and sat down to the table, and we sat down with them and ate right with them. We had our display all set out in the living room. We let the girls go look at the equipment while we washed up the dishes, pots and pans, and cleaned the kitchen up. Then, we went into the living room and I put on the demonstration for the girls. Eddie was sitting right next to the front door and when I got through with the demonstration, and just before I could start to close on them, there was a bang at the front door. One of the girls jumped up and said, "That's my boyfriend, I've got to go. He doesn't like to be kept waiting." She grabbed her coat, and headed to the front door, and just as she got there, Eddie grabbed her arm, and said, "Hey you haven't bought your set of Wearever yet." She said, "No, but I've got to go." He whipped out a blank contract and said, "All you have to do, is sign here." She said, "Yes, but I wouldn't know what I was buying. Eddie said, "That's all right, we'll just give you the same set that all of the girls are buying. They will be a witness to that fact." She said, "Yes, but I haven't got any money for a down payment." Eddie said, "Shucks, you've got $20.00 haven't you?" She said, "Yes." Eddie said, "Just give me the $20.00, and you can send me the other $70.00 later when you get paid.'" She pulled out a $20.00 bill, gave it to him, and signed a contract, and left with her date. The girls had invited another girl, so there were actually seven girls there that night. We sat there and we wrote up seven contracts for the largest set we had, the $360.00 set. We made $90.00 commission on each set there. When you get a bunch of girls together like that, they are somewhat like a bunch of sheep. If you sell one, you'll sell them all. If you miss on the first one, none of them will buy. And, if Eddie hadn't of been there by that doorway, I would have lost the whole deal that night. The next day, we took our wives out for a big steak dinner, to celebrate the occasion.

At Christmas time, my wife came out and joined me. Then, after Christmas, she went out to Ohio to visit her folks. A week later, I was supposed to drive out and join her. The day I was supposed to leave Ohio, I had two appointments. I had one in the afternoon and one in the evening. I kept the one in the afternoon, and thought I would just forget the one in the evening, and get an early start for Ohio. But, when I had completed the afternoon demonstration, I got to thinking that maybe I had better keep that appointment tonight. It was with two farm girls who were sisters. It was thirty miles in the opposite direction from where I had to go in Ohio.

I made the appointment at 6:00 p.m., and when I got there, the sisters let me in. They had invited another friend, so I actually had three girls there. Well, I sat there and put on the whole demonstration and none of the girls were really paying any attention to me. I was getting pretty fed up with them and figured that my time was just wasted. When I finished the demonstration, I had showed them everything except our coffee maker. I wasn't even going to show that to them, but then I thought oh well, I had showed them everything else, I will show them the coffee maker, too. I held up the coffee maker, and said, "This is our drip coffee maker." The visiting girl reached out, grabbed the coffee maker out of my hands and said, "This, I want." I reached out and grabbed the coffee maker back and said, "This, you cannot have." She grabbed it back again and said, "I'm going to have this." I let her keep it then, but I told her that she couldn't have that because it was my sample, and that I had to have it. She said, "You order me out one." I said, "There is a little catch to that. They are sold with the set; they are not sold separately. If you want the coffee maker, you are going to have to buy a whole set." Well by golly, she bought the whole set, just to get the coffee maker. Then, the other two sisters each bought a set right along with her. Well, I went back to Kalamazoo with $270.00 extra in my pocket, picked up my suitcase, drove all night, and got out to Zanesville, OH, where my wife was at, about 8:00 a.m. the next morning. I stayed there a couple of days with her and got rested up, then went on out to Pennsylvania to the Wearever factory and saw how they manufactured the cooking utensils. I came back to Ohio, picked up my wife, and went back to Allegan, MI. After another week, I put her on a bus and she went back to Illinois. I continued selling there until the first of April, when I had to get back to Illinois and go to painting. The last demonstration that I put on in Michigan was for three girls. I sold two of them a large set and the third girl wanted a set, too, but she didn't have the money. She was broke and out of work. So, I told her, "I'll tell you what I'll do. I'll fill out the contract here, and leave it with you. Sometime in the future when you've got the money you can just sign the contracts and mail them back to me in Illinois," I gave her a self-addressed envelope to use, too, and went on. I figured that I would never hear from her. But, six months later, I got a letter from Michigan and opened it up. There were the contracts and a check for $360.00. I sent the contract in to the company. You can just never tell what people will do. I was positive that I would never hear from her again.

My wife had been bothered quite a bit with flu and colds over the years. She decided that she was going out to Phoenix, AZ for her health. I pretty well knew why she wanted to go at that particular time. My cousin was leaving and driving to Arizona, and she wanted to go with him. So, I didn't say anything, I just let her go, knowing that I probably wouldn't see her back again, which was alright with me, too. The kids and I stayed on there with my aunt and uncle on their farm.

My old compressor finally gave out on me. And, not having the money to buy another one. I was out of the painting business. I was feeling kind of depressed and downhearted about the way everything had turned out. I left the kids with my aunt and uncle and went into Kenosha, WI. I took a job driving a cab and was put on the night shift. As I couldn't sleep more than three or four hours during the daytime, I would spend sometimes as much as eighteen hours at a time in the cab. Well, I was one of the top bookers and was making just barely enough money to exist on. The owner of the cab company hired his nephew to drive. The nephew came in and was bragging about how he was going to show everybody how to drive a cab. He started challenging me, wanting to make a breakfast bet, that if he booked more money during the night than I did, then I would have to buy his breakfast, or vice versa. Well, we made a good many breakfast bets, and I had a good many free breakfasts, as he never could beat me.

One night when I first started on the shift, I got a fare that took me to the outer edge of the town. Then, I was posted there until somebody out there phoned in and wanted to come downtown. I sat there until midnight without moving. My antagonist had been having a very good night. He had had about ten or twelve moves, while I was just sitting. So, he called over the radio to the dispatcher, and wanted to make a breakfast bet with me. I said, "Okay." Five minutes later, I got a call to go pick up a man. When he got in the cab, I asked him, "Where are we going?" He said, "Racine," which was about twenty-five miles from us. So, we went to Racine. I knew my fare off of that out of town trip would catch me up with the boss' nephew. After I dropped my fare in Racine, I stopped in a little restaurant to get something to eat. As

I was eating, I noticed two sailors eating there, too. I knew that those sailors had to be back to their base by 6:00 a.m. in the morning. But, their base was located about thirty miles south of Kenosha. As late at night as it was, it was about 1:00 a.m., I knew that they were going to have a time getting back to their base. I waited until they were finished eating, and they left the restaurant and started walking. I got in my cab and followed them. I let them get about three blocks from the restaurant then pulled up alongside them and asked, "You headed back to the base." They said, "Yes." I said, "I'm headed back to Kenosha. You guys get in the back seat, and I'll give you a ride back to Kenosha free of charge." This was something that we were absolutely not supposed to do. We were not supposed to solicit any fares or pick up and give anyone a free ride. We got back to Kenosha on the north side, and I talked them into having me take them to the south side of Kenosha. I called this fare into the dispatcher and told them that I was back in town and had just picked up a couple of sailors who wanted to get to the south side of Kenosha. On the way through Kenosha, I told the boys that they were never going to make reveille, because it was already 3:00 p.m. Anyway, I managed to talk them into hiring me to take them back to their base, which was another thirty miles out of town trip. So, I called that into the dispatcher and headed to Waukegan, IL. Well, the next morning, when I got my free breakfast, was the boss' nephew ever mad. At midnight when he made the bet, he had over $25.00 booked already, and he knew I only had a $2.50 booking at that time. I think he suspected that I had done a little hocus-pocus in order to get those two out of town trips. But, he didn't know and couldn't prove anything. There was a Jewish wholesale company there in Kenosha. I went in and talked to them and they were willing to give me a line of credit up to an amount of $1,000.00. At this time, I had acquired a big old nine-passenger Packard limousine, that had two jump seats in the back, and a glass panel between the front and back that could be raised and lowered. The back seat was almost big enough to set up housekeeping in. On my first day off, I dropped by the wholesale house, and loaded the back seat up with a lot of small toys (I mean small toys), and novelties, and headed for the countryside. I started setting me up a route. I would go into a store and talk them into letting me put in a line of goods, on a consignment basis. Then, I would come by once every two weeks and service the account. Whatever they had sold, I would replace. They would pay me for just whatever they had sold.

About this time, I started dating the lady that had bought our dining room set at our auction. Her name was Mary and we had known each other for several years. She had been a good friend of my wife's and had worked as a waitress with her for a couple of years. She was red headed and had kind of a fiery temperament, but, a very good person, and we got along very nicely. She had a boy and a girl in high school and was buying her own home, remodeling it, and working two or three jobs at a time, in order to pay for remodeling it. At this time, I was in debt to the tune of about $5,000.00, which I didn't have and couldn't pay at that time. I knew if I had time over a period of a couple of years, I could manage to get that paid off, but my creditors were not willing to give me that amount of time. So, I was forced into the bankruptcy court.

I hired an attorney in Elkhorn, WI, to put me through the bankruptcy. The bankruptcy court was in Racine, WI. As I had had to list all of my debts, I had included my debt to the wholesale company, which was about $600.00 at that time. Ordinarily, creditors do not attend a bankruptcy proceeding, but the wholesale company had a man there along with a deputy sheriff from Kenosha. As soon as the proceedings were over and before I had a chance to get out of the building, the deputy sheriff collared me, served a warrant on me, and arrested me for embezzlement. Well, my attorney told me, "You go ahead and go back to Kenosha, and I will meet you there at the sheriff's department." So, when I got down to the sheriff's department, I waited outside the building until I saw my attorney go in. Then, I went on in. He arranged to have me released on my own recognizance. I had had an open account with that company and had never handled any of their money, so there was absolutely no way that I could have embezzled anything from them. They were just mad because they were losing some money.

When my case came up in court, my attorney called only one witness in my defense, and that was the owner of the wholesale company. My attorney cross-examined him for over an hour. When he got through with him, he had a good enough case worked up against him to put him in jail. There were several laws that they had been breaking. The Judge said, "I don't see why you would want to railroad this man, because he is not an embezzler, there is no way he could have embezzled any money from you, and you just consider yourself lucky that I don't start prosecuting you. The case is dismissed."

Florence Reynolds, who lived in Williams Bay, WI, contacted me. I had put on a Wearever dinner for her and her husband and some of their friends. She was starting up in the hosiery business and wanted to know if I would be her salesman and agent. I was to get a 10% commission on everything that was sold. That sounded like a fairly good deal. I quit the cab company. I was tired of them anyway. I went to work for her and contacted a friend of mine in Walworth, WI, who was a good carpenter and had him make up display cases for us. The cases were two feet deep, four feet wide, and six feet high, containing several shelves for the hosiery. We started out small, because I had to get out and contact the storeowners and convince them to allot floor space to me for display racks, which was sometimes pretty hard to do. However, as time went on, I managed to build it up to 45 stores, which I serviced every two weeks. This territory covered quite an area, all of southern Wisconsin and northern Illinois. I had stops in Beloit, Janesville, Madison, Milwaukee, Racine, Kenosha, Burlington, Waukegan, Elkhorn, Delavan, and several other cities.

As you come west out of Kenosha on Highway 50 there is a double overhead bridge and there is a tavern that sits underneath the second one that has an outlet directly onto the highway. One miserable, sleety, icy night in January as I was coming down the bridge, I saw a car sitting at the edge of the road, waiting for me to pass, I thought. But just as I got down to him, he pulled directly out in front of me, and I hit him broadside. I didn't even have a chance to apply my brakes. That just totaled out the station wagon that I was driving. I wasn't hurt and neither was he. That was really a miserable night. I had to call Mrs. Reynolds and have her bring out another vehicle, then transfer my load of hosiery into the other vehicle.

Mrs. Reynolds wasn't too happy about the accident, but neither was I. Then she got me a good used van to drive and things went along good for a few weeks. I was north out of Hebron, IL and wanted to look at my road schedule, which was on a clipboard lying directly behind me. I reached around back and couldn't find it, so I turned my head and looked to see where it was. When I did this I automatically turned the steering wheel, too, and into the ditch I went. I didn't tip over but I took down four or five fence posts, I looked up and I was headed right for a creek. I didn't want to end up in that creek and ruin about $1,500.00 worth hosiery, so, I just stepped on the gas, gave the steering wheel a yank to the left, and went up the bank, made it onto the highway, slued around all over the road until I finally got control of the car again, and went on my way. I got a couple of miles down the road and I happened to think, "Spencer, you took out four or five fence posts back there. You need to get out and look at the right side of your van." I pulled off, stopped, and walked around the van to look at it, and sure enough, it had taken the right front fender and running board off of it. I just went on, as I knew there wasn't any reason to go back and look for the fender and running board, as they had be pure junk.

One of the stops that I had set up in Milwaukee was with a lady that ran a maternity shop. Her name was Dorothy Ryan and she was rather a remarkable seamstress. A woman would come in, wanting a maternity dress made, and Dorothy would take one look at her, pick up a bolt of cloth and her scissors, and start cutting, without even taking any measurements. In ten minutes, she would have a skirt cut out that would be perfect for her. I have seen her do that more than once. I started dating Dorothy. I know now that was the second worst mistake that I had ever made in my life. The worst mistake that I had ever made was in dropping Mary, who I had been dating for a year in Delavan. In my hindsight, I know that Mary would have made a wonderful wife for me.

One day when I was going into Rockford, IL, I went to pass a pickup truck. I was 2/3 of the way past him when, without ever looking, he made a left-hand turn, and hit me in the right side right on the passenger door. He just tipped me over and I went scooting along on my side in the ditch. I was blamed for the accident, because I was passing him at a crossroad, but he had never given any turn indication, hand signals, or otherwise. He certainly could not have looked before he started to turn, or he would have seen me. I was really disgusted, two nice vehicles totaled out in about six week's time. I thought if I was going to keep wrecking them, I would get an old clunker to drive. I went to the junkyard and they had an old 36 Plymouth four door sedan that they were just starting to junk out. They had pulled the battery out of it when I got there. I asked them, "Will that old clunker run?" They said, "Yeah it runs pretty good." I said, "How much do you want for it?" They said $50.00." I said fine you just sold it. Put the battery back in it." I got in and drove that old clunker away. It had a cloth top on it with a hole in it the size of a manhole cover and when it rained the rain just poured in on me. I drove that old car for about two years and put about thirty thousand miles on it, and never once had an ounce of trouble with it. One day I was going down the highway doing about sixty and I saw a wheel go spinning down the road and passing me up. I thought somebody's lost a wheel. I got just a little further down the road, and eased up on the foot feed, and I could feel the right rear end start to drop down. I thought, oh boy, I'm the one that lost a wheel. I don't know how, but I managed to pull the car off to the side of the road and bring it to a stop without rolling it. I got out and walked on down the road, picked up my wheel, brought it back and put it back on the car and went on my way again.

I had taken a bachelor's apartment in Williams Bay, which is where Mrs. Reynolds lived and where our warehouse was located. One morning I woke up at 6:00 a.m. and started to roll over to get out of bed and threw my back out. Boy, I could hardly move. It took me from 6:00 a.m. to 10:00 a.m. before I managed to sit up on the bed. I still had to get dressed and get about a block and a half to where my car was parked, then drive about twenty-five miles to get to my chiropractor at Elkhorn. I got there to see him at about 5:30 p.m. in the afternoon. Well, he gave me a good adjustment, and I walked out of there without any trouble. But, I never will forget that day.

My aunt and uncle were keeping my two children, Janet and Ellery. So, one day my aunt called and told me that Ellery had been kicked off of the school bus and would not be allowed to ride the school bus anymore. My uncle had to drive him to school and then go pick him up, which was no good, because my uncle had more than he could do to manage his farm. So, I went out there and asked my aunt, "What is the trouble? Why did they kick him off of the bus?" She said, "Well, they claimed that he pulled a knife on a girl and threatened to cut her." I said, "Something must be wrong. As far as I know, he doesn't even have a knife. Who was the girl that he threatened?" She gave me the girl's name. It was one of their neighbors that lived about a mile and a half down the road from them. So, I went down to the neighbors and asked them if they would mind if I talked to their daughter. They said, "No, we don't mind." They called her in and said that Mr. Spencer wanted to talk to her. She came in and seemed like a nice girl to me. I asked her, "Would you tell me just exactly what happened between you and Ellery?" She said, "Sure, he pulled a knife out of his pocket, and said, look what I found this morning. It was an old rusted up knife that was so rusty, you couldn't even open the blades on it. He never threatened me at all. He just said to look at what he found that morning." I asked her, "Would you mind going with me and telling Mr. Taggart just what you've told me?" She said, "Yes, I'd be glad to." So, we went to see Taggart, and she told him just exactly what she told me. And, as the consequence, Ellery was allowed on the bus again.

Another time my aunt called me, and said that Ellery had been kicked out of school, for being a troublemaker. And, they weren't going to allow him back in school at all, and I was going to have to send him to a private school. She also said that the school board had set a date, and they wanted her and me to be present, so they could tell us just exactly why they didn't want Ellery in school anymore. I said, "Fine, I'll be there with you." Well, come Wednesday night, when the meeting was set up, I picked up my aunt and went into Hebron, and went down to the high school where the meeting was going to be. We got there about a half-hour early and went in to talk to Mr. Taggart. I asked him, "What is all of this about Ellery being such a troublemaker?" "Well," he said, "The other day, Ellery picked a bad fight with one of the other boys, and we can't have that." I said, "Well, just how did the fight start, and what was it all about?" Taggart said, "Well, I have some notes here that I made at the time. Would you like to see them?" I said, "Sure." So he handed the notes to me, and I looked at them, and the first thing I read was, that Earl picked a fight with Ellery. The note went on and gave more particulars about the fight. I folded the notes up, put them in my pocket, and Taggart said, "May I have my notes back?" I said, "You sure can. I'll give them back to you right after the meeting." He didn't say any more, and we went into the meeting. There were six board members there, and one of them was Earl's father. We sat down and Taggart introduced each one of us separately. After the introductions, each board member got up and gave about a five-minute speech, telling exactly why they expelled Ellery from school and why I was going to have to send him to a private school. My aunt and I never said one word while all this was going on. When the board members were all through, Taggart asked us if we wanted to say anything. I got up, and I said, "I sure do. Each of you gentlemen have taken the time here to tell us all of your reasons for kicking Ellery out of school. I got here a little early before the meeting and had a talk with Mr. Taggart here. Mr. Taggart gave me some notes that he made at the time of the fight, and I would just like to read the notes to you gentlemen." I pulled them out of my pocket and opened them up, and started reading. "Earl picked a fight with Ellery. Now these notes were made at the time and all of you are claiming that Ellery started the fight, but, according to Mr. Taggart's notes, Earl started the fight." I pointed to Earl's father and said, "How come Earl hasn't been expelled from school? He is the one that was the troublemaker; he was the one who started the fight." Well, their mouths kind of hung open and they didn't have anything to say. Finally, Mr. Taggart asked my aunt and me if we would mind stepping outside the room for a minute while they had a private discussion. We walked out into the hallway and about five minutes later, Mr. Taggart came out to us and took us back into the room. The president of the board said, "Mr. Spencer, I believe we owe you an apology. Ellery has been reinstated, and you have our apologies." I said, "Fine, we'll go on home." That took care of that.

Mrs. Reynolds was a character. I was riding with her one day and we were going down the highway doing about sixty, when she decided she wanted to change her hose. I told her, "Fine, pull over to the side and I'll move over there and drive and you can change your hose." She said, "Oh that's not necessary, I can do it." Well, she changed her hose all right, while we were doing sixty miles an hour on the highway. I can't describe the contortions that she went through, but it sure scared the daylights out of me. Along about this time, the hosiery business was falling off and Mrs. Reynolds was forced to shut down. That meant that I was out of a job. I had kept up my membership in the carpenter's union and was able to get a job as a carpenter. I went to work for a big gravel company out of Chicago at their Algonquin, IL site where they were going to open up a new gravel pit. They were putting up a building there that would eventually reach up to 185 feet in height. Well, I was finally making some decent money again. Well, Dorothy had got herself into a financial bind and was just writing checks all over the place. I was making better then $1,200.00 a month at the carpenter job, so I had money enough that I was able to advance Dorothy enough money to get her checking account straightened out before the law caught up with her. Then, we got married, and she closed her maternity shop down. Well, I had seen an ad in the paper wanting a farm caretaker. I had never heard of a farm caretaker before, so answered the ad to find out what it was all about. There was a wealthy businessman in Chicago that had bought a 150-acre farm on the outskirts of Huntley, IL, and he wanted somebody to move on the farm and take care of his three horses, pigeons, chickens, and geese. He and his wife lived on the farm for the three summer months, and he wanted somebody on there for the other nine months to take care of the farm animals and keep things ship-shape. The deal was that we would get our rent free, and we could just move into their house, which was fully furnished, including all kitchen utensils, pots, pans, china, silverware, linens, etc. All we had to do was to bring our clothes, and move in, although, we did have to pay our utilities. So, I signed a contract with the man and Dorothy and I moved in. Dorothy had three daughters. One was nineteen and she chose to stay in Milwaukee, the second one was sixteen, and her third daughter was six years old. So, we had three girls - her two daughters and my daughter, Janet.

One year, my uncle gave Janet a thoroughbred black-angus bull calf to raise for her 4H project. She raised the calf up and then exhibited it at the county fair at Woodstock and won a first place blue ribbon with him. She also won a wristwatch, a $150.00 prize, and the right to take him down to Springfield to the state fair. Well, we took him down to the state fair and she didn't do quite so well with him there, but she did get a twenty-fourth place ribbon, the last one that they gave out. I'm no cattle expert, but I always believed that she should have gotten at least a second or third place with that bull. Where as far as I could tell, her bull was as good or better than any of the others there. But, then I wasn't a prominent farmer and the others had all been exhibiting animals for several years.

Janet was crazy about horses. When she was about eight or nine, I had bought her a Shetland pony, which she dearly loved. When she was about twelve or thirteen, we sold the Shetland and I bought her another larger pony, which was about three-fourths the size of a horse. It was a brown Scottish pony with a bobtail. I paid $200.00 for it, which was a small fortune at that time, but it was a good investment, because she just lived for that pony and was an excellent rider. In fact, I'd seen her ride that pony standing up on its back, for half of a mile or so.

A little while back, I had told you about the second worst mistake that I had ever made. Now, I'll tell you about the worst mistake that I had ever made. The worst mistake I ever made was in marrying Dorothy. The first week that we had moved into our new home in Huntley, we took over a little restaurant about twelve miles from Huntley. It was out in the country at a four corners of the highway called Allen's corners. There was a family there named Allen that owned a fair sized farm and had a couple of big shops and operated a big wrecker service. They had two huge wreckers and they specialized in semi-truck wrecks. I've known them to go as far as Ohio and Pennsylvania on wrecker calls, and then the other direction I've known them to go to Iowa, Arkansas, and as far as Nebraska for a wreck. I went out with them one night on a call. There had been a semi that went off of the road and turned over on its side about thirty miles away. This was at about 10:00 p.m. at night. The semi was loaded full of beer, and before they could even upright the trailer, we had to unload that beer and stack it on the side of the road. I was wondering what the heck they were doing. Well, one of the men began to dig a hole at the edge of the road. I found out about the time we got the truck unloaded, they had their hole dug. It went down about two foot below the foundation of the road. They ran a cable with a big anchor on it into the hole and hooked the anchor underneath the pavement. The reason for that was that the semis were so heavy, that even though they had a big huge wrecker, without that anchor they could tip the wrecker over when they tried to upright the trailer. Well, the whole job took about five hours, but they got everything back upon the highway, and hauled them back to their shops, which if they weren't too badly damaged, they would repair them. If they were damaged beyond repair, they would just put them in their junkyard.

Well, the Allen's owned the restaurant and it was like our house, fully equipped. All we had to do was lay in a supply of food, and open the doors. It was just a small restaurant, with six stools at the bar, and five tables that would seat four people. So, with a full house, we could serve up to twenty-six people. Well, Dorothy took over as the boss of the restaurant, which was all right with me, as I had my construction job to go to. And, our two girls were the waitresses. Dorothy did all of the cooking and I was the dishwasher, janitor, and handy man. We would get up about 4:30 a.m. every morning, and I would take her and the girls down to the restaurant and we would eat our breakfast and get everything in shape to open up. We would open up at 6:00 a.m. every morning as we had a fairly good breakfast trade at that time. I would do up any dishes or take care of any other chore, such as garbage, and at 7:00 a.m., I would leave to go to my construction job over in Algonquin where I'd put in my eight hours, then come back home, take a bath, get cleaned up, take care of the horses and other animals and livestock on the farm. I would get down to the restaurant at about 7:00 p.m. and would work until we closed at midnight. That made for some pretty long hours for me. But, I didn't mind, as I was capable of doing it. Then Dorothy informed me that I was supposed to pay the rent for the restaurant, buy all of the food for it and pay the girl's wages, all out of my pay as a carpenter. What money she took in at the restaurant was hers. I wasn't even supposed to touch the cash register, let alone, know how much she took in. About that time, I realized that the biggest mistake that I had ever made was in marrying her. She kept me tore up all of the time and had my nerves in such a frazzle, and I was so down hearted, that I started to cry. And it wasn't just for a little while, it was for two weeks. If one of the fellows on the construction crew spoke to me and said, "How are you today Spence?" I would just start crying and could not help myself. Well, after two weeks of deep depression, I finally got a hold of myself, snapped out of it, and came back stronger than ever. I knew then and there that I was never going to let myself get into that type of condition again. That marriage lasted three months. I moved out and took Janet with me. We moved into a little three-room apartment in Woodstock. It had two bedrooms and a living room. This was upstairs, and we had kitchen privileges. This worked out pretty fair for us. Janet wanted her pony. The county fair grounds was about 1/2 mile from where we were living, and I had done all of the painting there at the fair grounds for several years and knew the head administrator of the fair grounds fairly well. I talked him into renting us an empty stall at their horse barns. I took Janet out to my uncle's farm and we got the pony. She was just going to ride it into town, which was only about six or seven miles. So, I let her get started, while I visited with my aunt and uncle for a while. I waited until I figured that she was about 2/3 of the way into town and I started out after her. When I caught up with her, I stopped to talk to her for a few minutes. She wanted to turn around and take the pony back to the farm. Well, I couldn't figure out why the sudden change. Anyway, I told her, "Look, young lady, for a month I have put up with your begging and whining about having your pony. Now, we have all of the arrangements made and everything else, and you just take that pony into the fair grounds, and put in that stall that I rented." Well, very sullenly, she did. Well, after a couple of days, she seemed to straighten out, and she was very good about going out every day, and taking care of the pony.

Unknown to me, when Janet was riding her pony from the farm into town, and while I was visiting with my aunt and uncle, her mother and her new husband (my cousin), had been visiting up in southern Wisconsin, and had come down to visit some people in Woodstock. They had come along and spotted her along the highway. They had stopped and talked to her and told her that they were going back to Nebraska and would take her back with them, and she should take the pony back to the farm and leave it. I had never told her mother that she couldn't visit with the children, in fact, I had told her that she was welcome to visit any time, just so long as she notified me first that she wanted to visit with them. But, she couldn't do that, and of course Janet told them about Dorothy, so I guess the first one they went to see was Dorothy, and I guess they had quite a time tearing me apart.

Of course, I didn't know anything about all of this, but I sensed that there was going to be trouble in the future. I went down to the neighboring town of Harvard, IL, paid a firm of well-known, attorneys a $500.00 retainer to represent me in any problems that might arise. I don't know just what my ex-wife's plans were, but I think that they went back to Nebraska. Well life went on for about two months without anything happening, and Janet behaving herself. I still didn't know anything about her meeting with her mother. I came home from work one day, and Janet wasn't there. I didn't think anything about it; I just figured that she was up at the fairgrounds, taking care of her pony. But, when 7:00 p.m. rolled around and she didn't show up, I knew something was wrong, so I went up to the fair grounds to see if she was still up there. She wasn't there and neither was her pony. Well, I questioned one of the fairgrounds workers, and he told me that Janet had picked up her horse at about 9:00 a.m. that morning and had cleaned the stable out, and that they hadn't seen anything of her since then. Well, I thought then that maybe she had taken the pony back out to the farm and was out there with my aunt and uncle. So, I went out to the farm, but she wasn't there and they hadn't heard anything about her. So, I went back to town and went to the police department and reported her missing. Well, I previously found out where Dorothy was living. She had left the farm there in Huntley and moved in to a couple of rooms in an old farm house just outside Hampshire, which was maybe eight miles distance from the restaurant. So, I went down there to see her. It must have been around 9:00 p.m. at night when I got there. Well, she wasn't very pleased to see me. She wasn't even going to talk to me, but I can be pretty stubborn when I want to be. I just pushed on in to the room, and sat down on her bed. She just had two rooms there, both bedrooms, one for her daughter and one for her. I told her that I was there to stay until I got some answers. I kept asking her about Janet and she kept saying that she didn't know anything about her. Finally, I told her that I knew that she was lying through her teeth, and if she didn't level with me and tell me the truth about things, I was going to go to the district attorney and swear out a kidnapping warrant against her. Well, that kind of sobered her up a little bit. And then my questioning of her brought out the facts about her mother driving along on the highway and spotted Janet riding her pony into town. She also told me that Janet was staying with her next-door neighbor there, so I went over to the woman's house and asked for Janet, and the woman said she didn't know anything about Janet, and never had seen her. I said, "Look, I'm sick and tired of being lied to and if you don't produce her, I'm going into town and swear out a kidnapping warrant, and you'll be mentioned in it." Well, at that, she called Janet out and I told Janet to get her clothes and hat and come along with me. She said that she wasn't going to do that, and I said, "All right then, don't. You are still a minor and still my responsibility. I'll just go into town and get the police, and they'll come out here and pick you up." Then she decided that she would go with me. So, I took her on home to our rooms in Woodstock, but she was one very mad little girl.

Two, days later, she was gone again. So, I went back out to see Dorothy, and she said, "No, she isn't here." This time I believed her, but I asked her, "Do you know where she is?" She said, "Yes, she is with her mother up at Elkhorn, WI." So, I went back to Woodstock and got a hold of the district attorney, and swore out some kidnapping warrants for my ex-wife and her husband. Well, I don't know what really happened, but when they heard about the warrants, they checked in with the Elkhorn police, and then, all of a sudden, the warrants were dropped, and that was the end of it. I never did find out exactly what happened. But, I'm sure that there was quite a little bit of money that changed hands there. I also called my attorneys in Harvard, and told them about what was happening, and they just politely informed me that they were returning my $500.00 retainer. They couldn't represent me. They went back to Nebraska, taking Janet with them. I started to search for her pony. I was checking with all of the farmers east of town, because I knew she always had ridden out to the east, and I knew most of them there and had painted for most of them. But nobody had seen or heard anything of the pony. After a week of searching, I was talking to a seed salesman, who had dealt with all of the farmers, and I asked him to keep an eye out for the pony. He said, "Describe the pony to me." So, I did. He said, "I believe I know where that pony is. Two days ago, I was out west of Woodstock about four miles, and I think I saw it in a pasture out there, at least one that matches your description." So, I got directions from him as to where this pasture was. I went out there. Sure enough it was our pony. He was out there in a pasture with five other horses, practically starving to death. There was not enough pasturage there for one horse, much less six. The farmer she had left him with was a worthless drunk and wasn't about to take care of the horses. So, I went into town and rented a horse trailer, and went back out to pick up the pony. The farmer tried to give me a hard time, but when I showed him the sales papers on the pony, he let me have him, and I took him back out to my uncle's farm.

I had been talking a lot about working on a big construction job in Algonquin and now I'll try to tell you a little something about that job. It was a big gravel pit and we were putting up a huge building that was 40 feet wide and 100 feet long, and it would go up 185 feet in the air. Afterwards, we poured the cement foundations for the building that was in a rectangle. It was divided into six compartments. The concrete foundation was 30 feet high, and it started 15 feet below ground, and went up 15 feet above ground. Then, the next 20 feet was built out of 2 x 12 planks laying flat on top of another. Well, I believe that we had about ninety carpenters stationed around that foundation. Each man was responsible for an area about 6 feet long. We were each responsible for nailing down the 2 x 12 there in front of us. We would nail one nail every six inches in a zigzag fashion. We all started out with our regular nail hammer, but two days of that and we were all worn out. So we all got a two-pound sledgehammer. Now those hammers new, had a slightly con-curve head on each end of it, and when we finished the jobs, both ends of my little sledgehammer had a con-cave head on them at least 1/4 of an inch deep.

After about six weeks, we had that phase of the job done. We got the framework of the building up and we were working on the top two floors. Of course there were ladders going up to the top floors, and it would take almost a half an hour for a man to climb up the 180 foot level, and about that to climb back down again. That kind of got to be an old story, so we had the crane operator hook onto his headache ball, and two of us would get on top of the ball and hang onto the cable, and he would raise us up to the 80 feet level, where we would crawl off of the ball onto the ladder, and climb the next 100 feet. But, at least that saved at least 50 percent of our climbing time. That system worked out pretty good for quite a while until the inspectors came around one morning and saw us doing it, and they put a stop to that, claiming that it was too dangerous. We were flooring the two upper floors with three by twelve planks. Now those planks were so heavy, one man could not carry one by himself. Now to get those planks up to the 180 feet level, the crane operator would hoist them up to the 80 feet level. We would station one man on each floor, and he would be directly above the others below him. It took two men up on the 80 feet level to pull the plank in and unhook it from the crane, and they would up end it and

237

hand walk it up to the person on the floor above them. We literally man handled several hundred of those planks, weighing about 250 pounds each, up 100 feet without ever dropping a one of them.

As I said once before in the earlier part of the story, some of these events will be out of sequence.

After Janet left, I bought a used house trailer. It was 8 by 40 feet and I rented a lot in a trailer park about 12 miles east of Woodstock. I picked up Ellery and we went to baching it in the house trailer. After I left Dorothy, she kept the restaurant open for about three months and then closed it up. Actually she lasted about six weeks longer than I thought she would. I had several times suggested to Dorothy that we close the restaurant at 9 p.m. as there really wasn't enough business after 9 p.m. to warrant staying open. But, she wouldn't listen to me and insisted on staying open till midnight. As soon as I left, she started closing the restaurant at 9 p.m. as it was to small of an operation, and she wasn't making enough profit to hire help, dish washer and janitor. And I knew she didn't have the stamina to do all of that plus the cooking and everything. After she closed the restaurant, she took a sales job in a big department store in Elgin after Ellery and I moved into our trailer. I got to thinking that in all fairness maybe I should go and have another talk with Dorothy and see if we couldn't work something out. I didn't know where she was living in Elgin, but I did know the store she was working in. I went into the store, and when I found her, she was in the dress department and was waiting on a lady. There was a chair there and I sat down in it and never said a word, just waited until she was through with the customer and had a few minutes to spare. I tried talking to her but she wouldn't have anything to do with me. I didn't raise a fuss of any kind. I merely turned around and left.

I got back home to the trailer park about 4 p.m. and a half hour later, there was a squad car that pulled up and a cop got out. He came to the door and said, "I'm sorry, you are going to have to go with me, I've got a warrant for your arrest." I said, "My arrest, what for? I haven't done anything." The cop answered, "The warrant says here that you went into the department store in Elgin and raised a big fuss inside the store. You made a public nuisance out of yourself, and was harassing and threatening your wife, and embarrassing her in front of her customers." She must have gone to the police just as soon as I left the store, for them to get out here after me that fast. I knew that I would have to go with him and I told him, "Okay, just give me, five minutes to get my coat and hat on." I went in and told my son Ellery to go across the road to my neighbor, who was an elderly gentleman, and to have him to take you out to the farm, and to tell Uncle Jim what has happened to me, and tell him to meet me in Woodstock with his checkbook. So, they took me into Woodstock and as soon as we got to the police station, they didn't even take me inside, they just transferred me to another squad car, which took me down to the county line, where they met another squad car from Elgin, and transferred me over to that one. Well, they didn't take me into Elgin at all, they took me down to St. Charles which was a town about twenty miles south of Elgin. There they took me in and locked me up in a cell for the night. The next morning, they got me up at 6:00 a.m., gave me a little breakfast, put me in a squad car, and took me up to the Elgin police station. They transferred me over to the Elgin police, who didn't even take me to a cell, but took me straight to a judge's chambers, where my wife, district attorney, and the judge were waiting for me. The district attorney read off the charges to the judge. The judge told me, "Well, Mr. Spencer, you were a pretty busy fellow, weren't you? I'm afraid that I'm just going to have to assess a fine on you." I told him, "Well, don't I have a chance to put on a defense of any kind?" He said, "Well, yes, but I don't see where you have any defense to put on." I said, "Well, I would like to call my wife to the stand, and have her put under oath, so that I can question her." He said, "Oh, you can't do that; you can't put her on the stand. That's just not legal." So, the judge fined me $18.00, which was the exact amount that I had in my billfold. He also gave me strict orders not to go near my wife again and bother her. So, I paid the $18.00, and was wondering how I was going to get home. I walked out of the courtroom and there was my uncle and my son. My uncle wanted to know. "What in the world happened to you? I went into the police station in Woodstock and they told me that you were in Elgin, so I went down to Elgin, and they told me that you weren't there, and didn't know anything about you, or where you were, and for me to come back here at 9:00 a.m. this morning, and maybe they would be able to tell me something. So, I told him what had happened, that they had taken me down to St. Charles, buried me where no one could find me, so I would be sure to spend the night in jail. Talk about American justice. They never read me my rights, but of course, that was before the Miranda Law was enacted, and I was not given any opportunity to make a phone call, secure a lawyer, or anything.

I was still selling Wearever on a part time basis, and about three weeks later, I had an appointment down in Huntley, which was about eighteen miles from where I was living. It was about 10:00 p.m. when I started home, and about three miles north of Huntley, my car broke down and quit running. I managed to pull off on the side of the road, so it was completely off of the road. I hitched a ride back into Huntley, and went to the Huntley police station and reported to them that my car was broke down, and where it was sitting, and told them that it was just too late to get anything done about it that night. I also told them that first thing the next morning, I would get it taken care of. There was a deputy sheriff from the Woodstock office there in the Huntley station at the time I made my report, and I asked him if he was going back to Woodstock shortly. He said, "Yes, I'm about to leave."

So, I asked him if he would give me a ride back to my home at the trailer park, and he said, "Sure, come on." So, I went with him. When we got up to my car, I had to stop, so that I could get my sample case out of it, and then we went on. He took me back to the trailer park, which was about seven or eight miles out of his way, so I gave him a $10.00 bill to pay for my ride home, which he took, and wished me goodnight.

The next morning, I got up early, and had my neighbor to drive me down to Huntley. I went to the Chevrolet dealer in Huntley. He was the one I had bought the car from. I told him what had happened, and he said, "Sure, I'll send a wrecker out and pick it up." So, we went back to the car with the wrecker. I got out, and went over to the car and opened the front door, and as I did so, there was a piece of paper that floated to the ground. I picked it up and looked at it. It was a ticket that was ordering me to be in court on Wednesday morning. I asked the dealer, "You didn't see a ticket of any kind on the car did you." He said, "No, I never saw a ticket." He knew what I was talking about, but he actually hadn't seen the ticket. I said, "Good." I tore the ticket up, threw it away, and took the car into town and got it fixed. I had no intention of being in court Wednesday morning. Early Wednesday morning, I got in my car, went up to Elkhorn, WI, because I had a little business to take care of up there. I got back home at about 6:00 p.m., ate supper, watched a little TV, then went to bed. At about midnight, I was wakened by a lot of racket going on, lights flashing outside and a siren going off. I got up, and could see that there were two cops walking around the trailer, and another one pounding on the door. They were just making sure that all the neighbors were woke up and knew what was going on. I went to the door, opened it, and the cop roared out at me that they had a warrant for my arrest. He said, "You were supposed to be in court this morning and you never showed up." I said, "Okay, come on in. Give me a chance to get some clothes on, and I will go with you." He came in and shut the door, as it was cold outside. He stood there by the door, leaning on the heater. I told Ellery just to sit tight, that I would be back before morning. They took me back down to the police station in Woodstock, took me in and sat me down in the lobby, and said, "You just wait here." I said, "I want to see the Justice of the Peace that signed this arrest warrant here." They said, "Well, he is at home in bed." I said, "Well, he signed this warrant at 1:00 p.m. this afternoon, and you could have served it on me earlier this evening, and I'm entitled to be taken before the nearest judge at the time of arrest. By God, I want to see him, and I want him down here." They said, "We can't get him down here at this time of the morning." Well, I kept raising such a fuss, that they finally called him, and got him out of bed. He came down to the police station, came in and walked right past me, without even looking at me. I hollered at him, "Hey, you bastard, come back here." He turned around real surprised like, and said, "You talking to me?" I said, "Yes, you son of a bitch, I'm talking to you." I said, want to know what I'm doing here, and why I'm here." He said, "Well, you were issued a ticket and were supposed to be in court this morning, and you didn't show up." I said, "What do you mean, I was issued a ticket. I never saw any ticket." He said, "Well, it was put in the doorway of your car." I said, "Like hell it was. When we picked up the car that morning, there was no ticket on it and, I have two witnesses that would vouch for that." We had quite an argument. Finally, he said, "Well all right, you can go." I said, "Yeah, sure, I can go. What am I going to do, walk twelve miles back home? You brought me in here, you can just take me back." He turned to the sheriff and said, "Yeah, just have a squad car to take him home. But, we are going to check up on that." I said, "Just go right ahead and check." So, they took me home, and I went to bed again, which was about 4:00 a.m.. The next morning, my next-door neighbor came over to see me and said,

"You know, you almost burned out last night." I said, "What do you mean?" He said, "Well, I came past your place after they took you in, and I happened to look up, and dense-black smoke was pouring out of your smoke stack. I went in and your furnace was just red hot. It was turned up just as high as it could go." I said, "Oh no. That's the last time that I will ever invite a cop inside my house. He came in, and he was leaning there on the furnace and turned it up. I had left it on medium. Thank you for going in and turning it down."

That same day, the owner of the trailer park, came by and politely informed me that I had to get out. He wasn't about to have any criminals or troublemakers in his park. Well, I had never liked him to begin with, so it didn't bother me too much to move. I moved over to a trailer park over on the south side of Harvard, IL. Well, I had my troubles there, too. Ellery was big enough at that time to do a little work to earn a few dollars. Although, he didn't want to, I made him go out to the local golf course, and caddy. He caddied one summer and did fairly well. I would make him turn his money over to me. I was saving it in an account for him. I would allow him a few dollars every week for spending money. At the end of the season, I had $150.00 of his money saved up for him. and asked him if he needed any spending money, all he had to do was ask, and I would give it to him. So, one day, I came home from work. and Ellery wasn't there. Well, I had been home about five minutes, when the owner of the park came over and told me that the police had come and picked Ellery up, and that he was in jail over in Woodstock. There was an old fellow up in his seventies, that ran a small filling station on the north side of Harvard, and Ellery had gone up there, bought a bottle of coke, turned around and conked the guy in the head with the coke bottle, which of course, knocked him out, then, robbed the guy of $5.00. He probably might have got away with it, but, he had been in the place two or three times before, and the fellow knew who he was.

They were holding him under a $3,000.00 cash bond. In other words, I had to come up with the $3,000.00, not just a percent of it. Well I didn't have $3,000.00 at that time and couldn't raise it. Then, they sent him down to a boy's reformatory at St. Charles, IL. That was for a four-year term.

Well, that winter, I was out of work, so I answered a blind ad in the Rockford paper that was for insurance agents. I thought, well, insurance people seem to be doing pretty good, so why not? My boss' name was Joe Thompson. He was a college graduate and in his late twenties. Well, after a couple of days of training, I went out on my own. I called on one fellow who was in his sixties, and made my presentation to him, filled out the application, handed it to him to sign, and he wouldn't sign. He said that he would have to think that over a little bit, I said, "Okay." We just sat there quietly for about five minutes without saying anything, and I gave him the application again, and said, "Well, now that you've thought it over, you may as well sign it." And he did. So, I started out on the crew, and they had breakfast bets going around amongst themselves. They started betting with me. And, I began getting a lot of free breakfasts again. I don't believe that I ever lost a breakfast bet in my life. I called on a man whose name was John Henry. He was Irish, and I knew from the beginning that I was going to sell him a policy, and he knew that he was going to buy it. But, he was just giving me a hard time, all the way through. So, in the end when he had signed the first policy, paid me for it, and I was starting to put my papers back in the briefcase, he said, "Have you got anything else that you want me to sign my John Henry to?" I said, "Yes." I flipped over an application to him and told him, "Sign here." He signed it, I filled the application out, and he paid for it. His wife was laughing and said, "Maybe that will teach you not to be so dam smart."

Well, there was an elderly woman (she was about fifteen years older than I was) on the crew and she was a pretty good sales person. In fact, she was Joe's mother-in-law and somehow we started working together, and found out that we did better together, than we did separately. They had what we called a boiler house operation going. That was the way we got our leads. They had about fifteen girls working on the telephone, and each one of them would sit there and just go right through the phone book. Well, Joe had a stack of write in leads that the company had sent out to him. They were all from Chicago and suburbs. There must have been about three hundred of them, where people would write into the home office and ask for the insurance. When I found that out I told Joe, "Give me a bunch of those leads, and I'll go run them out." He said, "No, they are no good. There have been two or three people that have tried it. and they couldn't do anything with it." I said, "That's probably because they don't know Chicago and I do know Chicago. Just give me a stack of those, and I'll go see what I can do." So, he gave me fifty of them and said, "Well, if you do any good with those, I will give you some more." I said, "Okay." This was on a Monday morning, and I said, "I'll see you Friday."

I asked Mrs. Farmer if she wanted to go along with me. She said, "Sure, I'll go." Those leads were scattered all over the Chicago area. So, we did pretty well with them. The first week, we came in with over twenty applications. So, Joe gave me a few more leads. I said, "Why don't you give me the whole stack? I can separate these and sort them out, so that we are not going from one end of Chicago to another and putting a lot of miles on our car that is unnecessary. On Monday, we started out in Antioch, IL. We hit it lucky, and sold five policies to one man. Then, we went into Zion, where we sold three more to a person. Then, we went on into Highland, where we had a lead on an Italian family. We sold them four policies. As we were leaving and going out the door, the fellow's wife said, "Didn't so and so want some of this insurance?" He said, "Yeah, I believe he did." So, he gave me their name and address, and they were in the next little town down the line. So, we went and saw them, and wrote three policies on them. Before we left, they gave us the name and address of some of their in-laws who wanted some of the insurance. They were in the next town down the line. Anyway, it went on that way, and I think we wrote twenty-one policies, off of that one lead. We wrote forty-eight policies that week. When we came into the sales meeting on Friday, the secretary was processing a pile of applications, I said, "It looks like you've had a pretty good week." She said, "Yes, the crew has done pretty good this week, they have me swamped down, they actually wrote twenty-four applications this week. I said, "Well, I hate to do this to you since you are so busy, but here is forty-eight more." Well, after that, some of the others thought that they would try their hand in Chicago again. So, there were different ones that I gave a bunch of leads to. They went in and worked for two or three days, and came back without ever even selling a single one. Well, after that, we had the Chicago territory to ourselves, Chicago, and all of it's one hundred, sixty-eight suburbs all around.

We made all of our calls together, and we developed a pretty good system. If we were calling on a man, I would turn the pitch over to her, and let her make the sales, if we were calling on a woman, she would turn the pitch over to me, and let me make the sale. That worked out real well. We called on one lead that was a widow-woman whose husband had been a doctor. We rang the doorbell, and she came to the door. She really looked a mess. Her hair was all frizzly, no make up on, and in a ragged old housecoat. We told her who we were and what we wanted. She invited us in, took us into the living room, and said, "Sit down and make yourself at home, I'll be with you in a few minutes." She took off and went upstairs, and it was about forty minutes later before she came back down. But, what a change in a person; her hair was done up really nice, her face was made up, and she had on a beautiful see through negligee. Well, I made the sales pitch. I couldn't get her to sign it though. She had hinted two or three times, that if I would come back by myself that she would buy. Well, finally, I gave her a self-addressed envelope, and left the application with her, and told her that when she made up her mind, that all she had to do was send the application in to me. I didn't really think that I would hear from her, but a month later, I got her application in the mail.

Another lead that I had was the President of the B&O Railroad. I called on him, up in his big plush offices. It took me maybe a half of an hour, and I sold him four policies on him and his family. He called his secretary in and told her to make out a check for me, then he started telling me about his life with the railroad. About how he had started out as a section hand, and of everything that happened to him, as he was working his way up to president. I sat there for over an hour, listening to his stories. Finally, he said, "Well, I think the secretary ought to have that check made out by now." So, he gave me the check, and I went on my next lead. It was on a colored person only about two blocks from where the B&O offices were. It was a big, old tenement house, and the apartment was down in the basement. I went down there, and there were no lights in the basement. It was just as dark as midnight in there. I finally found the right apartment number, knocked on the door, and there was a woman that answered. I said, "Is Mr. so and so there?" She said, "No sir. He's not here. I'm just his girlfriend." I said, "Well, tell him that I'll call back later." Which, I never did. What a contrast in places, from big plush offices of the B&O to the dingy hole in the basement of a tenement house.

One of the leads that I had was on a Mr. King, of the Kingworld Distribution Company. I had no idea what he distributed, but I soon found out when I made my call on him. He was sole owner of a movie distributing company. There wasn't a single movie distributed to a theatre in the United States that didn't go through him. I imagine that I spent about three hours with him. He took out policies on himself, his wife, his father, his mother, his mother-in-law, and a couple of grandchildren. The total monthly premium for all of those policies came to $550.00. That turned out to be the largest monthly premium ever written. The company contacted me and wanted me to write up that sale for a training manual that they were going to have printed. So, I wrote the letter for them and it was printed in the training manual. It wouldn't surprise me if it were still in the training manual today.

Well, about this time, I was promoted to office manager. I was sent down to Decatur, IL, and opened up an office there. Well, Decatur was a pretty rough town. I had six telephone girls going, and I wasn't doing too well. I had only managed to hire two agents. Well, at the end of two months, I got notice from the home office that I just wasn't doing enough business to support six girls, and that I needed to lay three of them off. I thought to myself, I'm not doing enough business right now, but if I lay three girls off, I'm going to do a whole lot less business. Then, they will close the office up. So, instead of laying off three girls, I hired four more and put them to work on going through the phone directory. That worked out pretty well. Our business started picking up and the home office never said a word about my hiring four girls instead of laying three girls off.

While working in Decatur, I started having problems with my lower back, and I couldn't find a chiropractor that I liked in Decatur, so I started going to one in Champagne, IL, about twenty miles east of Decatur. Now this chiropractor was sort of a character. It was a woman and she was good. She was about six feet-two, big-boned, and must have weighed well over two hundred pounds, but didn't show it. I got along with her and I liked her very much. She was closed every Wednesday and open on Saturday. So, one day I asked her, "How come you are closed on Wednesdays? It seems to me, that if you would stay open on Wednesday and close up on Saturday, you would have yourself a nice two day weekend." She said, "Since you are from out of town, I guess I can tell you. Wednesday is my doctor's day." I said, "Oh, I'm sorry to hear that you are having problems." She said, "No, no, no, that's not it. I have every doctor in town coming to me for adjustments and they don't want their patients to know it. So, I just stay closed on Wednesday and they come in through the back door, to get their adjustments."

Well, I no sooner got the Decatur office functioning fairly decently, than they transferred me to Maywood (a suburb of Chicago). When I got there, I had to find office space to rent. There really weren't any decent offices to rent, but there was a large bank that had built a new building and moved into it, and they had their old bank building up for rent. I rented an office inside the building and picked out the bank president's office, as it was the largest one, and opened up for business. I was surprised, because I could have opened up a bank there. I had four or five people coming in there every day, wanting to make deposits, they didn't realize that the bank had moved, Some had wanted to rent safety deposit boxes. I guess I could have rented some to them, as I had a whole vault full of them. I was limited as to the amount of money that I could spend for office furniture.

They were allowing me just $5.00 a day, or $30.00 a week, so to start out with, I bought an old used desk for $15.00, a couple of chairs for $5.00 apiece. The desktop looked like the devil, so I had a fellow come in and refinish it, and that cost me $60.00, which I paid out of my pocket, then collected from my company at $5.00 a day. I got a couple of small tables and six chairs for the phone girls. I hired six of them and got them going through the phone directory. By this time I realized that Joe was deliberately trying to make things hard on me so I would quit. He was afraid that I was doing so well, that I would be moving up and taking his job. Well, I managed to hire about five agents and got them going so that they were producing enough to warrant keeping the office open.

I made one sales call there, sold the woman a $35.00 monthly premium deal, and when she went to pay me for it, she brought out a huge jug full of pennies. She started counting out pennies and realized that it would take her all day. She decided that this was going to be too slow. So she went and brought out another jug full of dimes, and said that she would pay me in dimes. She started counting dimes and decided that, too, was going to take quite a while. She then went and got a jug full of quarters and counted out $35.00 in quarters. I had to borrow a pail from her to carry them in, take them to the bank and cash them in for paper money.

I had one call to make, and it was on the fourth floor of an apartment house. These apartment houses all had electronically controlled doors. There were speaking tubes from the apartment down to the front door. You would ring the doorbell, and the person in the apartment would speak to you through the speaking tube. If they wanted to let you in, they would press a button in their apartment, and it would release the lock on the door. If they didn't want you in, then there was no way you could get in. Well, I recall my days of selling Fuller Brushes, where I never bothered the front doors. I merely went around to the back. There were stairs going all the way up to the fourth floor. I got up to the fourth floor and the back door was standing open, but the screen door was shut. I couldn't see into the apartment. I knocked on the door, and a woman hollered, "Come on in!" I opened the door and went in. I couldn't believe my eyes. There she was standing at the ironing board ironing some blouses, stark naked. She said, "Oh my God! I thought you were my girlfriend. What do you want?" So I told her what I wanted and talked to her about some hospitalization insurance, and she said, "Wait until I go get a robe on." Then, she stopped and thought for a second, and said, "What the hell, you've already seen me." So, I sat there, and sold her an insurance policy.

At the end of three months, I had the office running fairly smoothly. I was transferred again down to East St. Louis. I opened up an office down there. I moved down to East St. Louis and made up my mind at that time, that that would be the last office that I would open up. I was getting sick of this business. And, of course of these moves, I took Mrs. Farmer along with me, which Joe didn't like, because she was a good agent. But, Mrs. Farmer owned an apartment house in Belleville, which is just outside East St. Louis. She had an apartment that opened up just about then and we just moved into it. The place needed an awful amount of work, as it had been let go for several years. I started redecorating for her in my spare time. It had one living room ceiling that was painted a dirty rose color, it just made you shudder to look at it. I went down to the local paint store and introduced myself as a painter, and made arrangements to buy my paints at a discount. The storeowner said, "Oh, I've got a real good interior paint that is just the right thing for that ceiling of yours. It is a one-coat application. One coat will just cover anything. If it doesn't, we will furnish the paint for the next coat." Well, I got two gallons of white ceiling paint from them, went home, and we painted that ceiling. The next day, we went in to look at it, and when it had dried, you could tell that there was some white paint on it, but the rose was still burning through it. So, I went back the next day and got two more gallons of paint. The proprietor said, "I just don't believe this." I said, "Well, you better believe it. Why don't you come along with me and look at this thing yourself!" He said, "I think I will do that." We got there, and he agreed that the two coats did not cover it. So, I put the third coat on, and it made quite an improvement. But, that dirty rose was still showing through. I went back again, and got another two gallons of paint and told the storeowner, "Come along with me, I want you to see this." So he did. He agreed with me, that it still needed a fourth coat. Well, that fourth coat done the job, and was I glad. I was getting sick of painting that ceiling.

I got the office set up and going pretty good, so that I only had to be in the office for a couple of hours every morning. Then I would go back and work on the apartment house the rest of day. I don't believe that I ever mentioned the name of insurance company that I was working for. It was the Reserve Life Insurance Company. The home office was in Dallas/Fort Worth, Texas. The Reserve Life bought up another small insurance company in Cincinnati, Ohio, and they installed Joe as the president of it. When they did that I thought that I would get the Rockford office, but, no, they installed another person in it. It promptly fell to pieces, so they closed it down and also the offices in Decatur, Maywood and Belleville. We were all out of a job.

There were two brothers, Carl and James Smith, who had been area superintendents for the Reserve Life, and they were let go at the same time. They both went back to Ohio and opened up insurance offices. Carl had his in Dayton, Ohio, and James had his in Columbus, Ohio. Carl called me and asked if I wanted to come to Dayton and work with him? I told him "Sure," I went to Dayton and was living in the YMCA there. There was a pay telephone in the hallway right outside my room door. I went to it one night to call Mrs. Farmer down in Belleville. I picked up the receiver and as I did, someone said, "Hello," I said, "Mary?" She said, "Yeah, is that you Ralph?" I said, "It sure is, I don't know how this could happen, I just picked up the receiver – this is a pay phone and I haven't put any money into it nor dialed your number. She said I don't know either. I just picked up the phone and was going to make a phone call when you said hello. We talked for about a half-hour on the phone company. She told me she was going to move back down to Kentucky where she was originally from to take care of her mother, who was having ill health. I said, "Well, that is not to far from Ohio. Maybe I can drop down there sometime and pay you a visit." I worked for Carl for about two months. One day he asked me, would you go to Columbus and work for James?" I said, "I suppose I could." He said, "He called me up one day and asked if he could swipe you from me." So, I moved to Columbus. The area he had me working in was 90% colored and I just was not doing anything at all with them. At the end of two months, I was literally starving to death, and I mean that. I gave up my job with James and went down to Corbin, Kentucky (that is the original home of Kentucky Fried Chicken) and joined Mary, who was living with her folks about six miles out of town. She was selling insurance for another company, so I signed up with them too.

We went up to Frankfurt, KY, as that was where the home office of the company was located, and I had to take the state test in order to get my license. The company wanted us to move into Lexington, KY and operate out of there. We went to Lexington and started looking for an apartment. I went into a grocery store to get some cigarettes, and I asked a clerk, "Do you know of anyone who has an apartment for rent around town?" She said, "Well, yes. You go see Whitey," I said, "Who in the heck is Whitey?" She said, "I don't know what his name is, but everybody calls him Whitey. I can give you his address, just a minute and I'll look it up," She gave me the address, and we hunted the address up. It was in the best section of town and turned out to be a beautiful, two-story house. We rang the doorbell and Whitey came running down from the upstairs apartment. He was barefoot, with just a pair of slacks on, no shirt. We told him who we were and that we were looking for an apartment. He said, "You look like the type of people I want for a tenant. I was hoping for a middle-aged couple. I didn't want any kids in there. Come on, and I'll show you the apartment," He opened the door of the apartment and took us in. We could hardly believe our eyes at what we were seeing. The floors all had beautiful carpets on them, and the apartment was completely furnished with beautiful old antique furniture, with beautiful drapes and curtains on the windows. I said to Mary, "We sure can't afford something like this." She said, "Well ask him what he wants for rent, I would kind of like to know anyway." I figured he would say about $500.00 or $600.00 a month. I asked him, "Whitey, how much do you want for the apartment here!" He said, "Well, for you people, I'll take a hundred dollars a month. I was living down here and it was too much for me. I had the upstairs apartment, which was a lot smaller and just right for me, so I moved into it. I just want to get a couple in here that will take good care of the apartment. You appear to be the type of people that I want."

Perhaps I should explain something about Whitey here, before I go any further. He had come from a poor family, and was working in the grocery store as bag and carryout boy. There was one lady, who was a doctor's widow, that whenever she came into the grocery store, he would be very polite to her and go out of his way to help her, especially in carrying her groceries out to her car. This went of for some time when one day she asked him if he would come to work for her. He said, "What do you want me to do?" She said, "I have this big old home and I'm in it all by myself and I'm not as spry as I used to be. I would like for you to come and live there with me and take care of me. I'll even adopt you and when I die, I'll leave everything to you. I don't have anyone else to leave it to." He took her up on it. He moved in with her, and she adopted him legally. He took excellent care of her for four years, at which time she passed away. True to her word she left everything to him and at age 27, he found himself a multi-millionaire. Then he became Lexington's playboy with a series of girl friends, since every girl in town was setting her cap for him.

While he was a nice pleasant young man and while he was having a good time he never let things go to his head.

The day that we were to move into the apartment, we got there just about 12 noon and he was downstairs in the apartment. He had it all opened up for us, waiting for us and had a full meal cooked for us in the oven. He said, "I didn't think that you would want to go to a restaurant now." Not only was the apartment beautifully furnished with antique furniture, everything else that we needed to live with, was in the apartment, including bed linens sheets, and in the kitchen, pots and pans, fine china, sterling silver. All we had to do was move our clothes in. For the three months that we occupied the apartment, we lived like a couple of millionaires, all for $100.00 a month.

There was a beautiful old, roll top desk in the living room. I kept looking at that desk and kept thinking to myself, that is just exactly the kind of desk that would have a couple of secret compartments in it. I started looking for them, and it took me three hours of searching, but I finally found the secret compartment. However, there was nothing in it. In the dining room, there was a three cornered cabinet set in one corner of the room, filled with glassware. We were sitting there eating dinner one day when we heard a rapping in behind the cupboard. At first we thought it was some one knocking at the door, but when we answered the door there was no one there. When we sat back down, the rapping started up again. Mary said, "That's coming in from behind that cupboard there." I said, "It can't be. That cupboard is sitting up tight against that wall." But the more I listened to it, the more I had to agree with her. It was coming from behind that cabinet. We got up and moved the cabinet from against the wall and looked behind it, and there was absolutely nothing there. We moved the cabinet back in place, and the rapping started up again. I never was one to believe in ghosts and spirits, but there must have been some spirit there. When we asked Whitey about it he said that yes he had heard that rapping several times, but couldn't explain it. We had some leads in the neighboring town about thirty miles away, and there was a good highway running to it. We had been over this highway before, and when we got about ten miles out of town the highway was completely blocked off, and the construction crew had it all tore up and were in the process of rebuilding it. There was a big detour sign posted across the highway there with an arrow pointing to the left and there was a smaller two lane, concrete highway, that looked to be fairly new, and I thought, that for once we had lucked out. For once we were going to get a decent detour. We followed the highway for about a mile and a half and came to a bridge across a small river. the highway ended right there at the bridge and there was a gravel road on the other side of the bridge.

We went on across the bridge, followed the gravel road, which kept veering off to the right. After a couple of miles it turned into a dirt road. It was now veering to the left a little bit. We followed that for a little ways and it turned into a one-lane road, going across a grassy meadow, just two wheel tracks across the field. We began to wonder what the heck we had gotten into. But there was a farm right there and the farmer was out in the yard. I drove up to him and I asked him, "What the heck has happened to this road?" He said, "Oh, it ends right here, but you just drive on across the meadow here, and you see that little group of trees in the distance, you'll pick up the track over there." We drove across the meadow, it must have been 1/2 mile. We got over there to where the trees were, and we could see the tracks as the farmer had said we would. We followed the tracks for maybe 1/2 mile, and they turned into a one-lane dirt road, all this time the road kept curving around to the left, and after about 1-1/2 miles of the dirt road, it turned into a one-lane gravel road. On further it turned into a two-lane gravel road. In about a mile and a half we came right back onto that bridge, crossed the river and there was our two lane concrete highway, which took us right back to our starting point. The detour had made one big circle and wound right back at its starting point. We just quit for the day and went home.

Another time, we had a lead that was 25 or 30 miles from Lexington and was up in the mountains. We had the address with the name of the little town on it, and we couldn't find the town on the map at all. We could figure out approximately where it should be. We got down into the area, and we came up to a crossroads, and there was a group of men standing over on the other side, so I drove over across the road, got out of the car and went up to them and asked, "Can any of you gentlemen tell me where this little town is located?" I showed them the piece of paper I had the address written on. The first fellow took it and looked at it, and said, "No, I've lived here all my life and I never heard of that place." He passed it on to the second fellow, and said, "Do you know anything about this?" The second one said, "No I've never heard of it either. He gave it to the third one and he looked at it and said, "No. I've lived here all my life and I've never heard of it." He passed it to the fourth one, and he said, "Well, I've never heard of it either." He passed it to the fifth one, who said, "I've never heard of it either." He gave it to the sixth one, the last man, who said, "I'm sorry, I've never heard of it either." I said "Well thank you gentlemen." I took the note back from them and started back to the car, and the last man called me back, and said, "I do believe I know where that place is." I said, "Fine, I would appreciate it if you could tell me." He said, "You go down the highway a mile, and you come to a bridge across the river, and right on the other side of the bridge, you'll find a gravel road that leads off to the left. You follow it and it will wind up into the mountains there, and you will find the place. It is not much more than a post office and two or three houses. There is not even a grocery store or a filling station in it." We started down the highway, went down one mile, and there was no river, and no bridge. We went on another mile and no river and no bridge. We went on a third mile and no river and no bridge. We went on a fourth mile and nor river and no bridge. When we got to the fifth mile there was the river and the bridge. We crossed the bridge, and sure enough there was a gravel road leading off to the left. We turned on the gravel road and followed it back through the woods for about three hundred feet, and it ended right into a riverbed. By this time I knew that sometimes they used a riverbed for part of the road there in Kentucky, but I had to wonder which way do I go? Should I go up stream or should I go downstream, there were no signs. I thought, well I'll take a chance and go up stream. Sure enough, after about two hundred feet around a curve in the river, there was a road going on up the way. I followed it for about six miles and found the place.

Southern Kentucky was very poor insurance country. We had very few leads and half of them never panned out. Taking care of her folks, really turned into a full time job. Her mother became bed ridden, and she was a corker to take care of. Mary couldn't lift her so I had to take over the job of putting her on a bedpan. She would fight me all the time. She would cry out, "Oh the shame of it all, having to be put on the bedpan by a man." Then she would roll off of it deliberately and do her job in the bed. Then I would have to change her sheets, turn her over and clean her up. I made a pretty good male nurse there for about a year. We had no washing facilities and no running water. There was a huge copper kettle out in the backyard. I would fill it with water, then build a fire under it and get the water to boiling, bring out all the dirty sheets and dump them in there. Of course, I would put in detergent and take a long pole, and would poke them around in the pot until they were clean. I cleaned as high as fifty-one sheets in one week, and all of that was unnecessary, if that cranky old woman had had any decency about her.

It had a fairly large yard around the house, which had never been taken care of, and if people ever had any trash or junk to get rid of, they just threw it out in the front yard. I started cleaning the yard up and it took me a month to get that yard cleaned up to where I could mow it. I hauled off three dump truck loads of tin cans, whiskey bottles, beer cans, pop cans, horse shoes, pieces and chunks of iron, bolts and nuts; you name it and it was there in that yard. Of course, I took on jobs of any kind that I could do. One of them was painting a forest rangers tower on the top of a mountain. I had to climb a mile up the mountain, and then climb ninety feet up the outside of the tower, and paint my way down. There were three of us painting that tower and it took us two weeks to get it done. Another time, I spent three days helping fight a forest fire there in the mountains. That was really a job, because when you are working on the side of a mountain, one foot would be about a foot higher than the other one. We finally got the fire stopped.

One of the neighbors gave me three baby pigs. I told him, "You just keep them here until they are weaned from their mother. That will give me a chance to build a pen for them." I started to build a pen for them in the edge of the woods, which was about 150 feet from our back door. I went into the woods and cut down young saplings that were about two-inch's in diameter. I nailed them from one tree to the next. I never had to set in a fence post; the trees were so close together. I made it large enough, that I enclosed about 1/4 acre of land. Then I cut another mess of young saplings and cut them all up in 3-foot lengths. I drove a peg every six-inch's with 1-1/2 foot above ground and 1-1/2-foot below ground. I drove those all the way around the pen, and if you think that wasn't work you are crazy. Everybody told me that I was nuts for building that hog pen there. The stink would just drive us out of the house, and the pigs would be out of the pen and running all over the place, and I would be spending all my time chasing them. Well, as it turned out there was no stink and the pigs never once got out of the pen. Pigs are naturally a clean animal if they are given the chance to stay clean.

We had a neighbor woman that lived about half a mile or so from us. She had a son who was about 45 years old. He was just a no good drunk and had been all his life. Well, he woke up one morning, and said, "I've got the call of God." He was instantly reformed. He had a buddy that was as big a drunk as he was and he got the call of God too at the time. They both started preaching and were putting on a revival. The neighbor's son George was going to get married, and she invited me to the wedding. They were going to have the revival meeting first and the wedding afterwards. At first I declined, and wasn't going to go. Then I started thinking, Spencer old boy, you haven't a blessed thing to do that day, so why don't you go, it might be an experience. The woman he was marrying was a widow woman with five children. She was receiving a $500.00 check every month from ADC. What he was after was that $500.00 a month check. I went to the revival that night and to give the devil his due, George conducted the first half of the revival and did a half way decent job of it. Then he turned it over to his buddy, and he was one of these hell fire and damnation preachers. He started ranting and shouting, and after about five minutes, he stopped suddenly and said, "We are supposed to be saving souls, and I can see by the looks on your faces that you are all worried about the wedding, so let's have the wedding right now and get it over with." He called George and the woman up, and called her by the wrong name. He said to her, "Do you (so & so) still using the wrong name, take George here to be your husband?" She said, "Yes." He turned to George, and said, "Do you take (so & so) still the wrong name, to be your wife?" George said, "Yes." He said, "I now pronounce you man and wife. Okay, now lets get back to the revival and save some souls."

After the revival I was talking to the lady and she asked me what I thought about the wedding. I said, "Do you really want to know.?" She said, "Yes." I said, "All right, I'll tell you. I think George ought to take that girl and go into town and get themselves a marriage license, hunt up a legal minister and get married to her." She said, "Oh no. There was nothing wrong, that was a legal marriage."

Everybody else seemed to think so to. George was a pretty good husband for about one month. By that time he had control of her $500.00 monthly check, In Kentucky men have control of all the finances. He forgot about his call to God and reverted back to being a no good drunk like he was before.

Our neighbor invited us to attend church with her one Sunday. She was a hard shell Baptist. We figured that it wouldn't hurt us to go to church. So we went along with her. The minister put on a pretty good sermon. After the sermon was over, every one had gotten up preparing to go home, when our neighbor started having a fit, or at least I thought it was a fit. But, Mary said no, that she was talking in an unknown tongue. She was just shouting, raving and ranting, rolling on the floor, jumping up and down, waving her arms, and everybody was standing around in a circle, clapping their hands and urging her on. Of course, nobody was able to understand a word she said, because it was in an unknown tongue. That went on for about 15 minutes, then she finally calmed down. We took her home and she said she couldn't remember a thing about it.

The hillside, across the road from where we were living, was just covered with beautiful blackberry briars. But nobody ever went over there to pick them. I asked Mary, "Why is it that nobody ever goes over there and picks those blackberries?" She said, "That hillside is infested with rattlesnakes. If you go over there to pick those blackberry's you will get snake bitten for sure." I said, "Baloney." I took a couple of gallon pails and went over there and started picking. I picked 40 quarts of some of the finest looking blackberries you ever saw and never saw hide nor hair of a snake. Only one time, when I reached down toward the ground to pick a clump of berries, I heard a rattlesnakes rattle, I just said, "you can go ahead and rattle Mr. those are my berries." I went on and picked them. I never got bit, and I never saw the snake. I have learned one thing over the years that snakes are afraid of me. This may sound goofy but its true. Several times, I've seen snakes coming toward me, and I would stand still and watch them. They would get about eight feet away from me and stop, raise up, look me over, turn around and go the other way.

I guess that I failed to mention that right after I came to Kentucky, Mary and I had slipped across the border into Tennessee and got married. Her brother Tom Harmon lived about a mile down the road from us. He had a twenty-acre field of corn that he never got around to husking. I made a deal with him. For one third of the corn I would husk it all out and load it all up, and put it into his corncrib for him. Well, he went for that in a big way. He told me, "You'll never get that field husked out. It's to wet and muddy, you'll never get a wagon in there. You'll get tractor and wagon both stuck." I said, "I don't intend to take a tractor and wagon in there." He thought that I was nuts, but he said to go ahead. I went ahead and I husked that field out, I never took a tractor or wagon into it. I would husk out maybe fifty hills of corn and throw the ears into a pile, go on down the way and husk out another fifty hills of corn, and throw those into a pile. I went through the whole field that way. After I had the field all husked out, I pulled the tractor and wagon up alongside of the field, where I was on solid ground. I took a couple of gunny sacks and would sack up a sack full of corn then throw the sack over my back and walk out to the wagon with it, and dump it in the wagon. I cleaned the field up that way. It took me a little time, but then, at that time, time was all I had. I took his 2/3 down and cribbed it for him and took mine home. He was pretty put out about that. He never believed that I would get the corn husked and out of the field. He thought that I had really rooked him by taking 1/3 of his corn.

One day Tom asked me if I wanted a job working in a sawmill, that they needed another man where he was working. I said, "Sure." So I went with him the next day and talked with his foreman and hired on. At first they put me out road swamping. Road swamping was clearing brush out and making a roadway for the tractors to go through for pulling the logs into the mill. It merely consisted of cutting out any brush or undergrowth Just to make a lane wide enough for a tractor to go through. Of course they were all Kentuckians working there, and I was a dam Yankee from up north. I figured they would have their fun with me. They did not think that I would be able to do any of the work. I did a good job of the swamping and the foreman even told me that I was the best swamper that he had ever had. After about a week of that they pulled me off that and put me to working in the mill itself. They gave me the worst and hardest job there was there. They would bring a log in and the sawyer would cut a slab off one side of the log and the slab would come out on a endless belt and my job was to take that slab and throw it into a gully down below, where they would burn it. Ordinarily they would have two men working on the slabs. But they put me on the slabs by myself, figuring that I would not be able to handle all of the slabs and that I would make a fool of myself. I'll admit that it was strenuous work and I would be really tired by the end of the day. I know for a fact, that not one of them could have handled that job by themselves. That's why they had two men on it before me.

I worked with Tom in the sawmill for about three weeks, when another of Mary's brothers named Henry, asked me to go to work in his sawmill. As he made me a much better deal than what I had, I switched over and went to work for him. Well, we worked for about three days and the sawmill broke down. Upon examining things, we saw that whole sawmill was rotted out. Being the only carpenter there I got the job of completely rebuilding the sawmill. Henry was also a part time bootlegger and would take off for two or three days at a time and go down into Tennessee, and buy up a load of bootleg whisky and bring it back to sell. While he was doing that I had charge of the mill. Things worked out pretty good for a little while, but the big engine that ran the sawmill was old, and finally it broke down. There were no replacement parts to be had, so Henry just closed down the sawmill and forgot about it.

This was at the time that John F. Kennedy was campaigning for President and I think that I was the only Democrat in the county. Ordinarily I was a Republican, but I was 100% for Kennedy. Everybody else around there was a rabid Republican. They told me that no way possible could Kennedy win, and that there were not enough Catholics in the country to elect him. I tried to tell them that there would be a lot of other people besides Catholics that would vote for Kennedy, but they wouldn't listen to me. By the time that Election Day rolled around, I had taken several small bets. Of course I was betting on Kennedy. I collected well over $100.00 on my election bets. You talk about a whole county being disappointed and downhearted, that one sure was. Well, I guess as a matter of fact the whole state was, because it was a highly Republican state.

Mary's father was ordinarily a mild pleasant gentleman. He used to follow me around like a little puppy dog, wanting to help me. He and I got along real good, but he began going senile. One day I heard Mary scream, so I ran into the house, and there he was with his pocketknife out and opened up, threatening to kill Mary. I knew he was out of his mind, because if he had been in his right senses, he would not have dreamed of doing something like that. I started towards him, talking to him all the time. I could see that he wanted to listen to me, but wasn't sure whether he should or not. He was standing in front of the davenport, and I got close enough to him that I reached out and grabbed his wrist and pushed his arm up, and pushed him down on the davenport. Ordinarily I would not have had any trouble holding him down but as it was he had the strength of three men. I had him flat on his back on the davenport I was sitting on his legs and had his arm pinned down, and managed to twist his arm enough that he dropped the knife. I told Mary, "Get in the car and go down the street and get the neighbor. I don't know how long I can hold him this way." She ran out, got in the car and drove about 1/4 of a mile to the nearest neighbor and brought the man back with her. He got there just in time, because I was completely worn out, trying to hold her dad down. He took over and held him down and kept talking to him, and it was just a few minutes until his senses came back to him, and we could turn him loose. I picked up the knife, went out on the back porch and threw it out into the woods as far as I could throw it. My brother-in-law Tom came by and Mary told him what had happened. He just jumped all over me and said, "You manhandled my father, and nobody does and gets away with it." I told him, "well it kind of looks like I did." He took off just as mad as the devil.

Mary had a third brother, Frank that lived in Cincinnati, Ohio, and he was a foreman in a factory there. He thought that he was really a big shot. About two months before, Frank's daughter married a young preacher. It wasn't but about three days, when here came the three of them - Tom, Frank, and the preacher. I met them at the door. They said, "We've got to have a talk with you." I said, "Fine, come on into the kitchen and we will talk. Tom and Frank followed me into the kitchen, but the preacher walked around the side of the house to the back door where he just lounged around there. I asked him to come in, but he wouldn't do it. I knew what was up. Tom and Frank were going to beat up on me, and the preacher was out there by the door in case I made a run for it and he could stop me. They started to berate me about manhandling their father, and I told them, "What was I supposed to do? Just stand there and watch him slit Mary's throat? Because that was what he was going to do. "Well, that stopped them a little bit when they thought about it that way. They knew that I was right. They said, "You've got to give him his knife back." I said. "Sorry. I can't do that." They said, "Well we'll just take it from you and give it to him." I said, "No, you are not going to take it from me. Because I don't have it." They said, "Well where is it?" I said, "I took it and threw it out into the woods. It is out there someplace and if you want it, you can just go out there and find it." I also told them that while Frank was here, they had better look into a nursing home for their folks. Tom said, "Oh no, my folks are never going to go into a nursing home." By that time they had quieted down some and left, taking the preacher with them. Well, it wasn't but a couple of days, when I read in the local paper, that there was a canning factory up in Mendota, IL that was hiring help through out the area and would furnish free transportation north for anybody that wanted to sign up. I told Mary, "This is it. I'm going to sign up for that. I know that they pay a fairly good wage, and they have housing there. I can live right on the company property there. I'll just work the season out, save my money, and come back after you, and we will get out of here." Two days later I was on a bus with about forty other men from around there, and was headed for Illinois. When we got up to the plant at Mendota, they had small hutments there that sleep six men, and they had a cafeteria in the plant, where you could eat your meals. The company would deduct the meals from your pay. I worked for three months there for them. I had about $1,200.00 saved up but there was another contractor in Mendota that came along and offered me a job with him, but I had to start right away. So, I thought, I could always use the extra money. I called

Mary and told her what the situation was, that I was going to work for this fellow for a little while before I came back. I worked for him for almost three months and accumulated another $1,000.00 in savings. He had an old stake body truck, it must have been about twenty years old. But it was in good running condition. He wanted $250.00 for it and I bought it from him. The heater in the truck was old and rusted out. It couldn't be repaired and I couldn't get another heater for it. This was in December and I headed for Kentucky in it, and the temperature was below zero.

I believe that was the coldest ride that I ever made in my life. I stopped at every filling station that I came to and it would take me about a half an hour to get warmed up. Then I would go again for another twelve or fifteen miles, until I reached another filling station. I kept that up until I crossed the Ohio River at Cincinnati. After that it warmed up considerably and I made the rest of the trip without any problem. It was about two weeks before Christmas at that time and we planned to leave after the first of the year, for Illinois. We took her father and mother down to Tom's house, and told them. "Here you are, now you can take care of them. We have taken care of them for a year." One week later, Mary's folks were in a nursing home. We waited until after the first of March to head north to Illinois. When we went, we took one of our neighbors with us. He was married and had three children. He had been out of work for quite awhile and I assured him that we would find work up there. So, he went with us, and he and Mary drove Mary's car, and I drove the truck. Of course the truck was piled high, but we had every thing securely fastened down and made the trip without incident until we got just west of Chicago. On interstate 90 I ran out of gas in the truck and pulled it off to the side of the road. In those days when I traveled, I always carried a five-gallon can of gas with me. I got the gas can off the back end of the truck, poured the gas into the truck tank, then the truck wouldn't start.

We got a chain out and hooked onto the truck with Mary's car. I knew that there was nothing wrong with truck's motor, it was just that we had run out of gas. We pulled it a short distance (about fifteen feet) and it started. Now at that time a State Trooper pulled up and stopped us. He said, "Did you know you are breaking the law? It is against the law to pull a vehicle. You have to call a wrecker service for that." I told him, "Sir, we are not pulling it. All we did was to pull it fifteen feet to get it started, that's all." I said, "I ran out of gas, and after I put the gas in, it wouldn't start, so we pulled it for fifteen feet to get it started, that's all." He said, "Where did you get the gas?" I said, "Well I had a spare can on the truck, carrying it with us for this purpose." The trooper stood there scratching his head, and finally said. "I guess you can go." I knew I could because there wasn't anything he could do. We hadn't broken any laws.

We made it into Mendota and decided our best bet was to buy a house. We bought an old house that was pretty well run down and started to remodel it. It took George and I about six weeks to get it in livable condition. The living room floor was oak flooring and some one had driven at least 500 finish nails all over it. Before we could do anything with the floor, I had to spend three days with a hammer and nail punch, driving those nails down into the floor, so we could sand it afterwards. We finally got moved in and George said, "I need to get to work. I need to send some money home." I said, "All right. I'll tell you what we will do. Years ago, when I was painting out of Delavan, there was a little red headed school teacher out of Chicago that owned a big girls camp out on Delavan Lake, and I used to do all of her painting. She should be out at the camp about now, so let's go and see her. I'm sure we can get some work from her." So, we headed for Delavan Lake. When we got to the girls' camp, she had just gotten there the day before. She said, "I sure am glad to see you, I've got a lot of work for you." It was just as if I had not been gone for a week let alone ten years. She said, "All six of the cabins need painting, the caretaker's house, the machine shed and boat house need painting. On top of that, the water tower is all fouled up, and we can't get any water out of it. I said, "Fine, I think we can handle all of it." We went back down to Mendota. I had enough funds left so that we were able to buy the tools, brushes and other equipment that we needed. I borrowed an old twenty-foot extension ladder and headed back to Delavan Lake. The first thing we tackled was the water tower. I started to get out on the roof of the tower to crawl up to the hatch, and as I did I could feel the roof start to sink down. I backed down the ladder and went to see the schoolteacher and told her, "The first thing that we are going to have to do is to tear the top off that tower. I started to get out on the roof to go up to the hatch and it just started to go down with me. She said, "Well, whatever. I have to have it for the girl's showers." We went to work and tore the roof off. Before we built a new roof for her, we got inside and cleaned it out thoroughly, made sure the drains were all opened up, and the sidewalls were all soft and rotted. We went into town and got a load of hard maple flooring and put a new floor in it, and we took and relined the walls with the maple flooring. Finally, we built a new roof on it. Her water tower was back in action and ready for use again. It took us three months to do all of the painting she wanted done. As I didn't have any spray equipment we were doing it all by hand with brush's. When we walked away from that job, we went back to Mendota and I had a check for over $5,000.00 in my pocket. Of course, after the expenses were paid half of that was George's. He rented an apartment in Peru, IL, and sent his wife money to come up and join him. She hired a cab in Williamsburg, KY, and her and the kids came all the way up to Mendota in the cab. It only cost them about $350.00, which really wasn't bad, for that was an eight hundred mile trip and the cabby had to turn around and drive back home. Between painting and carpenter work, we managed to keep fairly busy. George stayed with us for about a year until he got homesick and went back to Kentucky.

Once while we were living in Mendota, Mary's daughter Doris and her husband Joe came down to pay us a visit. Now Joe was my first insurance boss and was mad at me mainly because I had taken Mary, one of his best agents, away from him. We were sitting in the living room playing cards and Joe was sitting next to me. He kept ragging me and I put up with it for a while. Finally, he made me good and mad, I didn't say a word, just got up and wrapped my arm around his neck and pulled him out of the chair, out the front door into the yard, threw him down on the ground and was sitting on him. Of course he was trying to get away from me. Doris and her mother came running out into the yard. Doris reached down and rammed her fingers into my mouth, and was trying to tear the roof of my mouth up with her fingernails. I grabbed her wrist and pulled her hand out of my mouth before she could do any damage. I poked Joe in the stomach and knocked the breath out of him. Then I got up and made a dash for the back door, pulled the screen door shut behind me and hooked it, I shut the back door and locked it, and went through the house to the front door and locked it. I left every body standing out in the front yard. Then I called a friend of mine and told him to get over here, I was in trouble and needed a friendly witness. Then I called the police. Joe got his breath back and came to the rear door and found the screen door hooked. He jerked the screen door night off its hinges and kicked the back door in, breaking out not only the door but the doorframe too, and came after me. I grabbed him picked him up and twirled around over my head two or three times, threw him down on the floor and sat down on him again. About that time, my friend and the police came in. Joe got up and was raising cane. The police were standing there trying to talk to Joe and my friend snitched a pair of handcuffs off of one of the cops and hand cuffed Joe's hands behind his back. Joe was still ranting and raving and the police saw that they couldn't talk to him, so they took him out and put him into the rear seat of the squad car. Of course there were non-door handles in the back seat of a squad car, and the doors electronically lock, so he couldn't get out. But the back window was down and he actually tried to dive headfirst through the window. They took Joe down to the police station, and I went right along with them and swore out charges of breaking and entering against him. Joe had a considerable amount of money on him and was able to post a cash bond, so they turned him loose. He and Doris went back to Rockford and we were never bothered by him again.

Mendota turned out to be a very poor place to start up a business in, as the people there are very clannish, and you almost had to be a lifelong resident before you could earn a living. We had already bought a house there, so I tried to make the best of things. To give you an example of what I was up against there, there was just one painter in town, and I know for a fact that he was booked up ahead for four years in advance. The town and that area really needed another painter in a bad way. I contracted with one party to paint his house. It was a huge old two story-house, and needed a lot of preparatory work before it could be painted. I quoted him a price of $1,500.00, which was really a good price for the work that had to be done. I came by three days later to start work on the job, and he came out and wouldn't let me start. He said the other painter had given him a price of $650.00 for the job and that I was way over charging him. Well, I was not over charging him, as I knew the cost of the paint alone was over $600.00. The other guy just couldn't stand a little competition and was willing to do the job at a loss, because he had to lose money at that price. I managed to get some work around there, but if I really got hard up, I would go north up around Woodstock, and I could always pick up all the work that I wanted.

Mary was becoming senile like her mother and became almost impossible to live with. She was accusing me of having an affair with a woman that I didn't even know, didn't even know she existed, and a lot other stuff along that line. So I packed up my clothes and moved into a hotel and operated out of the hotel. By this time I had acquired another air compressor and spray equipment.

While I was living in the hotel, there was a group of Mormons living in town, two of them contacted me and tried to convert me to Mormonism. They would visit me in my hotel room and talk to me for hours at a time. I was interested, for as a teenager I had dated a Mormon girl and they had tried to convert me, and I had read the book of Mormon at that time. Well, I hesitated to commit myself and they told me that they were going to build a new $100,000.00 temple in Ottawa, IL and they would give me the general contract for it, but I had to be a member of the church in order to get the contract. I more or less considered that to be a bribe. I knew that as a member of the Mormon Church I would have to tithe 10% of my earnings to the church. That in itself would bring the money available for construction down to $90,000.00, I thought, no, I'm not a general contractor, I am just a painting contractor. I don't know anything about blue prints or how to read them. I really don't know anything about construction costs, and I could just wind up losing my fanny if I took that job. So, I just told them "No thanks. I'm not interested."

I had hired an old fellow there in Mendota. He was a good person and a good worker, but uneducated. He couldn't read a ruler. He knew what the inch marks were on it, but that was all. I devised a method where he could make an accurate measurement with a ruler. I pointed out to him that between the inch marks there was one big mark, which meant a half-inch, and between them two smaller marks, which meant 3/4 or 1/4 of an inch. I would tell him that I needed a two by four, two feet, three inch's and one big mark and one small mark. That he could understand and he could get it right. It just took a little patience. I had taken on a repair job on a big old house that had built in gutters. The guttering had rotted out all around the house and I had to tear it out and re-build it. There was just no way of using modern gutters on it. It took us two weeks to get that gutter torn out and rebuilt. It was just awful slow and tedious work. I don't think I'll ever take another job like it. I took Mike and we went to Aurora and painted that farm. We finished up about the 5th or 6th of November. We loaded every-thing up and headed back to Mendota and on the way, the state police stopped me. They looked the truck all over and were just looking for something that they could write up a ticket on me. I had my air compressor hooked onto the rear end of the truck, and had my ladders on top of the truck, and they extended 3-1/2 feet past the rear end of the truck. The state law required that if you have anything extending 4 foot or more past the end of the vehicle, that you had to have a red flag on it. They got out their tape measure, and measured the ladder, which was only 3-1/2 feet over, and finally after about a half-hour of fiddling around, they wrote me a ticket for not having a permanent license plate on my compressor. Well, I had pulled air compressors for a good many years and had never had to have a license for the air compres-sor, and had never heard of it.

When I got back to Mendota I went to see the JP there that had jurisdiction, showed him the ticket, and tried to tell him that there was no such law. He shut me up, and told me that was just a new law that had been passed, and fined me $10.00 and costs which was $8.00. I paid him the $18.00 and forgot about it. The next spring I had to be in the state capital of Springfield for some reason, I forget what it was now. I needed a new truck license, so I went into the state license bureau and bought my truck license. Then I happened to think, and I told the fellow, "Well, I guess I need a permanent license for my air compressor to. "He said, "Well, I guess we could give you a permanent license for it if you want one, but we have never issued a license for a air compressor out of this office as of yet." I said, "Oh. Well, last November 5th the state police stopped me, and they issued me a ticket for not having a permanent license on my air compressor. That cost me $18.00." he said, "Wait just a minute, I am going to call someone, and I want you to talk to them." The party that he called was the head of the state police. I told him my story, and he said, "There, is no such thing as a license plate or permanent license for an air compressor at all. Those cops must have been ticket happy. Do you happen to have his name and badge number?" I said, "No, I don't have his name or badge number, but I can tell you exactly where it happened, what day it happened, and what time it happened." He said, "I think that will be good enough, I can check the records and find out who it was and I'll give them a talking to. If anything like this ever happens again, you just tell them to get on their radio and call me.

I got tired of living in the hotel and decided to buy a new house trailer. I went down to LaSalle-Peru and rented a house trailer there. I figured that I would move everything into the rented house trailer, then go buy my new one, and park it right next to the rented one, then it would be a simple matter, to move things from one trailer to the other. I went down to Hannibal, MO and purchased a new Princess trailer for $1,800.00. It was ten feet wide and sixty feet long. I made arrangements for them to deliver it and went back to Peru. While I was gone the rented trailer had burned up completely, and I had absolutely nothing left except my car and the cloths that I had on. Now this was just two weeks before Christmas and I hadn't taken out any insurance on my belongings, as I figured they would only be in that trailer for a week. The next day I went in to see my insurance agent, and he had a big laugh. He said, "I heard that you burned up and didn't have any insurance." I thought, that's real nice of him. So I went over and contacted another insurance agency, and transferred all of my insurance to them. The park owner had a *junk* dealer to come and pull the framework of the burned out trailer to their junkyard. I had a brand new aluminum stepladder that I had paid $39.00 for and had it stored under the trailer, but, there was no sign of it either. I went out to the junkyard and asked them about it, and they said that they had it and that it was part of the salvage deal. I said, "Like the devil, it was part of the salvage deal." They tried to give me an argument, but at least I got the ladder back from them. There are all kinds of people in this world, you don't even have to look for them, and they will find you.

There's a factory in Sandwich, IL that manufactured Cheese Puffs. I got the contract for painting the inside of the factory, and when I finished and the owner paid me off, he also gave me ten cartons of the Cheese Puffs. I ate Cheese Puffs for a year after that. I also painted and roofed a two-story house in Sandwich. It was a rental property and the owner didn't live in it. As time went on, they had a rainstorm and the owner called me up and told me that the new roof was leaking. I said, "I really don't see how but I will come over and look at it." I went over, got up on the roof, examined it thoroughly, and couldn't see any sign of a leak anywhere. I reported it to the owner. The next time that it rained, he called me up and said that it was leaking again. I told him that I had examined the roof before, and that there was no place that it could possibly be leaking. I said, "No, I am not going to come over this time, but I'll tell you what, the next time it starts to rain, you call me and I'll come over then and crawl up in the attic. I'll examine the whole attic while it's raining." So, it went on for about a month, then I got a call from them one morning, saying, "Its starting to rain over here now and it looks like it will be a pretty good rain." I said, "Fine, I'm on my way over." When I got there the renter was home and I asked him to show me where it was leaking. They took me into the

kitchen and there was a chimney that ran from the basement up to the top of house, and the ceiling around the
chimney was soaking wet. I said, I examined that on top
of the roof and I know that it is not leaking around the
chimney. I've got to get up in the attic and find out where
that leak is. Where is your crawl hole?" They didn't want
to tell me, but finally they did. It was in their bedroom
closet. I went in there and opened the door of the closet.
It was jam packed full from the floor to the ceiling. I
guess they thought I would take one look at the closet
and forget about it, but I didn't and started to pull the
stuff out of the closet. I completely emptied it, and had
stuff all over their bed and the floor. Then I crawled up
into the attic and examined the whole attic thoroughly, especially around the chimney and could not find as much
as one wet spot, The tenants wanted the owner to re-
decorate the whole house for them, which he wouldn't
do. What they did was to soak the ceiling by hand. Need-
less to say, after that they did not get their redecorating job.

We were visiting in Rockford with Mary's daughter,
Doris. Once when we were sitting around the kitchen
table, drinking coffee and talking, Doris was standing
beside me. She was a fairly large girl in her thirties and
started smarting off to me. I told her, "You better watch
your mouth or I'll turn you over my knees and give you
a paddling." She said. "Yeah, you and what other army?"
I never said another word, I just reached up and grabbed
hold of her arm, and yanked her down over my knees,
clamped my legs around her legs, put my elbow in the
small of her back to hold her down. Turned her dress up,
pulled her panties down, and gave her a paddling. Her
mother was sitting across the table laughing her head
off. I took Doris by surprise. Other wise I would not
have been able to do that. She was a good sport and didn't
get mad at me. But she did have a lot more respect for
me after that.

This next episode happened about two years previous. Joe and Doris lived in a big two story, seven room

house. This was before he was made president of the insurance company in Cincinnati. They bought a house on the other side of town. They had checked with the movers and the movers wanted $1,500.00 to move them. I told them to forget about the movers, that I could get them moved for about $250.00. When moving day came along, I went down and rented a U-Haul truck for $150.00 and I had Joe to get some other volunteers from the insurance crew to come and give us a hand. There were five of us there to do the work at 9 a.m. I backed the truck up to the front door of the house and we started to work. We took all of the bedrooms first, as they were the last ones to be unloaded, then the living room, kitchen and dining room as they were the first ones to be set up. Nothing had been packed, not even the dishes. We did all of that as we went along and by 5 p.m. that day, we had the new house completely set up, rugs in place, furniture all set up, even the pictures on the walls, stove and refrigerator all set up in the kitchen, and Doris was cooking supper for the crew in her new kitchen. With volunteer labor, the total cost $185.00, for the truck and gas.

As I said before, some of these incidents are going to be out of sequence, so here are a few of them that should have been included somewhere along the line before.

One time when I was living with my uncle, he had a forty-acre wheat field that was so full of wild mustard that you couldn't see any of the wheat. I thought I would do him a favor and go and clean up that mustard out of that field. I had to pull each mustard plant up by hand. I would start at 6 a.m. in the morning, work two hours and come in for breakfast and then work until noon, take an hour off for dinner, go back to work, and work until supper time, take an hour off for supper, then go back to work and work until I couldn't see any longer. It took two weeks of working like that to do it, but I got every mustard plant pulled up out of that field, and there never was any wild mustard in that field again.

My uncle always kept his calves in the barn during the winter months, and he would usually clean the barn about two times a week. One day, one of his Black Angus calves got out of his pen, and we were trying to get him back in his pen. He was at the far end of the barn and my uncle grabbed hold of his tail, and the calf just took off, he dragged my uncle the full length of the barn, right through one of the gutters which hadn't been cleaned in three days, before my uncle could let loose of his tail.

Over The Hill at Forty

For about ten years I had been on the outs with my family. None of them knew where I was or what I was doing, except my Aunt Chloe. I had always kept in touch with her and she always knew where I was and what I was doing, but none of the family ever thought to ask her if she knew anything about me. During this time, both of my younger sisters had gotten married, and I had no idea who their husbands were, or what they were like. My folks had sold their home in Delavan, Wis. and bought a small house down in Brooksville, Fla. where they were spending their winters now. In the spring and summer they would come north and visit with my aunt and uncle for a short while. Then they would go over to Muskegon, Michigan and stay with my youngest sister Annabelle. Annabelle was a biology teacher at the high school in Muskegon. As my folks were getting along in years, I decided that it was about time that I made peace with my family. My other half sister, Eileen, had married a young fellow from Ohio who she had met at college, where she had gotten a degree as a librarian and he had gotten a degree as an electric engineer. As soon as they had gotten married, he had gone into the army and they were stationed up in Alaska near Anchorage for three years. At the end of his third year in the army, he took his discharge and they came back down to the lower states, and he got himself a job with McDonald Douglas Aircraft, out in Los Angeles where he would spend the next 41 years working for them. I lived in my new trailer for about two years in the trailer park in Peru, IL. I decided that I might as well move back up north, because I was spending most of my time working up there. I had my trailer pulled up to my uncle's farm, and parked it there on the farm but did not live in it. I just moved in with my aunt and uncle again.

At one time my uncle had been quite sick, and was in the hospital. The doctors had told him that the best thing he could do was to go home and put all of his affairs in order as he only had about two weeks to live. Well, he didn't believe the doctor and he went to a chiropractor, in Delavan, WI. 'he chiropractor straightened him out, and he lived for almost twenty years afterwards.

As my uncle was getting on up in years at that time, and couldn't really take care of all of his farm work, I was doing was doing a good deal of the farm work for him. One winter we remodeled the kitchen and living room. My uncle had a nephew of his who was an expert carpenter come in and remodel the kitchen for him, while I remodeled the living room. They had had bees in the house for years that they had not been able to get rid of. I started in the living room by tearing all of the plasterboard off of the ceilings to get it ready to put up new sheet rock. When I tore the ceiling down, I found that the bees had a honey comb in between six of the rafters that extended all the way across the ceiling to the far side of the room, about fifteen feet. Well, this was odd. It was in the wintertime and was about zero outside. I left the front door open and the bees would come out of their hives and head for the outside, hit that cold air, and it would kill them instantly. They would just drop straight down. I went out to the corncrib and got a scoop shovel and had my aunt scrub it up real good. Then, my uncle and I went into the living room and he would hold a big washtub up, and I would take the scoop shovel and go in between the rafters and scoop the honey down into the washtub. We got over three hundred pounds of some of the finest honey you ever tasted. When we finished the job, my uncle paid his nephew union wages and gave him half of a beef as a bonus, but he never even said thank you to me for my work. One day I was shoveling corn out of the corncrib into a wagon to take over and grind up for meal for the cattle. When my uncle came out and watched me for a few minutes, he said, "That's not the way to do it, here let me, show you how." He was under doctor's orders not to do any work and not to get out in the cold at all. He took the shovel and started shoveling. I watched him for about five minutes, then I told him, "Uncle Jim if you are going to do this, I will get out of here and go into the house. If you want me to do this, you get the hell out of here and let me do it." Boy was he mad. Nobody had ever talked to him like that before. He slammed the shovel down and stomped into the house, and it was about a week before he would talk to me again.

One day in June I had a couple of the neighbors in to help us. They were running baled hay up into the haymow, on a grain elevator. I think that we probably put 300 bales of hay into the mow that day. Out of that, we lost just one bale from the elevator, and it just so happened that I was walking under the elevator, when that one bale came down and hit me right on the top of my head. One bale that we lost that day and I had to be underneath it when it came down. I didn't say a word, I just walked over to my car, got in and drove 25 miles to my chiropractor's home. Because this was on a Sunday and I knew he wouldn't be in his office. When I got there I told him what had happened, He said, "Do you think that you could drive another ten miles?" I said, "I reckon that I can."

He said, "Good, then lets go over to my office, and I'll take care of you." Well, we did, and he did, and I went on back home to work. This chiropractor was a young fellow and was just getting started up. He just had his office open two evenings during the week and on Saturday. The rest of the time he was head instructor in the Lombard School of Chiropractic. When I first started going to him, he had just charged me $4.00 for an adjustment. Years later, when I finally moved away, he was getting $25.00 an adjustment. Whenever I started getting a cold the first place I would head for would be the chiropractors, and they would knock it right out of me. One day I came down with a bad cold and I knew Doc. would be at the college in Lombard, so I went to another chiropractor in Woodstock and he gave me an adjustment. He worked on my neck. He gave me a crack in the neck, and when he got through, it felt like my neck had a U turn in it. I didn't say a word then, I just walked out and got into my car and drove down to Lombard, and went into the college. I asked for my doctor and he came out. I told him what had happened. He examined my neck and said, "That's not good, but I think I can help you." He took me back to the examination room, stretched me out on a table, and went to work. Ten minutes later he said, "I think we have you straightened out." I asked him what I owed him. He said, "Nothing. The college is paying me. While you're here would you like a tour through the place?" I said, "Sure." So he gave me a guided tour through the whole college. That included the morgue, where they had six dead bodies stacked up on top of one another. I think he thought that I would get sick at the sight of those dead bodies. But, I had seen many a dead bodies during the war, and they didn't bother me at all.

My uncle told me that he had some friends that lived about three miles away that had a set of farm buildings that they wanted to get painted, so I went over to see them. They were three brothers, all bachelors, and they had an old maid sister who was keeping house and cooking for them. I had never seen such buildings as they had there. The main cow barn was 185 feet long, sixty feet wide and thirty feet high on the sides, and sixty feet high in the gable end. They had a corncrib that was twice as large as any corncrib I had ever seen, with a big cubicle on the top of it. They had a hog barn that was as large as an ordinary cow barn, a couple of huge machine sheds, and two, two-story houses on the farm. They wanted everything painted. The buildings were all in bad condition and looking at them, I knew that I would have to hand scrape every square inch of them. I contracted for the job. I knew that it would take me at least three months to do it. I was working by myself at that time. The oldest of the three brothers was the boss, and I knew that he thought I would get half way through the scraping and give it up. If I quit he wouldn't have to pay me for the work that I had done as it was a contract job. Then he could call on another painter, and tell him to look, they had the scraping half done and all of my work would be free gratis to them. Well, I fooled him. I not only got the scraping all done, but I finished up all of the painting, too. I completed the job. But when I started to work on the farm, I knew that I would need a sixty-foot ladder to reach up to the gable end of the barn. One day I spotted an ad in the Woodstock paper of a sixty-foot ladder for sale. So, I went in to see about it, and the person who had it for sale was a Mr. Louton. He had a small paint factory in Woodstock. We went out to look at the ladder and it was a wooden ladder with three twenty foot sections, and the bottom section had a 4 foot spread, and each section was so heavy, it was all I could to pick up and move one section. Louton was asking just $30.00 for the ladder so I bought it from him. Mr. Louton was a very friendly man and he gave me a guided tour through the factory. As a result I started to buy most of my paint from him. He had a special formula for outside white oil paint. It was the best outside white paint that I had ever seen. There would be times in the years following, that I would buy six hundreds gallons at a crack. By buying that much at a time, Louton gave me a special price on it, I enjoyed dealing with him because if I ever had any questions, I could go to him and he would explain every thing to me.

I took my ladder out to the farm. When I went to work on the gable ends of the barn, it would take over an hour just to get the ladder set up. I would set the bottom section up first, then set up the second section, move it onto the bottom section, run it up a couple of rungs, and take the third section and set it up, and set it up into the second section, and then I would have to grunt the whole works up. It would take me five minutes to grunt those sections up one rung, and when I got the second section up as high as it would go, I still had to grunt the third section up as high as it would go. I just barely got the job done when cold weather set in. Since I didn't have any interior work to do, I took a job in the R.C. Allen Typewriter Plant. In there I ran a punch press, punching out parts for a typewriter. While working there, I bought a typewriter for myself, and also an adding machine that they made in another plant up in Michigan. Two years later they closed the plant and moved it to Japan.

I contracted a job in Evanston IL, which was about sixty miles from Woodstock. It was for the Evanston Curling Club. There were two big Quonsets huts joined together in the center. The building was 150 foot long, 40 foot high and 80 foot wide. They furnished the paint for it, which was white enamel that I believe, cost them about $20.00 a gallon. I believe that I used 150 gallons on that job. I had my dad helping me, and I had him doing all the groundwork while I did the climbing and spraying. Since it was to far to drive back and forth to Woodstock every day, we stayed in a motel for the week that it took me to do the job. We finished up on a Saturday afternoon and I got all loaded up and headed home. I was driving the truck and my dad was driving the car. It was late in the evening as I came through McHenry, IL with about twenty miles to go, when I noticed a squad car drop in behind me. Well, I thought I'll just make sure that he doesn't have anything to stop me for. So I was careful not to exceed the speed limit. He stayed right behind me for about twenty miles. We were only about a mile and a half from home and it was dark now, when I heard his siren go off. He pulled me over to the side of the road, and I couldn't imagine what he was stopping me for, but I soon found out. I didn't have a taillight on the compressor. My dad had stopped, but when he saw the cop get out of the squad car, he took off and went on home. Well, the cop said," You've got to have a taillight there. You can't drive it with out a tail light, or you will just have to park it on the side of the road until morning." I said, "Mister I only have about one mile to go to get home and I'll be off of road." He said, "I'm sorry but I can't let you go without a light on there." I said, "Now you just tell me, how in the dickens am I going to put a light on there." He said, "Well, get one of your flares. You are supposed to have flares." I guess he was hoping I didn't have any flares, so he could write me up for that too. I finally found them. I took one and was going to fasten it to the top of the truck rack on the back of the truck, and he said, "Oh no, it has got to be on the compressor," Well, the compressor was solid metal with a rounded top and no place where you could possibly fasten a flare. I took the flare down and handed it to him, and said, "Here you go fasten it on for me." He took the flare and went back to the compressor, kept walking around it and studying it for about ten minutes. There was no way to fasten that flare on there, so he came back, gave me the flare, and said, "Well, I guess you will just have to fasten it on the truck rack here." I did and he let me go on. When I got home I asked my dad, "Why did you take off? Why didn't you stay there with me? I thought for a while, That I was going to have to park and leave it there until morning, and then I would have had to walk the rest of the way home." He just couldn't give me any good reason for leaving.

My uncle's farm hadn't been painted for about thirty years. He wanted it painted, so I painted it for him. I had to give all of the buildings three coats in order to make them look half way decent. I trimmed them all out in white. There was a big barn, a milk house, hog barn, corncrib, and a large machine shed. I painted all of those free gratis. My uncle did furnish the paint, but never offered to pay me ten cents for my labor. It only took me three weeks to do the job.

That year I became acquainted with Ed Krause. He was an excellent mechanic and was operating out of a little two-stall garage at that time. Later on, he was to build a new garage for himself which was 150 feet long and 60 feet wide, with doors wide enough and high enough to take in a big semi-truck. It was equipped with all of the most modern machines and tools. He also had a lane through there where he tested trucks. From then on, he always did all of my mechanical and repair work and really took good care of me. One day in November, I was operating the punch press in the typewriter factory, when the foreman came by and said that I had an emergency call and that I could take it in his office. It was my aunt and she told me that my uncle had had a heart attack and had just died. I told my foreman what was up. He told me to go ahead and take off, and not to come back to work until after the funeral.

The next year my sister Ilene, from Los Angeles, was visiting with my aunt and me. She wanted to go up to Delavan to our old hometown and visit some friends up there. I said, "Okay. I'll take you up there." Now this was in 1967 and it was 22 years after the war had ended, and in all of that time, I had never met another man out of my old division or heard one word about it. We got about five miles north of Hebron, IL. Headed for Lake Geneva and I spotted on a telephone pole, a big triangular sign with a 10th Armored Division insignia on it, with arrows pointing down another road. I said, "What in the world is going on? That was my old army division," So I took my sister up to Delavan, dropped her off, and came back and started down the road that the sign pointed to, and pretty soon I came to another sign that pointed up another road so I turned on it. I got back up to the south shore of Lake Geneva and ran out of signs. I passed a little group that looked like they were having a family reunion, I stopped and got out of the car, and started over towards them. A couple of fellows came out to meet me. I asked them, "Are you the bunch from the 10th Armored Division?" They said, "Yes. Who are you?" I said. "I am Ralph Spencer from Hebron, IL, and the 10th was my old army division. I've never met a man nor heard a word about the division in twenty two years." They informed me that they have a reunion every Labor Day weekend and this year it will be in Louisville, KY. They were just a bunch out of Chicago planning their trip to the reunion. I had them write down all of the information about the reunion, about where it was going to be, and what hotel it would be in, etc. I told them that I would see them at the reunion. That Labor Day weekend, you had better believe that I was in Louisville, KY, and so were the bunch that I had met at Lake Geneva. They all gave me a regal welcoming, and I really had a great time that weekend.

That weekend in Louisville started me to thinking I hadn't had a vacation in ten years and Expo 67 was on at Montreal, Canada. I had just finished a good sized farm job, and I had over $1,500.00 to play with, so I told my aunt, "I'm going to go up to Expo 67, but I hate to go by myself. Do you know of anyone who would like to go?" She said, "Yes. I'll go with you." I was really surprised, because she had done very little traveling. We packed our suitcases and took off. I decided to make a real trip out of it, so we went up through International Falls, MN then followed the lakeshores down around for two thousand miles to Montreal, Canada. When we got there we rented a room with a French family near the sight of the Expo. I was really surprised at my aunt when we started the trip. She suggested that we should share a motel room, that it would be foolish to rent two rooms. So that was what we did. If the room only had one bed in it we shared the bed. She slept on her side and I slept on mine. We got along just fine. We stayed a week in Montreal and spent five days at the Expo. It was really an experience. We left Montreal and went up to Quebec, Canada. While in Quebec we hired a fellow with a horse drawn carriage to give us a guided tour around the city.

At that time, there was a prominent Senator in Washington D.C., who had a beautiful blond daughter that had married a big colored man. It was quite a scandal. My aunt had just been reading about them in the paper, and it said they were on a honeymoon somewhere. She was talking about them and said, "I wonder where they are at now?" I said, "Do you really want to know?" She said, "Yes, I'd like to." I said, "I can tell you." She said. "How do you know where they are at?" I said. "Just take a look at the carriage next to us." And there they were. We went on north in Canada for a ways and then crossed over into northern Maine. I told my aunt, I have an old army buddy and we were as close as brothers were. Now I am going to look him up. She said, "Do you have his address?" I said, "No, but, I'll find him." She said, "I doubt that. You would be wasting our time." I said "He originally came from Raymond, Maine, and there is bound to be someone there who knows him." We got into Raymond and I started asking around for Lloyd Huff, but no one seemed to remember him. I was about ready to give up, when one old fellow said, "Yeah I remember him. I can tell you where he is at, too. You just take Highway 205 here south for about 30 or 35 miles. He has got a small roadside garage right on the side of the highway just this side of Gorham." I thanked him and we went on down the highway. Just before we got to Gorham, I spotted his sign and it said "Huffs Garage." We pulled in and stopped. I went into the garage and asked for Lloyd. The fellow in the garage said that he wasn't there right at that time, but that he would be back shortly. I said that I would just wait for him out in the car. About a half-hour later, I saw him pull into the front of the garage in a small wrecker. He opened up the wrecker door and another fellow came up and started talking to him. I walked over and he was looking down at the ground. I said, "I'm looking for a fellow by the name of Lloyd

Huff." He turned his head kind of sideways and looked at me, and said, "Spencer?" I said, "Yep." It had been 25 years since we had seen or heard from each other. He got up and we gave each other a big bear hug. He said "Come on inside and bring your aunt with you and sit down in my office. I still have some work to do here, and it will take me about an hour. Then we will go on home." We went in and sat down and waited. In about 45 minutes, he came out and said, "Okay just follow me." We followed him on into Gorham. He had an upstairs apartment that he lived in and said, "Come on up and meet the wife." So we went up. He opened the door and walked in, and his wife was there fixing supper. The first thing he said to her was, 'Honey, who was I talking about all of last week?" She said, "Why your old army buddy, Spencer." He said, "Well, meet Spencer." I think you could have knocked her over with a feather. We had supper with them and visited for a while. They didn't have a guest bedroom, so we just called down to a nearby motel and reserved us a room there. The next day he picked us up and gave us a guided tour around the country. The main sights that he showed us were three covered bridges, which had historical significance. From there we headed on home. We stopped in two or three places in Ohio to visit relatives and friends. My aunt wanted to visit Mamie Huffman, who had been a next-door neighbor of hers, and I also knew her quite well, as I had worked about four months for her husband as a farmhand and in their roller skating rink. She had been head of the draft board at Pomeroy, Ohio. She was the one who was actually responsible for my being drafted. They had made a fortune in the dairy business in Illinois and when they retired, they moved back down to their home in southern Ohio. They lived in a little town named Chester where she was the queen bee of the local society. When they moved back to Chester from Illinois they had been fairly wealthy, and they had a big over grown son nicknamed Sonny who they had set up in about twelve different businesses and he had failed in all of them. That left them almost poor people again. Her husband had died, and she had been forced to give up her fine home in Chester, and was living in a small house trailer in the woods outside of Chester. When I lived with them I hadn't dared smoke a cigarette inside of her house. We finally located her trailer and she invited us in. I felt kind of sorry for her, because it was quite a come down for her. I thought to myself I'm just going to see what she does, and I pulled out a pack of cigarettes and took one out. She said, "Just a minute." She got up and started looking in her cupboards and came back with an ashtray for me. She didn't mind my smoking in her house at all now. We went back home and got there in about one month from the day we left. Before we had started on our trip to the Expo 67 I had just contracted with a farmer who owned two farms and they both needed painting. For three years I had been trying to get his work, and I was supposed to start his job at the time that we started our trip. I had called him and told him that I was sorry, that I hadn't had a vacation in ten years and that I was taking one now, and that I would start the work as soon as I got back. He was as mad as a wet hen about that and said, "Like the devil you will. You don't have those jobs anymore." Well, he was true to his word. He wouldn't even speak to me after I got back. It took me five years, and I finally got his work again, simply because he couldn't find anyone else to do it.

At that time as a sideline I was selling a line of sterling silver and fine china. One night in Woodstock I had a young lady with me that I was training to be an agent. I just could not line up an appointment for us and I did want her to see a demonstration put on. I thought to myself, that there was one girl here that I had sold a large set of Wearever to and that she was building a large hope chest. So I said, "Let's go call on this girl." I told the lady with me to wait in the car and I would see if I could talk my way in. I rang the doorbell and the girl came to the door. She recognized me and she said, "I'm sorry you can't come in. I split up with my boy friend and I've sold off my entire hope chest. I'm not going to start another one." I told her, "I have a line of fine china that I know you would enjoy seeing. I have a young lady here that I'm breaking in, and she needs to see a demonstration put on. If you would let us come in and put on a demonstration for you, I guarantee you that I will not try to sell you anything at all." She said, "Well, under those circumstances, all right." I went out and got the girl and the sample kit, and went back in and put on the demonstration. When I got all through, I packed my samples up, said good-bye to the girl, and headed for the door. She said, "Wait a minute. Where are you going?" I said, "I told you that I would guarantee you that I wouldn't try to sell you anything, So I'll just be on my way." She said, "Not so fast, I want that china. So I sat down and believe it or not, I wrote her up for $900.00 worth of china. She was back in the hope chest business in a big way again.

The owner of the china company wanted me to take over as the superintendent of the southern part of Wisconsin, and the northern part of Illinois. But I had too much invested in my painting business, and as superintendent, it would have been a full time job. I could have made pretty good money at it, but I really didn't want it. I told him that I knew of a party that would make them a good superintendent. She was up at Williams Bay, Wisconsin. I told them about Mrs. Reynolds and that I had worked for her in the hosiery business. I told them that she was a good sales person and would probably be interested in the position. He told me to go see her and if she was interested to go ahead and hire her and train her. Once I had her trained, then he would see about making her superintendent. I went to see Florence and she was looking for a sales position of some kind. When I explained to her, she was very interested. But I told her that she would have to work with me until I had her trained. Then the owner would make her a superintendent, which put her, over me. In other words, I just hired my own boss. She worked out pretty well with them, and stayed with them for about three years.

Things went along pretty good for a while. It was about seven years after I left and divorced Mary, that I met another woman by the name of Marie Wolf. She was from Marengo, which was about 20 miles distant from my aunt's farm. We hit it off pretty good together, and after about three months when her divorce became final, we got married. This was in January and at that time she was working in a mousetrap factory. She managed to get two weeks leave and we left for California to visit my sister and her husband in Los Angeles. On our trip we went south about 90 miles and picked up Highway 66 and followed it all the way across country to Los Angeles, about 2,000 miles. We had pretty decent weather for the whole trip, until we crossed the California border. About fifteen minutes after we crossed the border, it started to rain, and it rained and rained. We got to my sisters in Woodland Hills (which is a suburb of Los Angeles) and it was still raining. The main reason I wanted to go to Los Angeles on our honeymoon, besides visiting with my sister and her husband, was to go to Disney World. Well, it rained for three days and nights, with no chance to go to Disney World, and Marie had to get back to her job in a week's time. So we headed back, and this time we took the southern route home. We went down through El Paso; then from El Paso to Texarkana, Texas. At Texarkana at one of the restaurants that we ate at, the owner had a huge cactus plant in the restaurant. She gave us a small shoot and told us that when we got home, just to plant it in a small pot and it would grow. So we did that and it started growing and it grew right straight up without any arms or anything. It was triangular in shape, and it was just six years old and four-foot high before it started putting out any arms on it. It was eighteen years old when Marie died. It was twelve feet tall with hundreds of arms of branches on it. We had it in the living room and there were two years that we used it as a Christmas tree.

After returning from our honeymoon, I moved in with Marie. She had an upstairs apartment in a large two-story house in Marengo. At the time she was just renting the apartment, but about three months later when she got her settlement from her ex-husband, we decided that it would be a good investment to buy the house, which was on the market for $26,000.00. She went ahead and bought the house and paid for in cash, so there was no mortgage on it. It had two apartments downstairs and one apartment upstairs. It had a large three-car garage, which was unfinished. It had no doors and no windows in it and it had a dirt floor. About three months after buying the place, the downstairs tenant moved out and we moved down into the downstairs apartment on the west side of the house and rented the upstairs apartment. Marie wasn't happy with the apartment the way it was, so, I completely remodeled the living room, kitchen, bathroom, and two bedrooms. I stripped the rooms right down to the wall studs, insulated the walls and put up new sheetrock. The bedroom, which wasn't very large had no closet in it. So it became a little smaller and I put in a nice clothes closet along one wall. It made for rather a small bedroom, but it was adequate and we got along okay. The living room had a twelve-foot ceiling in it and we lowered it to nine foot. In the kitchen, she had her son James come in to tear out all the cabinets and build completely new cabinets for her. In the bathroom, we tore out all the old fixtures, including the tub. We put in a new tub, new stool, and new sink. It took us about 4 months to get all of this done. I put in new carpeting in the living room, bedroom and hallway, which I laid, and we put in a new tile floor in the bathroom and kitchen, which I also put down. We hired a plumbing firm out of Harvard to do all of the plumbing and to put in the new tub, sink, stool, and new kitchen sink for us. The plumbing firm gave us a pretty good bid on the new fixtures and did a good job on the installations. We paid them off without any problems. There will be more about this plumbing firm a little later on. After we got the apartment straightened out, I went to work on the garage. The first thing I had done was to get her son Jim to help me. The first thing we did was to pour a cement floor in the garage, plus a nice wide approach on the east of the garage. It was 12 feel wide so I could get my air compressor up on it and park it there. Then we put the windows in the garage. We put two overhead doors up on the east end and one on the southwest end of the garage. Then I put a dividing wall in the garage, with a small doorway going from one section to the other. But I am forgetting one important part. Before we poured the cement floors we dug a ditch from the house to the garage and through to the north side of the garage. Then we ran a gas line from the house to the north side of the garage so I could put in a furnace, and heat the garage. The southwest section we used as a garage for our car, in the east section, which would hold two cars, I used for a shop. I built shelves for storage space along three sides of it, and all along one side in the garage side. We had plenty of storage space and we used all of it. Then I painted the whole thing, two coats of white on the inside of it and three coats of white on the outside of it. I even ran the gas line through the north wall of the garage and brought an outlet up on the outside of the garage, with the idea in mind that I would build a workshop along the north side of the garage for Marie. Then we poured an eight-foot wide slab of concrete along the whole north edge of the garage. I never did get the shop built for Marie. But the slab came in handy for me to store my ladders on. After I got all that done I started on the basement of the house. We had rented the other downstairs apartment to an elderly lady, and there was a rickety old stairway going down into the basement from her apartment and we were afraid that she would try to use that stairway and fall and hurt herself. I floored over the top of the stairway and made a walk-in closet for her. The basement wasn't much. It was only about 12 foot by 20 and it had a dirt floor and stone walls all the way around it. I saved up all of my used five-gallon paint pails, until I had one hundred of them. I started to dig the basement out behind the furnace, which was a dirt wall, using the pick, picking the dirt loose, then I would fill my pails up with the dirt. When I got my hundred pails all filled, I would carry them all up outside and load them onto my truck. Then I would truck them out to a land fill, where I would empty my pails out and carry them back to the basement again and start all over. There was no way possible to put an elevator into the basement to move the dirt outside. After digging back about ten feet I ran into another rock wall. They thought that I never would get it done. Now everybody thought I was crazy for doing this. The foundation of the house had rock wall built up and they were all kind of crumbly. I would knock out a portion of the foundation, cart all of the stones, concrete and cement out. Rocks that were to big to fit into my pails or to heavy to pick up and carry outside, I would dig a hole in the floor and bury them. Then I went into Rockford and bought 400 cement blocks and trucked them back home. I got Jim to come back in with me, and we dug a trench, and poured a cement footing, and then he laid up a new cement block foundation underneath the house.

I never did get the basement completely dug out. It was about the 14th year of our marriage when I started excavating our basement. But I had a large section of it done. A section about 40 by 50 foot dug out, and a new foundation under about half of the house when Marie died of Lou Gehrig's disease and I sold the house.

Some time before my marriage to Marie, while I was still living with my Aunt Chloe I had taken my son Ellery in with me and gave him a full partnership in the business.

He was married and had a small girl named Michelle and a boy named Edward Raymond. They were living in

Hebron and he was working in a factory in Woodstock and practically starving to death. I taught him the painting business and the roofing business, and a few things about carpentry. He had a few brains and learned the business quickly.

His wife Margaret became jealous of me, and said that he was always talking about me and was always with me, and he wasn't paying any attention to her. One day when we were at his home in Hebron, cleaning up some equipment, she came out of the house with a 22 rifle, threatening to kill me. I kept talking to her and kept her attention, and while I was doing that, Ellery slipped around behind her, clamped both of his arms around her and knocking the rifle out of her hands. I picked up the rifle and unloaded it. He was still holding her and she was as mad as a wet hen. He finally let her go, and she took of screaming, and headed towards the business district with Ellery after her. He finally caught up with her and got her quieted down. But the neighbors really had something to talk about for a few days.

One time I sent Ellery into town for some materials that we needed. This was about 10 a.m. And I expected him back before dinnertime, but dinnertime came and went, and about 3 p.m. he finally showed up. He said, "Boy it sure is great to have a job where you can take off and have a leisurely lunch, watch a ball game on TV, and not to have anybody chew you out about it." Well, I didn't say too much about it to him, but I thought to myself that this was not going to happen again. It wasn't too much later that he came up with a brilliant idea. He said, "I think that it would be real nice if the firm would have one member with a college degree." I said, "I guess it would be, but I don't think it will be." He said well, I thought that I could just go on to college and the business would pay all of my college expenses and pay Margaret so she could live decently, and I would get a degree." Now maybe I could have done that, but by the time we paid for his tuition, books, living expenses and furnishing Margaret money to live on, I wouldn't have cigarette money left. I told Ellery that it sounded like a pretty good idea. But, fair was fair, and until the business was big enough to warrant an expenditure like that, I think we will just go on the way we are.

Once we were working on a big old house and had to replace a large picture window. I told Ellery to go ahead, go down to the lumberyard and get the glass and put it in. I was working on the other side of the house, I figured that it would take him about an hour and a half to replace the window. But the afternoon passed and it was getting close to quitting time, and I hadn't heard anything from Ellery, so I thought I would go around to the other side of the house and see how he was coming along. He was just fitting a pane of glass into the window and about that time it broke. He said, "Damn." I asked him, "What in the world have you been doing all afternoon? You should have had that put in and glazed up two hours ago." He said, "Well, that's the fifth one I have tried to put in there. They have all broke. I don't know what's causing it." I said, "I can tell you in a hurry. You are trying to put a single strength glass in there aren't you." He said, "Yes," I said. "Why in the world after you broke the first one, didn't you come around and tell me what happened. Go down to the lumber yard and get a double strength pane of glass, and you won't have any further trouble." He said, "I didn't know that there was any such thing as a double strength glass." He got the double strength glass and it went in without any problem.

One day I needed a certain type of wrench that we didn't have. So I just went and picked one up for about $15.00. When I told Ellery about it, he just blew his stack. He said that he was sick and tired of the way I spent his money without telling him about it. I said, "Why don't you and Margaret come over to the house this evening? I've got something I want to talk over with you." So, after supper they came over, and I sat them down at the kitchen table then sat down with them. I said. "You say you are sick of the way I spend your money?" he said, "Your dammed tooting I am." I said, "That's fine. From now on you can spend your own money, and I'll spend mine. As of now this partnership is ended." That kind of set him back on his heels. But that's the way it was; I was tired of his ways and I had had it. We had one barn that we had contracted for. I told him he could have that job and use the equipment to do it, and it would give him a little bit of a stake. But that when he had that barn done, that was it and he was on his own.

With the profit off of that job, he had enough money to go ahead and buy a new compressor for himself and the spray equipment that he needed to start running me competition. Which was all right, because there was plenty of work for both of us. I had one farmer that I had been painting for for several years. Usually he painted one coat every two years, but this time he had let it go for over three years. It was peeling pretty bad and needed a through scraping, and then two coats of paint on it. The farmer thought he would play it smart and called Ellery to give him an estimate. Ellery told him sure he could do the job, and that one coat would be plenty. I guess Ellery thought he would be smart and make a small fortune out of the job. He evidently cut his paint to thin, and one coat didn't even begin to do the job. He wound up putting three coats on it and it cost the farmer a lot more than what my estimate was. The next time that I met the farmer, he told me what happened, and that from now on he was going to stick with me. I told him, "I'm sorry, you tried to under cut me there with Ellery, and actually Ellery had no business talking to you about that job, because you were my customer. So, I've had it. You can find another painter.

There was a fellow that owned a large insurance company that bought a farm about six miles west of Marengo. He was quite a character. He had two big fancy houses on the place. He lived in one and his son lived in the other. He had a wooden fence along both sides of the road. All told, there was over a mile of it. It was painted white and was peeling pretty badly. It took me over a week to scrape the fence all down. It took four days to paint two coats on it. It took 150 gallons of white paint. I just left all of the spray equipment on the truck bed and the compressor hooked on to the rear of the truck. I had 150 feet of hose from the paint pot to the gun, so I could reach 150 feet behind the truck and then 150 feet in front of the truck, and cover 300 feet that way, then move the truck up and cover another 300.

He had a large cow barn on the other side of the highway with a large corncrib, hog barn and a couple of machine sheds. He wanted me to paint the buildings all up, but then he only wanted me to paint the sides facing the highway. He said, "Forget about the back, they can't see it from the highway." I refused to do it that way. I told him, "If I can't paint the whole building, I won't paint any of it." It made him kind of mad but he finally agreed. We went ahead and gave him a proper paint job on the buildings. Then he wanted the cow barn painted on the inside. He had the ceiling and sidewalls all sided up with wood. which had never been painted. And they were really messed up with manure. We had to go in with the steam cleaner and steam clean everything first, then paint every thing two coats of white. When we got through, it really looked nice. He also needed a new roof on the big barn and the corncrib. And again he just wanted to roof the side of the buildings that could be seen from the highway. The backside could be rotted and falling down, just so it looked good from the highway. Again, I refused to do the job unless I could re-roof the whole building. We had another argument, but he finally came around to my way of thinking. When working on the roof, I would get up early and be on the job by daybreak. I would work until 10 a.m. And then I would quit, because by that time it was to hot and the shingles would get soft, and you couldn't handle them without marring them all up. Then, when it started to cool off in the evening about 5 p.m., I would go back on the job and work until dark.

The next events will be out of sequence. But I just happened to recall them. I painted a lot of silo domes, which were usually metal. I would line up two a day and paint one in the morning, and one in the afternoon. I would get $35.00 for one silo dome, and by doing two a day, I made $70.00 a day, which at that time was pretty good money. These silos were anywhere from 40 feet to 60 feet tall.

Also the acid from the silage would eat the concrete up on the inside of the silos, so I used to get inside the silo and take a wire brush and brush the inside of the silo down, then I would spray the inside of the silo with tung oil, which was acid resistant, and it would help prevent the erosion of the concrete.

In my time I have painted boats, cars, trucks, farm wagons, houses, barns, grain elevators, factory's, water towers, one airplane, and myself, but never a train.

One time I contracted to paint a large grain elevator. It went up 120 feet in the air and covered almost two-acre of land. I had my own cherry picker by then, but it was only a 40-foot deal. It handled the low work, but the other 80 feet above that was something else. I went in to the north side of Chicago to a firm that rented out cherry pickers, and rented one with a 90-foot boom on it. The rent was only $1,500.00 a week, which the elevator picked up. So that got us up 90 feet but there was still thirty feet to go that we had to do by hand. I had picked up a deluxe model of a boson chair. It was made out of steel with a steel seat and arms on it and steel brackets overhead to hoist it by, where the usual boson chair was a single piece of board in a rope sling. At one point, I had to paint the bottom of a catwalk, which was a good 120 feet above ground, and the only way I could get at it was to use this bosons chair. So I rigged up a block and tackle with a rope running from the chair to the ground, where it was fastened on to a truck. If I wanted to be raised up my assistant would signal to the truck driver and he would move ahead very slowly, and my assistant would signal to him when I wanted him to stop; when I wanted to be lowered down he would back the truck up. I was swinging in the air about 115 feet above ground when the rope broke. I came down in one big hurry. Fortunately I was above another steel catwalk, and only fell down 15 feet. I did the only thing possible that I could do to protect myself and that was to throw my hands and feet up into the air. When I hit that cat-walk, I hit my head against the steel framework of the boson chair and was knocked out. I was only out for two or three minutes. But, when I came to the truck driver was up there beside me to check on me. He was sure that I was dead. Outside the bump on my head there was nothing wrong with me. Fifteen minutes later I was back working again. But this time I used my head and done a little thinking, and figured out a way to get at the bottom of that cat-walk without using the bosons chair.

At this time, they were building a million-bushel bin, which I hoped to get the job of painting after it was finished. But, this was not to be as they bought their own spraying equipment and had their own men paint it. The first time that they filled it up with a million bushels of shelled corn, the blamed thing collapsed and they had a million bushels of shelled corn to clean up off the ground plus all the wreckage from the bin. Of course the grain elevator sued the contractor. Naturally he was fighting it. I never did find out what the out come was, but I know that five years later, they still had not settled anything.

Along about this time my wife contracted Lou Gehrig's disease, which is a disease of the muscles. It starts off with the very smallest muscle giving out, and then the next bigger one, and so on, until finally the last muscle is gone. It took us nearly two years to find out exactly what was wrong with her. None of the local doctors nor any of the Chicago doctors seemed to know. Finally we read about a doctor out in western part of

Iowa who was well known for his work in Multiple Sclerosis. He didn't even examine her, he just took one look at her and said, "I can tell you what is wrong, she has Lou Gehrig's Disease,"

These next incidents are all concerning Marie's progressive illness over the next five years. The first year, she managed to hobble around with a cane. By the second year she was confined to a wheel chair. I got her an electric Rascal scooter. Whenever she took it downtown, she insisted that I follow along behind her in case something happened. She would go just as fast as she could, not thinking about me at all. I would have to run to keep up with her. It got to the point where I had to hire help to look after her. I had my business to take care of, and most of the time I could get a nurse's aide anywhere from $5.00 to $8.00 an hour. But occasionally, when I couldn't get one of them, I would have to use a nurse from the local Hospice. They charged $18.50 an hour, and I was only making $15.00 an hour for my labor, so it was not a very profitable deal.

Once when she had a seizure, I couldn't get hold of the local doctor, so I called 911 and they sent an ambulance to take her to the hospital. First thing, the paramedics started to give her oxygen. Giving oxygen to some one having Lou Gehrig's Disease was a sure way of killing them. I had a devil of a time convincing them that giving her oxygen was the wrong thing to do. I knew that I hadn't thoroughly convinced them, so I rode along with her in the ambulance to make sure they didn't give her oxygen. We got to the hospital and they took her to the emergency room, where a nurse's aide promptly wheeled in an oxygen tank and started giving her oxygen. I yanked the mask off and told the nurse's aide that she was not to have oxygen, period, that it would kill her. She was pretty put out about me giving her orders, but I made her take the oxygen tank out of the room. I went out to the nurse's desk and answered their questions and filled out their forms for them. I happened to look around and there was that same nurse's aide wheeling that oxygen tank back. I stopped her again, and by this time Marie had come out of her seizure and was okay. The ambulance was still there so I had them load her back up in the ambulance and we went home.

Now Marie was in the emergency room about a half-hour, and never saw a doctor. The only one to attend her was that nurse's aide. After about a week I got a bill from the hospital for $585.00. They had things itemized. The doctor's charges were $150.00, the nurses labor was billed out at $40.00 an hour for three hours, plus the charges for oxygen and other medication. I took the bill and went back over to the hospital and got hold of their business manager. I asked him, "What do you pay for a nurses aide?" He said, "Twenty dollars an hour." Well I showed him the statement, and I pointed out to him, that she was not attended by a nurse, but by a nurses aide, and they were charging me $40.00 an hour for a registered nurse. I said, "That nurses aide was the only one who looked in on her. You are charging me for three hours and we were only in the hospital for a half an hour. You are charging me $150.00 for a doctor and she never saw a doctor, period. You are going to have to make some radical changes in this bill before I will even think about paying it. "He thought about it for a while, and he finally said, "If we just accept what Medicare will pay us for this. Will that be all right with you?" I said, "Actually, No. But I will go along with that."

At that time I was sponsoring a bowling team and bowling on it. I had to hire somebody to stay with Marie, and counting my bowling fees, it only cost me $35.00 a night to go bowling. During the third year of her confinement, I was just so wound up emotionally, that I was about ready to have a nervous break down. So I made arrangements with Sharon, who was Marie's daughter-in-law, to stay with her and I flew out to Maine to visit an old army buddy of mine. Now this was just after Christmas and before New Years and probably the wrong time of the year to make a trip to Maine. The two weeks that I spent with him did me a world of good. I was able to carry on when I got back home.

My aunt Chloe Fuller was up in her eighties. She had given me her power of attorney, so I could handle her business for her. I'll have to go back in time to tell you about my aunt and uncle. They never had any children of their own. My uncle's sister had a daughter named Ruth. When she was five years old, her mother and father were killed in a car accident and my aunt and uncle took her in and raised her. She is grown now, is married and has a son. She and her husband had taken over three acres of my uncle's farm and built a new house there, so they would be handy to look after my aunt and uncle. After my uncle passed away, her husband took over her business affairs. One of the first things he did was to draw out $30,000.00 of her money. He used $15,000.00 of it to remodel my aunt's house, which she really didn't want done. The other $15,000.00 was put into a joint bank account with their name and my aunt's on it so that they could write checks on it whenever they wanted to without asking her. He took care of my aunt's taxes and always managed to file them late, so she would have a $50.00 penalty to pay. She was pretty put out about this.

At this point, my aunt asked me if I would take over and handle her affairs for her. I told her that I would, but she would have to give me her power of attorney, that way it would be legal, and Ruthy and her husband couldn't do any thing about it. So that's what we did, without informing Ruthy, until the power of attorney was legally enforced. Boy, were they mad about that. Ruthy's husband Cal came over to see my aunt when I wasn't there. He had some papers there that he wanted her to sign and he told her that if she would just sign those papers and if I tried to embezzle any of her money, he would be able to stop me. Well, she had the good sense to refuse to sign any of those papers without me and her attorney being present. In going over her records, I kept seeing entries made where Cal and Ruthy had paid her interest money, but there was no record of what they were paying interest on. I went, over and I asked Ruthy, "What are you paying interest on?" She said, "That's none of your business." I said I'm afraid that it is. I have to now in order to keep her records straight." Finally after about half an hour's argument, she finally told me that's for the money we borrowed to buy a car with." I went back and I told my aunt and she said, "I wondered where they got the money to buy that car." I decided to look into that joint bank account they had with her. I took my power of attorney, went to the bank, and asked to see a complete record of that account, and whether there were any withdrawals made from it. They were very reluctant to do it, but they had to. And there it showed where they had drawn out $5,000.00 to buy the car with, and other regular withdrawals. Well, I kept thinking about that, and I told my aunt, I'm going down and close out that account." And she agreed with me. But evidently the bank must have informed Ruthy that I had gotten a complete statement on the bank account because when I went in to close it out there was only $700.00 left in the account. My uncle had had a fairly large account at a savings and loan in Marengo which was still in his name. So with my aunt's permission, I went over there and had that account changed strictly into her name. While I was talking to the president of the savings and loan. He said, "We have a new deal going on here that she ought to take advantage of, it pays 14% interest and the other account that she has her money in only pays 6%. We did a little figuring, and by closing out her old account she would lose $800.00 in interest money, but in six months time in the new account she would double that. So I had them to go ahead and change her account over.

When my uncle passed away, he left the farm to Ruthy, but my aunt had the use of it through out her lifetime. My aunt had a will drawn up in which I was the chief legatee and left Ruthy a brass bed that she had, $200.00 to her church and some other minor bequests. She told me that she didn't want her will to go though probate that I should just take care of it. When she finally passed away that is exactly what I did. I paid out all of the requests just as she had stated in her will, and of course what was left was mine. Evidently Cal and Ruthy did not know anything about the account in the Marengo Savings and Loan, as my uncle had kept that secret and my aunt had never said anything to them about it. At the time of my aunt's death, that contract still had about nine months to run, in order for her to collect the full amount of interest, without losing a large amount for early with drawls. I knew that if I went to the savings and loan, and told them about my aunt's death, they would immediately freeze the account and I would have to put her will through probate in order to get it. So I never said anything about her death to them and just let it ride. At the end of nine months, I went into the savings and loan and took my power of attorney papers with me, and told them that I wanted to draw out that money in cash, and that my aunt knew all about the deal, and had okayed everything. They were very reluctant to give it to me, and tried to talk me out of drawing it out, wanting me to reinvest with them again, I told them, "Sorry, no. I had a deal going that I needed the money for and that my aunt knows all about it, and has okayed it and everything." They finally broke down and paid me the money. I walked out of there with $45,000.00 in my briefcase. Of course, at the time of my aunt's death, my power of attorney was over.

As I was in the process of going through bankruptcy, for the second time in my life, and since no one knew I had that money, except the officials of the savings and loan, I knew that I had to hide it some place where it couldn't be found, I went into Kenosha, Wisconsin, which was about seventy miles away, and rented a safe deposit box in the bank there under a false name, and stashed the money away. I knew it wasn't the honest thing to do, but I couldn't face going into retirement broke. And that was exactly where my wife's illness had left me financially. This brings me into retirement, and I am just remembering a whole lot of events that happened, that I haven't covered yet. I guess I will go ahead and list them, although they will all be out of sequence. As my aunt was up in her sixties when I moved from Mendota back up north, I had parked my house trailer in her back yard and it was sitting there empty. We had a septic tank put in and we had the trailer hooked up so it was livable. At first we rented it out to Ruthy's son, who had just gotten married, so that there would be some one there close to her during the day who could check up on her, while I was at work. They lived there for about a year and a half until he got a job down in the southern part of the state. Then they had to move down there where his job was.

I had two brothers working for me, and their names were Robert and Jeffery Smart. We were working on a large farm job, and I told the boys to go ahead and paint the front end of a large corncrib. They got the equipment set up to start painting, which took them about a half hour, and I looked over there and saw that they hadn't set up a ladder yet and were just standing there looking at the front of the corncrib. I walked over and said, "Lets get the ladder up and start painting, I'm not paying you boys to just stand and look at the corncrib." They said, "Yeah, but it's covered with bees." I said, "Well, so what? You just go ahead and do your work, and let the bees do their work, They won't bother you." Well now, they just didn't believe that. I said, "Well I'll show you then." I took and set the ladder up, right through the center of the swarm, and said, "Give me that gun." I took the hose and tied it to my waist and started to paint and made my way up, painting on the right side of the ladder right up to the top painting right through the swarm of bees. Then I changed hands, took the gun in my left hand and painted my way down on the left side of the ladder right through the swarm of bees again. When I got down to the ground, I unfastened the hose, handed it to Bob and said, "Now its your turn. You see, I didn't even get a single bee sting." Well, he was still a little hesitant about it, so I told him, "Well, you go ahead and do it, and I'll give you a dollar for every bee sting that you get." Finally he got nerve enough and went over and moved the ladder then painted his way up one side of the ladder, just as I had, and down the other side and when he got back down, I asked him, "Well, how much do I owe you?" He studied for a second and said, "You know what? I never even got a single sting," His brother Jeff would not do it and I didn't try to force him. But I did kid him a lot about being afraid of a bee. It was just two weeks later that we hit the same situation on another farm, where there was a swarm of bees around the barn, and Jeff was just walking past the building and a bee swooped down and stung him on his hand. I didn't know and Jeff had never told me that he was allergic to bee stings. It wasn't about a half-hour that his hand was so swollen that he couldn't work at all. I sent him home and to a doctor. It took two weeks for his hand to get well, so he could work, Believe me, I never kidded him about being afraid of a bee again. If we had a job where there were bees about, I would find a job for him to do far enough away from them, so I was sure he wouldn't get stung. Jeff quit and started working for himself.

At that time I was working for a contractor, who was building up a large subdivision About thirty-five mile southeast of Woodstock, and the homes that he was building ranged in price from $250,000.00 to seven or eight hundred thousand dollars homes. I was doing all of the exterior painting and interior decorating. One day, Jeff came to me and wanted to know if I would buy out his business because he wanted to move out to Phoenix, Arizona. I said," Now I just might. What kind of shape is your van in?" He said. Well it is in real good shape."

The vehicle that Bob was driving was a case of a wreck looking for a place to happen. I agreed to buy him out so that Bob would have a decent vehicle to drive to and from work. He could leave his car at home for his wife to use. I got several good leads from Jeff and I got his van. I had agreed to pay him $1,500.00 for the works. I had paid him $500.00 down, and when I got the van I found out that it was in even worse shape than Bob's car. So five hundred dollars was all I ever paid Jeff. I more than made that back off of leads he had furnished me. I went into Rockford and bought a brand new Ford pickup. This was the only vehicle in my lifetime that I ever financed. And, I done that because Bob had agreed to buy it from me and he would make the monthly payments. I would keep the title to the truck until he had it paid for and at which time I would sign it over to him. Things went along pretty good for about a year. It was fall of the year, and my work had eased up, and I had laid Bob off for a little while, and he was working at a temporary job in Huntley, which was about ten miles south of Woodstock. His wife was visiting her folks in Hebron when my aunt called me up and said that my trailer had just burned up. I drove over to my aunt's and sure enough the trailer was nothing but a burned out hulk. I think that I had better take time here and explain that after Ruthy's son moved out of the trailer I had rented it to Bob for $100.00 a month just to have somebody there to look after my aunt. Everything was gone. I knew that it would be quite a blow to Bob as he was just beginning to get on his feet financially. As I had burned out once myself and lost ever everything, I knew exactly what Bob was feeling. And knowing that he would have to rent another place and pay both the first and last month's rent, before he could move in, and have to buy all new furniture. I knew that he didn't have any savings of any kind whatsoever, I gave him $500.00 and told him that it was just a loan and that I expected him to repay me as soon as he was able to which I knew it would be some time the next summer. Three weeks went past and I hadn't heard a word from Bob.

I drove over to Hebron to see her folks, who incidentally were cousins of mine, which actually made Bob some kind of shirttail relation. They told me that Bob had moved and was up in Wisconsin some place. I said, "Would you mind giving me his address so I can contact him?" They didn't know his address or how to contact him. I knew that they did know and that they were lying to me. I let things slide until after the first of the year, then I went back over to see her folks again. They still didn't know where he was, so I told them, "He has got my truck, and he hasn't been making the payments on it as he agreed to." They said they didn't know anything about that. I said, "Fine, I'm going to report the truck stolen to the Sheriff's department. The truck title is in my name, and it is mine until he has it paid for. His license and insurance are coming up shortly, and he won't be able to get a license up there in Wisconsin and without a license he can't get insurance on it. So you had better tell him to get that truck back down here to me." About six weeks later he did return it to me. He brought it over to the house when I wasn't there. Then he put some sand into the gas tank so I had to clean out the gas tank, the gas line and the carburetor before I could even get it started. So much for helping people out.

Once after Ellery went to painting for himself, he made a deal to paint a factory in Hebron, and in the contract the owner was to furnish the paint. He told the owner that he would need 160 gallons of paint to do the job. The paint was a special shade of blue, which was a special mix and couldn't be returned. When he got the job done, he had sixty gallons of paint left over. Rather than tell the owner that he had made a mistake of sixty gallons on the paint, he just loaded it onto his truck and brought it out to the farm and stored it out there, which is something that I would not have done. I would have owned up to it, and told the owner that I would absorb the cost of the paint myself. Ellery quit painting and went strictly to roofing. He worked for a while for a professional roofing firm. They really taught him the roofing business and I hate to admit it, but he wound up being a much better roofer than I ever was. He was working on a job about a mile away from where I was painting a set of farm buildings. The sheriff came by and said, "Did you know that Ellery has been hurt?" I said, "No, I didn't know anything about it." He said, "Yes. He is in the hospital with a broken arm, broken leg, and a broken rib. His scaffold collapsed and dropped him about twenty feet to the ground." I went down to where he had been working, thinking that I could gather up his tools and equipment and load them up and take his truck home for him. When I got there it was easy to see what had caused his scaffold to collapse. He had fastened one bracket into a rotten corner post. It held up all right, and he had loaded four bundles of shingles onto the scaffold, but when he got up onto the scaffold himself it was just too much. The bracket pulled right out of the building.

Banks

Everybody knows that banks are a good place to keep your money and to do business with. Well, I have got a few tales for you. There are two banks in Woodstock, right across the street from each other. I opened up a business account in one and a personal account in the other. They both told me that it was poor business to have an account in both banks, that I should just deal with one bank, which is a bunch of hooey. Every businessman that I've ever known has had accounts in two if not three or four banks. If a teller makes a mistake and you catch it while you are still at the window, they will correct it, but if you walk away from that window and then come back and tell them that they have made a mistake, they wont do anything about it. One day I got a letter from my bank saying that two weeks ago a teller had made a mistake and had over paid me $200.00 and would I please refund that money to them. I've always made it a practice when the teller counts out any money to me, I count it right along with her, then when she hands it to me I recount it again. I knew that there had been no mistake made to me. The teller undoubtedly made a mistake and overpaid some one $200.00, but they didn't know who it was, and they were just trying to collect it from me. I checked all of my records, and I could find no place, where there had been a $200.00 error. Now every bank has a slush fund for that very purpose. If some one makes a mistake, they can take the money out of the slush fund, and I told them that they would have to dig into their slush fund. I had never gotten that $200.00.

Another time I deposited a $5,000.00 check in my business account. This was about 4 p.m. I went across the street to the other bank and wrote a check for $500.00

to be deposited in my personal account. The teller took the check and went into the back with it, came back in fifteen minutes, and said, "Sorry, we can't take this check. You don't have funds in the other bank to cover this." I said, "Lady, I just got through depositing $5,000.00 over there in that account. Don't you tell me that I don't have the funds in that account to cover this check. She said. "I just called over there and they told me that you don't have any funds in that account." I told her, "If I don't have any funds in that account, then I don't have any account over there. You call them again, and tell them to check their records again." So, she did, and about twenty minutes later, she came back and said. "Yes, you are right. They just hadn't got that posted today, It will get posted tomorrow. We just figured that you were trying to kite a check." I said, "That is one thing that I absolutely don't do. If I don't have the money in an account, I just don't write a check.

Another time I deposited a $5,000.00 cashiers check, in my account, then I sat down and wrote out about $2,600.00 worth of checks to pay bills. Every one of those checks bounced, all six of them. I went into the bank, and I said, "What is the big idea of bouncing these checks." They said, "You'll have to talk to the head book-keeper." I said, "get her out here so I can talk to her." She came out and I asked her, "What is the idea of bouncing these checks?" She said, "Well, Mr. Spencer, if that check you deposited bounced, then you don't have enough funds in your account to cover these checks," I said, "Woman, what are you talking about? I deposited that check, I didn't write it." She said, "Oh." I said, "Not only that, that was a cashiers check." She said, I'm so sorry Mr. Spencer, that was my mistake." I said, "Yes it was your mistake, and what are you going to do about it?" She said, "Just have them put the checks back through and we'll cash them." I said, "No. First of all, I want you to write a letter to each one of these six businessmen and tell them that it was your mistake and not mine. That made me look like the devil to those men." She said, "Oh, we can't do that." I told her, "Lady, you are going to do that or I'm getting into my car and drive over to my attorney and sue you and the bank for defamation of character." Believe me they wrote the letters. And I also told them that I was going to check with each one of these people to make sure that they got those letters. I just drew $2,600.00 dollars out in cash and went around and paid each one of those bills in cash and telling them about the mistake the bank had made. One of them for $850.00 was to Mr. Louton of the Louton Paint Company. Well, he wouldn't accept my money, he said, "I merely sent the check back through, and told them that this man did not write bad checks." I thanked him for doing that.

After I got married for the fourth time and moved to Marengo, I opened up a third bank account in the Marengo bank. Then after two months I went in and borrowed $1,200.00 dollars from the bank. I really didn't need it, but I wanted to establish my credit with them. I repaid them with interest a month before the note was due. Of the other two banks in Woodstock one would only loan me $400.00 on an unsecured note, and the second bank would loan me $1,000.00 on an unsecured note. I had several times made loans at both banks in Woodstock. I had always repaid then on or before the due dates. Almost every time I went into one of the banks I hear that sorry old story, that I should consolidate my banking and deal with just one bank. I kept thinking to myself, that they might have a point there. I thought I would test them out. I would see who would give me the best service, the most cheerful service, and the most cooperation, and that would be the one I would deal with. I went to each bank, and applied for a loan, one for $400.00, one for $1,000.00, and one for $1,200,00. Now, I didn't need that money at that time, and if they would grant me the loans, I wasn't going to take them. But, they all three got together, and all three of them refused to loan me any money. They figured that I was going to pull some kind of a scam on them. I thought that if they didn't want to do business with me, I didn't want to do business with them. I went up to Harvard, which is a small town 12 miles north of Marengo. I went into the bank there and I asked to talk with the bank president. He was out of town, but the vice president a Mr. Smith took me his office and said, "What can I do for you?" I said, 'I'm looking for a bank that I can deal with and get some cooperation out of. I told him the story about the other three banks, and how after I had made several loans with them and repaid all of the loans on or before the due dates, and how they always harped on me to consolidate and deal with only one bank, and how I had decided to test them out and see who I could get the most cooperation out from. That they all refused to make a loan to me. He shook his head, and said, "I never heard of such nonsense." I made arrangements with him to open up an account with them, where by I could get an unsecured loan for $5,000.00 with them. And also, if I should happen to put a check through and there wasn't sufficient money in my account to cover it, that they would go ahead and honor the check, and they would notify me and I would come in and straighten the account. I banked with them for over fifteen years. One time I had made a mistake in my checkbook, I had written out a check for $450.00 and instead of deducting it I had added it to my total. Then I had written a check for $850.00 and lacked $485.00 of covering it. They honored the check and Mr. Smith called me and told me what had happened. He told me to come in and to bring my checkbook with me and they would go over it and see if we could get this straightened out. So, I did. It didn't take the bookkeeper but about five minutes to find my mistake, where I had added instead of subtracting. We straightened my checkbook out, and I borrowed $500.00 from them, and paid them back the $485.00, and then paid off my note.

When I first moved from Kentucky to Mendota, IL. I opened up an account in the Mendota State Bank and got along pretty well with them. I had a hard time keeping busy in that area. It seemed that you almost had to be a third generation resident before people would deal with you. Well I went north to Delavan and went out to see my little redheaded schoolteacher that had the big girls' camp out on the Island in Delavan Lake. I did a very large job for her and she paid me off with a $5,600.00 cashier's check. I got back down to Mendota and went into the bank to deposit the check to my account. It just so happened that the vice president of the bank was working in the teller's cage.

He refused to accept my check for deposit. I said, "What the devil do you mean that you can't accept this check? This is a cashiers check." He said, "We don't know that it's any good. We will have to hold it and then check with the Delavan bank to make sure that it is good." I said, "Just never mind, and just let me have that check back." He gave me the check back. I took it, turned around and walked across the street to the other bank, which I had never been in before. I was an absolute stranger to them. I presented the check to the teller and told her that I would like to have cash for it. She looked the check over good and reached into her money drawer, and started counting out the cash to me. I took the money and went back over to the first bank. I asked the teller to check my bank balance for me, and to let me know how much it was. When she did, I just wrote out a check for the total amount and said that I wanted it in cash and to close out my account. Then I went back across the street again to the second bank and opened up an account with them. I deposited everything including the $5,600.00.

Three months passed, and then the scandal broke. It made headlines in all of the newspapers around there. The vice president of the Mendota State Bank had embezzled $55,000.00 from the bank. He was the one who had refused to cash my cashiers check. I guess the reason he refused to cash it was because there was no way he could get his hands on any of that money. At the time he was indicted for embezzlement, he and his wife were planning a trip to England. In a statement that he made to the papers, he said he just didn't see why they wouldn't let him and his wife go to England. He was from one of the socially prominent families in Mendota. They set up a committee to collect money for him to help pay back the $55,000.00 so he wouldn't have to go to prison. They actually made a door-to-door canvas through out the town. They called on me and wanted to know if I wanted to donate one or two hundred dollars to the fund? I said, "Sorry, there is no way that I will donate money to that fund. Just let the bastard go to prison, because that is where he belongs." Well, he did go to prison, and actually had to serve three months. Of course he was on probation for five years after that and was forbidden to work for any bank or financial institution.

A new bank opened up in Marengo, and I had done all of the painting and decorating on the inside for it. It had young fellow by the name of Myzrk as bank president. He was a likable fellow with a good personality, but he made one big mistake. He wrote and published a book telling of all the ways that banks had of doing business and of all the ways they managed to cheat and chisel their customers. He got drummed out of the banking business for that. That was quite a book.

I needed a pickup truck. I decided that this was one time that I was going to have a new vehicle. So I went truck shopping. I finally found what I was looking for in a town about 35 miles east of Marengo. It was a new International 3/4-ton pickup with heavy-duty springs. I had them build a ladder rack on it for me. It was painted a shade of green that I really liked. I thought that I was getting the cream of the crop, but was I ever wrong. Now this was a brand new truck and it only had four miles on it when I got it.

The first week that I had it. the water pump fell off. Of course I lost a day's time while the truck was hauled into the garage and the pump was repaired, which was not a easy job, because a couple of the bolts holding the water pump had broken off and were still in the block. They had to be drilled out and new threads put into them. The next week I was in Hebron with it and parked at the curb. I got in, started it up, put it in reverse and started to back up, and I felt the right front side of the truck raise up in the air and then drop back down again, and I thought what in the world. I got out and took a look, and two of my shock absorbers had fallen down. I wired them up so they wouldn't drag on the pavement and took it back to my friend Ed in Woodstock. He put on four new shock absorbers for me because the others weren't in to good condition. I really forget what else went wrong with it. I think that I had some trouble with the steering and the brakes. For the first six weeks that I had the truck. I had it in the garage for at least one day a week having it repaired. Of course there was a warranty on the truck, but because I didn't take it to the dealer I bought from, it wasn't any good. I paid for all the repairs myself. But finally I got all the bugs out of it and I drove it for the rest of the time that I was in business until I retired.

Once about three or four years after I had bought the truck, somebody had hit me in the driver's side and had smashed in my door panel. About a week after I had the door panel fixed, I parked the truck on the far side of the street, across from the driveway to my house, and I got into my cherry picker, which was parked in the driveway, started it up, put it into reverse, and went to back it out into the street, and wouldn't you know, I backed right into the pickup and smashed the door panel in again. I never bothered to report that to the insurance company. I just went and had it fixed again.

That year I painted up the down town district of Marengo. I painted every store front and some of the buildings, with the exception of three buildings. There was a foundry just two blocks behind our house in Marengo. Once while I was eating dinner, I heard the city fire alarm go off. I heard the fire trucks go past the house about a block away, and I told my wife that it must be pretty close to us. We went outside and took a look. The foundry was just blazing up. The whole thing was on fire, and it was a big building too.

Well, I secured the contract to clean up the foundry and repaint it. I had three men beside myself working on it. It took us a little over two months to do the job. I believe that I bought up every wire brush in town, and we wore them right down to a nubbin. They had a mechanic who would tear a machine down to its basic parts, and we would have to clean the parts up for them, and the mechanic would reassemble the machine and we would repaint it. We also had all of the ceilings and sidewalls to clean and repaint, about half of them had to be rebuilt. Along towards the end, we were coating the roofs with our aluminum roof paint. It had a tar base and went on very heavy. It took a special spray gun to spray it. I had the paint pot set up in front of the office doors. We were going to move the paint pot to a different position, and I had to disconnect the hoses on it in order to move it. We had to maintain a 90-pound pressure on the pot in order to spray with it. I thought that I had drained the pressure off of the pot and I started to unfasten the material hose, and when I got the hose almost off the pressure just blew it the rest of the way off, and ten gallons of aluminum paint blew right up into my face. It just covered me from head to foot. I shut the machine down and went home to get cleaned up. I cut across the tracks, because it was only a block that way. I got home and got a large sheet of brown wrapping paper and laid it down in the drive way in front of the back porch. I figured that if the neighbors wanted to get an eyeful they could just watch. I stripped down naked and left my cloths on the paper, then I went into the house took a bath and got cleaned up. After I was dressed again, I went outside and wrapped my cloths up including my shoes and threw the whole mess into the garbage. They weren't worth trying to clean up. That all took about an hour, and then I went over to the foundry and had to clean up the mess in the driveway, which took another hour. By that time it was quitting time and I went home for supper.

My wife worked in the mousetrap factory. She assembled mousetraps. The first winter of our marriage work was a little slow, so I went and got a job in the factory too. Only I was on the maintenance crew. There was one other fellow on the maintenance crew with me. We got along pretty good and managed to keep the place cleaned up, until, one day, the factory brought in a huge new stamping press. It only cost them $60,000.00 for the press and that was back in the days when the dollar was still a dollar. The superintendent came over to us and said that he wanted us boys to move the old press out of the way and set up the new press and wire it all up. Well, neither one of us were electricians, although we both had done a little electrical work, but that ran mainly to wiring in houses. We asked the superintendent to cut the electricity off to the factory while we were changing it over. He said, "Absolutely not. We would have to shut the whole factory down. We have got a lot of orders to be filled." Well, there was only 60,000 volts going through that transformer. We went ahead and disconnected the old drill press. And you can believe me that we were mighty, mighty careful. We got it moved out and moved the new one into place and managed to get it connected to the transformer and never got so much as one shock from it. How ever I wouldn't be here telling this story if we had gotten a shock because one shock would have killed us. After we finished that job, we both quit. We had, had enough of that factory.

There was another factory out on the edge of town, which was called Arnolds. They manufactured magnets of all types. They had a building there that was over 200 feet long and at least 100 feet wide. It was two stories high, and was an all brick building and they wanted it painted. Of course it had a lot of windows all the way around it and the trim on them had to be painted. About half of them had to be re-glazed. They wanted a special pink color and, of course, the paint had to be specially mixed to obtain the shade of pink that they wanted, which I hated and thought it looked awful.

I drew up a contract for a total of $9,000.00, as I figured it would take three hundred gallons of paint to paint it two coats. I had checked with my friend Ken Louton, who had the paint factory in Woodstock. He told me that he could mix it for us for $10.00 a gallon, so 300 gallons of paint would be $3,000.00 just for the paint. Then there was a world of preparatory work to be done, in glazing the windows, and scrapping the woodwork, etc. The windows would have to be masked out with paper, or if we painted over the windows they would have to be cleaned by hand with razor blades. They approved the contract and told me to go ahead and do the work. I started the men to glazing windows and scraping the woodwork. I went to Woodstock and told Ken to go ahead and mix-up the 300 gallons of paint, which he did. We had worked for a little over two weeks and had all the preparatory work done. I had picked up the paint from Louton and had it on the job, when the superintendent called me into his office and said, "I don't know how to tell you this, but we are going to have to call off the paint job. We just got orders from the home office to cut down on all of our expenses, and painting was one way we could cut on our expenses. I told him, "Hey, I've got a signed contract with you, we have done all the preparatory work, all the windows are glazed, all the scraping has been done, and I have 300 gallons of paint sitting out there that I can't return. I've got two weeks wages for four men that I've already paid out, and you tell me that you are canceling the job?" He said, "Well, I know.

It is not something that we want to do, but when the home office says you do something, you do it. But make out a bill and we will buy the paint, and we will get off on that basis, and maybe next year we can go ahead and finish the job." I thought that if this was what they are going to do to me, then I am going to make them pay for it. I made out my bill, and the total came to $6,800.00. I turned it into them. Well, the next day, I got a call from the superintendent and he wanted me to come see him. When I got there, he took me into his private office and said, "You know, we were mistaken in trying to cancel the paint job, and we are going to go ahead and finish the job all up. He just apologized all over the place to me. Then he said that Mr. So & So would like to speak to me, too. So, he took me over to his private office, and he apologized all over the place to me, and then he said there was another man that wanted to see me, he apologized to me and sent me over to another person and he apologized to me. Before we got through there were six different ones that apologized to me. So we went ahead and finished the job. That was a big plant and they employed over three hundred people. They had a big parking lot in front of the plant and another parking lot about a block and a half away from the plant.

When we started spraying their workers had all been warned to park their cars in the second parking lot which was a block and a half away, but there are always some who just don't pay any attention to what they are told. There were about twenty of them who parked their cars in the lot right in front of the plant. Of course, there was a lot of over spray on their cars and they were pretty mad about that. They were going to get together and sue me and I told them, "No, they would not sue me, because I would clean up their cars for them." They were giving me a hard time when the superintendent came out and told them. "Now, you men were told to park your cars in the other parking lot. It is your fault that you got over spray on your cars here. I know a firm that cleans cars and I'll have them to come in and clean your cars for you at company expense." That satisfied them. Then the superintendent told me, "Now that's going to cost us $200.00 to have those cars cleaned up, and I think that you should absorb that amount." I said, "All right that sounds good to me." I couldn't have cleaned the cars up for under a $1,000.00 and I knew that I would get more work from them in the future and when I did, I would just add that $200.00 dollars onto my estimate and they would not know the difference. Later they called me out and I did a large interior paint job for them. That ran almost $5,000.00 Then another time they had a metal roof that needed to be coated and several large tanks to be painted with this roof coating. The tanks were all rusty and in poor condition, and had to sand blasted first before we could paint them.

Once when I was living in Mendota, I had a fellow call me up and wanted to know if I was interested in doing a paint job in East Moline, IL, which was about 85 miles from Mendota I said, "Sure, I'm always interested in work." He told me who to go see and I drove down to East Moline. I went in and talked to the man and he was more than glad to see me. He took me through the plant and showed me what all had to be done. This was a huge old building, that must have been over sixty years old, and it had 16-foot high ceilings in it. The place had never been cleaned up since it had been built. There was black grease on the ceilings that was 1/4 of an inch thick and also on the sidewalls too. Now, they made licorice there in that factory. The health authorities were on them about getting the factory cleaned up, or they would close them down. I told the fellow, "You are going to have to close the factory down anyway because these ceilings and side walls will all have to be steam cleaned, and even then I don't know if we could get every thing off, and it would be one hell of a mess while we are doing it. He said, "Oh no, we don't need to clean them. We'll just paint right over that grease. I already have the paint. All you have to do is just come in here and put it on." I thought if that's what he wants, okay, so I made a deal with him. This was in the fall of the year and I pulled my rig and gear down to East Moline and rented me a hotel room. I had to wait until they closed the factory down at night before I could start working there. The first night I had the place to myself. There wasn't even a janitor there. While there were fans going, which I thought should be turned off, but nobody told me about them and I wasn't about to go punching buttons, because I knew they had a batch of candy cooking in the ovens over night. So I went ahead and sprayed. I worked until about 5 a.m. the next morning, then shut down and went to my hotel room to get some sleep. About 7:30 a.m. the phone in my room rang. It was the superintendent of the factory. He wanted me to get down there just as fast as I could, because they had a big problem. I got out of bed, got dressed and went down to the factory. I walked in and sure enough they had a big problem. With the fans going, my over spray had gotten into everything, even the ovens where the candy was cooking, and the whole day's production was ruined. They had to tear all of the machinery apart and clean it and reassemble it again. I told the man that I thought that the fans should be turned off, but there was no one was there to turn them off and that I wasn't sure how to turn them off, and that I wasn't going to punch buttons with out knowing what I was doing. The man asked me if I had insurance to cover this. I said, "Heck no." He said, "Well, we're fortunate. Our own insurance will cover it. But you're going to have to cover all of the machinery up before you paint." I said, "If I have to cover up all of the machinery here, that's all that I'll get done, and I will not get any painting done. I will go buy some plastic drop cloths and give them to you, and you can pass them out, and have each man cover up his own machine at night. Then they can uncover them in the morning. He said, "That sounds like a fairly good idea," I went out and bought the drop cloths, and they probably cost me about $50.00. I took them back to the factory. Then about 11 a.m. I finally got back to bed. When I got to the factory at 5 p.m. that afternoon, the machines were all covered up, the fans were all turned off and there was a janitor on duty there all night long as long as I was painting. I went ahead and painted the place, and much to my surprise, I painted right over that thick, heavy grease and two coats of it, brought the ceiling and sidewalls to a white, enamel looking finish. Well, I finished the job without any further problems. When they paid me off, they gave me a large carton full of licorice (red, black and white) to take home. We ate licorice for a year after that.

A friend of mine, and also a competitor, called me up one day and told me that he had a job that he would like for me to help him out on. I said, "Well, what is it?" "Well he said, "I have an outside movie screen that needs to be painted, and I really need a couple of men who really know what they are doing, to do the painting. I said, "OK, we'll give you a hand." When we got over there, the screen was 60 foot high and 60 foot long. The bottom edge of the screen was 15 foot above the ground, which made the screen itself 45 foot high. He had a swinging stage there. It wasn't one of the newer motor-ized stages, but it was manually operated. We had to climb up the back of the screen to the top of it, get our block and tackle located, our ropes all threaded through the blocks, then we crawled back down to the ground, pulled the stage up by hand, then climbed back up the back of the screen again, crawled over the top of the screen and let ourselves down onto the stage. Then we could start painting our way down. The fellow I had working with me had never worked on a swinging stage before, and for that matter, neither had I. But I had seen others several times working on them, and I had talked to them, so I pretty well knew what we could or could not do. I told him that if anything happened, you couldn't lean against the screen at all. Because if you did, it would push the stage away from the screen and you would fall. He started to walk over to his side of the stage and when he did the stage wiggled a little bit, and he started teetering, and the first thing he did was to reach over and lean against the screen. I grabbed the ropes on my end of it and hollered, "Get off that screen." Now he managed to grab onto the back rail of the stage. The stage came back in against the screen where it belonged. That scared him enough that he was mighty careful not to lean against the screen again. It took us four days to paint two coats on the screen. And we never had any further problems.

Well work, was a little bit slow. I got hold of my friend that was selling paints and asked him if he knew of any jobs I might get. He said, "No, but I need another man in the territory. I can give you a job selling paints." I said, "Well that's better than sitting around idle." I knew that he was making an excellent living at it. Our main customers were factories, cities and counties. I stayed with it for three months. I made enough to cover my living and expenses. This friend was a model railroad enthusiast and he invited me over to see his model railroad. When I got there, he took me down into the basement and I couldn't believe my eyes. He had that basement (and it was a big one) completely, covered up with his model railroad. He had a line of tracks running up into his garage, which was about half-full, and he had plans of filling up the rest of his garage with it. It took five operators to operate it. He had whole towns, built up, water tanks for steam engines. He had mountains with tunnels running through them. He had several switchyards scattered around. It was just unbelievable what he had built up there. Now he had built every bit of this himself, including the five switchyards and all of the wiring that went into it. I believe that he had over 500 pieces of mobile equipment.

About one mile directly south of my aunt's farm, there is an 800-acre dairy farm that was owned by an old Hungarian widow. Now she was a corker to work with, but she was fair and honest. They had an extra large dairy barn that had stanchions for a hundred heads of cows. I painted them for her twice over the years, and in that time I saw the her convert the dairy barn to a pig barn for a new tenant, and it must of cost her $50,000.00. Later on, after the pig man left, it was reconverted back to a cow barn. Finally the old lady died and left the farm to her daughters who lived in Forest Park, which was a suburb of Chicago. Shortly after the daughters inherited the farm, it was in need of painting again. They knew of me and knew that I had been their mother's painter for years. But instead of calling me, they called out four other painters to get estimates from them. All four of them took a look around the farm, and politely informed them that they were not interested. And each one of them told them that if they wanted it painted, to call me. They had a city attorney in there handling the farm for them, and he had told them not to call me, but to call in three or four other painters and get estimates from them. Well, they finally decided that since I was the only one in the area that would touch that big a job, then they had better call me.

I went out and made my estimate and drew up a contract for $9,000.00, which they finally signed after taking it in and having their attorney to look it over. So, I told them fine, and that I had another job that I was on and had to get it finished, and it would be about two weeks before I could get started down there. I finished up the other job, and we pulled our rigs out to the farm. We were getting set up to start working, when they came out and called me over. They wanted to know if I had insurance. I said, "Certainly I've got insurance. I wouldn't dare stay in business one day without insurance." She was reading off of a piece of paper, and she said, "Do you have insurance for this?" I said, "No. Let me see that piece of paper." She handed it to me and I looked it over and there were twelve different types of insurance listed there, some that I had never heard of before, and none of them really necessary. She said, "Well, you can't start work here until you have all of this insurance. Our attorney has given us instructions not to let you start to work here until you have all of this insurance." I said, "Well, I've painted this place twice before, for your mother, and never had any of this insurance and got along just fine without them." They said, "Well, if you don't want to get this insurance, then we'll just have to find someone else." I said, "Well, don't be in such a hurry to count me out. I'll see what I can do about these," I went back to my men and told them to wrap things up and take the day off. I went in and had a talk with my insurance agent. He got a laugh out of them and said that there were some there that he had never heard of himself. I told him, "Well, draw me up a contract to cover me on each one of those deals there." So, he did, and the total premium came to $1,500.00. He said, "You're not going to have much profit out of this job, are you?" I said, "Oh yes, I will, because I'm going to take this out and show it to them and get started working out there. Then, I can come back in here tomorrow and cancel these all out. I'll pay just one day's premium on them. Which is exactly what I did. I worked and finished the job up with no further trouble from them. The premium for the one day cost me $50.00.

One day, my wife handed me the paper and said, "Look at that ad there. I think that is something you ought to get into." I took the paper and read the ad, and I have to admit, it did sound kind of interesting. There was a company in Detroit, Michigan that was selling franchises for a cleaning operation. They had developed an acid with which they cleaned brick buildings and most other kinds of buildings, too. I told her, "The ad sounds good, but I'll think about it for a while." Well, it went on for two weeks and she kept after me that I should go to Detroit and see about it. Well, I contacted the company by phone and found out that they were charging $7,000.00 for a franchise, but that included all of the equipment and an initial start up quantity of acids. They were going to have a school for new dealers in two weeks time. Well, they really had me interested. So, I sent them an initial payment of $1,500.00 and agreed to come out to Detroit to the school. Two weeks later, I took my son Ellery with me and went out to Detroit. We got ourselves a hotel room and went to school. The company was paying for our hotel room and meals, and they did put us through a good schooling. There were seven of us attending the school. At the end of the schooling, I paid them the remaining $5,500.00. We loaded my pickup with the acid and equipment necessary to do the work. Then, we came on home. I worked with that cleaning business for nearly a year, and never made one penny out of it. I could see where it would work and a person could make good money out of it in a large city like Chicago, Detroit, New York, or Los Angeles. But, out in the country, it just wouldn't work, or at least I couldn't make it work. Well, that year I not only lost the $7,000.00, but another $3,000.00 or $4,000.00 that I could have earned if I had been in the painting business myself.

Shortly after that, I took on a franchise for selling and installing barn cleaners. However, that didn't cost me any money, and again, I never sold a barn cleaner, although I did sell a lot of parts for them.

One time, while I was still living in and operating out of Delavan, I contacted with the Crane Plumbing Co. They had a large farm just about half way between Delavan and Geneva, which they had converted into a nursing home for their workers. Of course the Crane Company was strictly union and I was non-union. So, on the second day that I was working on the job, the manager came out, and said, "You know, we never thought about it, but are you union?" I said, "No, I'm not." He said, "Well, we are completely union, and we don't dare let you work out here. If one of the patients come out here and found out that you are non-union, they could have the union to call a general strike against us." I said, "Well, we don't want that, do we?" He said, "No, I'm sorry, but you'll just have to quit work." I said, "Oh no. Instead of quitting, I'll just join the union." He said, "Well, now that's using your head." Well, I went into Lake Geneva and got a hold of the business agent for the painter's union. Well, they only wanted a $500.00 fee for joining, so I asked them, "Is there some way that I can go ahead and do that job out there, until I can get the money to pay you?" He said, "Well, I can get you a work permit for $10.00 "I said, "Fine." So, he drew up the papers, and I took them back out and showed them to the manager. He said, "Just fine. Go ahead and go to work." Well, I finished the job all right, but I never paid the union a penny. They were a good outfit to work for and I did all of their painting for several years. And, they never again asked to see my union papers again, and none of the employees ever came out and asked me about it. So everything went along fine. They had built a sunroom onto the main house and it was about twelve feet wide by thirty feet long. They had put in special ultra violet glass in all of the windows and the storm windows, too. A small eight by ten pane of glass only cost $300.00. But, the patients could sit in there in the wintertime, and get the value out of the ultra violet rays. In a corner of the building I found a stack of these ultra violet windowpanes. There were fifteen of them stacked up there and that was $4,500.00 worth of glass. That was extras that the contractor ordered out and didn't use. I went to the manager and started to tell him about the panes that I had found and he stopped me and said, "I know what you are talking about and I don't want to hear about it. Why don't you just load those on your truck and take them home with you and just forget about where you got them?" I said, "Okay."

I was doing some inside painting on one of the barns when I opened a door, mostly out of curiosity to see what was in there, to a room in the back end of the barn. Two player pianos were stored in there. They must have been there for two or three years, as there was almost 1/4 of an inch of dust all over them. They both had rolls in them, so I sat down and tried them, and they both worked. So, the next time that I saw the manager, I asked him what they were going to do with those player pianos out there. He said, "We don't have any use for them. If you want them, just take them." While we were loading them onto my truck, he came out and said, "Come here a minute." So, I went over, and he took me into another room, and said, "You might as well have these, too." There were over three hundred music rolls in there. He said, "They won't be any good without the pianos." So we loaded all of them on, too. I took them into the shop, cleaned them all up, and as the woodwork didn't look too good, I gave both of them two coats of enamel and divided up the rolls. There were about one hundred fifty to each piano. I put an ad in the paper and sold them both for $150.00 apiece. Later on, they donated the big barn to the theatrical company for a theatre. They had to move that barn about five miles up the highway. The barn was so long, they couldn't get it around the corners, so they just cut it in half. Then they moved each half up to the new location and fastened them together again.

Once when Ellery was working with me, he got the idea that we should expand and go in for some really large jobs. I told him, "Okay. I know of one. Why don't we go and see about it?" He said, "Where is it?" I said, "Ft. Sheridan, over near Waukegan. I was told that they had about one hundred fifty large two story houses that they wanted bids on for painting." Well, that really hepped him up on it. So, we took a day and went over to Ft. Sheridan, saw the Colonel that was in charge of them, got the specifications, which called for three coats of paint, each one to be a different shade. That was so that the inspectors could drive by, and know that you have put on three coats. When I got through with the estimate, I figured that we would have to get about $180,000.00 for the job. Ellery said, "Hoo boy. We get that, we can both afford a new Cadillac." I said, "All right now, there are a few things to be considered before we sign any papers here. First of all, this is a government job. The government, jobs are all strictly union and we are non-union. If you'll read the terms of the contracts thoroughly, you will find that we have to put up a $50,000.00 deposit, to guarantee completion of the job. If we don't complete the job, we don't get paid, and we lose the $50,000.00. Besides, we have to be on mighty good terms with the inspectors, because if we are not, they can refuse to pass on our work, and make us do it over again. Not only that, we would have to employ three crews of about twelve men per crew. We would have the payroll to meet every week. We would have insurance to pay on the crews, we would have to pay in Social Security, and withhold income tax on them. Also we would have to buy about 3,000 gallons of paint. Also, we would have to buy two more air compressors, plus painting equipment for both of them. We would have to hire a fulltime accountant to take care of the paper work. Sure, on a job like this you can make a lot of money, or you can lose your fanny on it and wind up in the bankruptcy courts. If you want to go in for this (I handed him the contract form) there it is. I don't want any part of it." Well, that kind of ended his ideas of grandeur.

One time I painted a large church in Marengo. It was a wooden building painted all white. When I got through it looked just fine. A year later the president of the church board of directors called me up and said, "I want you to come over and look at the church with me," When I did, there were whole areas of the church that were black with mildew. He was very unhappy with it, and for that matter I was too. He wanted me to come back and have the church sand blasted and repainted all at my cost. I told him, "I'm sorry, I can't do that. That's mildew on there. I'm not responsible for that. That can happen to anybody at any time." He said they were going to have a church board meeting the next night at 7 p.m. He told me that he wanted me to be there and try to explain that to the board, because they are going to want to sue you. I said "Okay, I'll be there."

I went over to Woodstock to see my friend Ken Louton, as it was his paint that I put on the church. I told him what the story was and asked him if he would go along with me to the board meeting. He said that he sure would, but that he would come early so he could examine the mildew on the church. I told him that would be fine. We met that evening with the church board. The chairman said that he had talked with a chemist and he told me that there should have been a mildew resistant additive put into the paint, which evidently they didn't do. I told him that I thought that his chemist was mistaken, but I wouldn't try to explain or to tell him why, that I would let Mr. Louton explain it. I told them that he just happens to be a very good paint chemist and owns the company that manufactured the paint. Ken got up and asked the chairman of the board, "Was the chemist you talked to a paint chemist?" He said, "No, he was just a chemist." Ken said that there were several different varieties of chemists and that they can only be experts in only one line, Ken said, "I did put a mildew additive in the paint, and I always do. There are some kinds of mildew that the additive doesn't affect. I've been over to the church and examined the mildew, and this is one of the varieties that there is no known protection against. Now I've known Mr. Spencer for several years, and I know that he does not do sloppy slip shod work. He gave you a first class paint job there. There is no way that he nor my paint can be held responsible for that mildew. Now you can go ahead and sue us, but if you do, it will be a long drawn out affair, in which you will have about a 20% chance of winning. Now you paid Mr. Spencer $5,000.00 for the job and if you sue us, your attorney fees will probably run about $7,000.00 or $8,000.00. And if you lose the case, which I firmly believe you will, we will turn around and sue you for damages. Thank, you gentlemen, come on Ralph, I think its time we left." So, I got up, and we walked out of the meeting. And that was the last we ever heard about it.

Louton had just a small paint factory and only employed six men. He manufactured a product called Tuff Coat that he had invented and held a patent on. This was a product that was used on brick buildings, cement buildings or almost any kind building. There was a fine mesh netting that you had to put on the building first and then the Tuff Coat was applied over it, and it made excellent protection against salt water and sea air. He sold the product worldwide. He showed me a picture of one building in Singapore. It was a ten-story building and he had covered the entire outside of the building with Tuff Coat. He even had kits made up that you could use inside the house. If you had a crack in your wall, you could cover the crack with it and it would permanently seal it. I never did know just how he used it, but he had a small elephant and had a special made trailer to haul it in, and his sales men used to use it for advertisement and demonstration of the Tuff Coat.

Once there was a fellow who came to see me and said that he had a farm up near Whitewater, Wis., and that he wanted me to paint for him. For some reason, I was a little leery about dealing with him. I told him that I was extremely busy, which I was. I had just started a large farm job over near Janesville. I had advised him that he should find another painter. He wouldn't have any part of that and said that he had heard of me, that I had a good reputation, and that he wanted me. He said that he would just wait until I was free. He came over to the Janesville job about three different times to see how we were doing, and to remind me that I was to come over to his place after we got done with this job. I went up to see him and to make an estimate for him. He said that he just wanted one coat of red on the barn and that he didn't want any trim. He just wanted everything red. He said that we could even use a cheap paint. I told him that I didn't use cheap paint, that I used good paint. So I gave him a price of $450.00, and he signed a contract to that agreement. When we got up there to start his job, he had his nose in every paint pail that we opened up to make sure we had a good paint, then he wanted two coats, and then he wanted everything trimmed out in white, and, last but not least, he wanted the name of his farm painted across the end of the barn. So, we went ahead and we gave him a first class job, and gave him the two coats, and the white trim. It took me three days just to print the name of the farm across the end of the barn. I gave him a bill for $950.00 and he blew his stack. He said, "I got your contract where you said you would do it for $450.00. "I said, "Yes. That was for just one coat of red paint, no trim, and no printing." Well, he wasn't about to pay it. I said, "Okay. I'm not going to argue with you." We loaded up and went on to the next job. I went to see my attorney, and we sued him for the $950.00. That's the only time in my life that I have sued anybody. I think that I would have been better off if I had forgot about him completely, because the only ones who made any money off of the deal, was my attorney, his attorney, and the judge. I would have been money ahead, if I had just accepted the $450.00, and he would have been money ahead, if he had of paid me the $950.00. He was a Kentucky Hillbilly.

As I said before, some of these incidents are going to be out of sequence, so here are a few of them that should have been included somewhere along the line before.

One night, I came home to my uncle's farm. It was about 2:00 or 2:30 a.m. as I approached the driveway, I saw some headlights come on about 1/4 of a mile down the road. A truck pulled away, and went on down the road. I didn't think much about it at that time, I just went on in the house and went to bed. When I woke up the next morning, I kept thinking about that. I told my uncle, "I'll bet you that we had rustlers here last night." I told him about the truck lights coming on and the truck pulling away. So, after breakfast, we took a walk down the road along the fence line and sure enough about a 1/4 mile down, there was a big gap in the fence where the wires had been out. But fortunately, I came along just in time to scare them away before they had a chance to load any animals up.

After my aunt died and I had seen to it that the terms of her will was followed out exactly as stated, I hired a moving van, loaded up all of her furniture and things, took them to Marengo, and stored them in my garage. At first, I thought that I would have an auction, but then after thinking about it, I knew that I would have to pay the auctioneer about 1/3 of what we made. I decided that I would be better off if I had a big garage sale. So, that was what I did. I advertised in several area papers. So, I did really good in a three day sale, I took in over $6,000.00, which is probably about twice as much as I would have if I had had an auction.

At one time, my wife gave me a ten thousand-piece jigsaw puzzle for Christmas. It was so big, I couldn't work it in the house. I took it out in the garage, set a 4 x 8 piece of plywood on a couple of sawhorses and went to work. I had pieces all over that garage. It took me just about a week to get the pieces sorted out. I really had a time with that puzzle. It took me over three months to do it.

At one time I did a lot of hooking and in '76, for my bicentennial project, I made a flag seven feet long and four foot high. There was $85.00 worth of yarn that went into it, and 130 hours of work, and 40,000 knots in it. I entered it into the county fair and it was the only object of its kind in its category, and they gave me a pink ribbon on it that was fourth place. I asked them why they didn't give me a blue ribbon on it. They said, "Oh you had it finished off wrong" I asked them, "Well, just how then would you finish it off." They couldn't answer that, because they didn't know how it should be finished off. Another time my oldest sister Vinetta had given me a small kit of needlepoint. Now I had never done any needlepoint and wasn't particularly interested in it. But, after it had lain around for about three years, I decided that I might as well do it. I had no idea of what the correct way of doing needlepoint was, I just picked it up and went to work. There were several times that I had to take part of it out and do it over again, but I finally got it done. It was a picture of a tiger, about eight by ten in size. Once when my younger sister, Eileen was there visiting us, she told me that I ought to do like some big football player, I don't remember what his name is, but he was famous for his needlepoint work. I said, "Oh." I went into the bedroom and got this piece of needlepoint that I had done, and come back in and threw it into her lap. I said, "Is this what you mean?" Her mouth fell open, and she looked at it and said, "Did you do this?" I said, "I sure did." She said, "Where did you go to school to learn needlepoint?" I said, "What do you mean, go to school, I just picked it up and did it." She said, "Well, I'm going to school to learn how to do needlepoint. I don't believe that you just picked that up and did it. You had to learn somewhere." I said "Yeah, I taught myself." I think she still doesn't believe me that I just picked it up and did it.

Once in 1948, while I was manufacturing mink cages and nesting boxes, I had six men working for me. I was sponsoring a bowling team and two of the men were on the team. At that time, I was not a bowler, I was just sponsoring a team. The men liked to have their pay in cash. I guess that maybe they didn't trust my checks. So every Friday morning, I would go to the bank and get the money to meet the payroll. Now I usually picked up three or four $100.00 bills, which I paid out to them, There were two banks in town. One was the State Bank and the other was the Citizen's Bank. I was dealing with the State Bank and went in at 9:00 a.m. and picked up the money for my payroll. I got 3 $100.00 bills and at 10:00 a.m. two masked men walked into the Citizen's Bank and held them up and got away with a fairly large amount of money, mostly in $100.00 bills. At 5:00 p.m. I paid my men off and each of the two boys that were on the bowling team got a $100.00 bill, They naturally tried to get the $100.00 broken down at one of the stores. That night in the middle of their second game, the chief of police and two deputies came in and arrested the boys. They wouldn't even let them finish up their bowling game. They were sure that they had the two bank robbers. They took them down to the jail and interrogated them. Naturally, they told the police that I had given them the $100.00 bills. So, the police came after me. They were sure that I was the ringleader. I told the chief of police, "Look, I went to school here, graduated from the high school here, spent the war years fighting the war over in Europe, came back here, established a home and business, and you think that I would be such a damn fool as to rob a bank here in town? I got those $100.00 bills this morning at the State Bank. All you have to do is check with the teller there and I'm sure that she will tell you that I have been in the habit of picking up several $100.00 bills every Friday with which to pay my men." I gave them the name of the teller and then I told them, "Right there is a phone, just pick it up and call her right now." He said, "Well, it is kind of late to be calling her, so, we will call her in the morning." I said, "No, you call her right now. Those boys are not going to spend the night in jail, and neither am I." So he called her, and she verified the fact that I had picked up those $100.00 bills. And she said, "In fact, I even wrote down the serial numbers of them. Hold on just a minute, I stuck the notation in my purse. I'll go get it and give you the numbers right now." So he copied the numbers down, and I said, "All right, let's go down to the jail now. I'm going along with you." They had taken the bills from the boys and locked them up in a safe. So he got the bills out and compared the serial numbers, and they matched up perfectly. He said, "Well, I guess you boys are off the hook. You're free to go." I said, "I think you owe those boys a big apology." So, he very grudgingly apologized to them, and then we all went home. They never did catch the bank robbers and the local papers played it up big, in telling that how the robbers had overlooked the stack of bills worth over $5,000.00. Well, one week went by and next Friday the bank was held up again. The robbers told the tellers that they were after the $5,000.00 that the other guys had overlooked.

That winter, I worked in the bowling alley setting pins for the next three months. Now if you think that's an easy job, then you are badly mistaken. This was back in the days before the automatic pinsetters came out. I didn't start bowling until I was about 45. I was bowling in Woodstock, sponsoring a team and bowling on it myself. When I started out, I had a 110 average, but, in a couple of years, I had brought that up to about 150, which I maintained from then on. By the third year I had put together a championship team, so what happens? One week before the season started, they all deserted me and went over to another sponsor, and they did win the championship that year. I had to get along most of the year with three bowlers, and was lucky to have them. Naturally, we wound up at the very tail end. I sponsored teams and bowled on them for the next fifteen years before I finally managed to have a winning team, and I don't think that you could have a closer deal then what we did. We went right to the final game of the season, and we were tied with the team that we were playing. We were pretty well tied up all through the game and were tied up going into the 10th frame. The last bowler on the other team had a strike and a spare in the tenth frame. He had a strike and nine pins in the tenth. I was anchorman for our team, and in the tenth I had a strike and a spare. We won the game by one pin. It was that close. Another time I was bowling in a moose tournament in Elgin, IL, when I managed to chalk up eight strikes in one game. My total score for that game was 175. Another time, I bowled in the Chicago Tribune tournament of Beat the Champ, and I managed to beat him by about five pins. Of course, I was bowling with a handicap, and he was bowling from scratch.

In 1947, shortly after I had opened up my little box factory, I became acquainted with a fellow named Bultman. He was a trucker and had a shop set up on the northeast edge of Delavan. He had three semis, one of them was a large flatbed truck, and he had a large planing mill set up there. I was talking to him one day and he wanted to know if I wanted to take a trip to northern Michigan because he was going up there after a load of lumber. I said, "Sure, I'll go along with you. I need quite a little lumber for my shop. Maybe I can buy half the load, and you buy half of a load." He said, "That sounds like a good idea." He told me that he wouldn't charge me anything for hauling the lumber down providing that I would help him to clean out his lumber after we got back down here. I told him that it sounded like a pretty good deal to me. From then on, we made about one trip a month up to the sawmill in northern Michigan. After about our third trip up there, he asked me if I wanted to buy in with him. He said that if I had $3,000.00 he would sell me half interest in his whole business. That included his semis and the planing mill. I wanted to, but I just could not raise the $3,000.00. I knew he was intending to build up a lumberyard, and he needed the $3,000.00 for buying some more land and to put up a couple of buildings with it. That was just another lost opportunity for me. I just couldn't take advantage of it because of the finances. In 1998, when I went back there to my school reunion, I passed his lumberyard, which was on the southeast edge of town, and it was a huge, big, multi-million dollar yard, new buildings, new equipment in there, and I could have had a 50% interest in that if I had just had $3,000.00 back in 1947. Once a year in the latter part of October or first of November, he would take his flatbed up north, and load it with Christmas trees. When he got back to town with them, he would invite me over and I could have my pick of the trees. So, I always had a beautiful Christmas tree.

Over the years, I made six trips to Europe with our tour group from our army reunion organization, and Les Nichols always headed them up. In 1995, Les took a group over for the fiftieth anniversary of the Battle of the Bulge. When we got over there, the Luxembourg's and Belgium's were ready for us. Every city that we went into had a big reception for us. And while Metz, France wasn't included in our routing, the mayor of Metz heard that we were there, and put on an impromptu reception for us. He came over to Luxembourg City, latched on to us and insisted that we come over to Metz. So that day, we had two receptions, one in the morning and one in the afternoon. All told, we attended eleven receptions on that trip. At the reception in Bastogne, we all got a pleasant surprise. They awarded us all the Belgium Croix de Guerre, which means cross of war. It was the highest honor that Belgium has for soldiers. Later, at the reception in Luxembourg City, we were also awarded the Luxembourg Croix de Guerre. At one town in Belgium, after the reception, we had to march from the reception hall out into the country for about a mile and a half to see a monument there commemorating the Battle of the Bulge. Well, there were one hundred twenty-two of us on the tour, and we made quite a parade going out to the monument, and had the town band leading us. At one point we passed a pasture where there were about a dozen cows grazing, and when they heard the band, their heads perked up and looked at us.

They all came over and lined up in a line along the fence and stood there watching us as we went by. That was quite a hike for that bunch of old retreads for we were all up in our seventies.

In 1996, Les took another group over into Europe, and we went along with him. My sister Eileen and her husband Dean went with me. They had been with me on the 1995 trip. We flew into Amsterdam, Holland. While in the hotel in Amsterdam, I wanted a cup of coffee, so I went into the restaurant and ordered a cup. They brought me out a little tiny demitasse cup. It had about one swallow of coffee in it, and they only charged me $5.00 for it. I didn't drink any more coffee in that place. If you think that you've seen bicycle riders here in the states, you should go to Amsterdam. There are over one million bicycles in that town, There are only about a half of a dozen of the old windmills left in Holland. We went out and went through one of them and it was quite interesting to see all of the works on the inside. From there we went out to the Flower Marts, which was about twenty miles out of Amsterdam, and that is quite a sight to see. It was a one-story building, about thirty feet high, and at the very least, it is one mile square. Try and imagine one room a mile square. They are continually adding on to it all the time, and it is completely filled up with cut flowers. It is something to see, I tell you. They ship those flowers by air all over the world.

From there we went and boarded a cruise boat for a cruise up the Rhine River, which we all enjoyed very much. When we got into Sierek, France, we tied up to dock on the river shore. A bunch of us took a big tour bus into the city, which was about fifteen miles from there. We went to a shopping district there where they didn't allow any busses, cars, or vehicles. The driver had to park the bus about a half of a mile away from it, and we walked from there uphill to the business district. The place was just lined with stores of all types. We all split up and each one went his own way. We agreed to meet at

4:30 p.m. in front of the post office. I never was too much for shopping, so I got back to the post office about 3:30 p.m., and there were four or five other fellows there, so we stood talking for a little while, when a thought hit me. I'm a stamp collector, and that's a post office there. This would be a good time to get some stamps. So, I told the fellows, that I was going into the post office to see if I could buy some stamps for my collection. Also, I told them that as the group gets assembled and takes off at 4:30 p.m., would one of them come in and get me. They said that sure, they would do that. So, I went into the post office, got into line and waited my turn at the window. I tried telling the clerk who couldn't speak any English and I couldn't speak any French that I wanted one stamp of every kind that he had there. Finally, when I got him to understand what I wanted, and I got my stamps, I looked at my watch, and it was 4:45 p.m. I thought, boy, I hope the group hasn't taken off without me. But, when I got outside, there was no sign of them. Well, I went back into the post office and finally found someone who could speak a little English and asked them where I could find a taxicab. They told me that I had to go back down to where they parked our tour bus. So, I walked down there, which probably took me another fifteen minutes, and saw no sign of the bus. It was gone. I flagged down a taxi and asked the driver if he could speak English. He said that sure he could. I told him fine, that I was off of a cruise ship that was anchored along the shore there on the Rhine River. I asked him if he knew where that was. He told me that he did. I got into the taxi and told him to take me down there to the ship. When we got to the Rhine River. there was no sign of the ship there. So, he just kept going on down the way and there was another dock, but no ship there, then there was a third one, but no ship there. Well, we got to the fourth dock, and there was a ship.

As I got out of the cab, there was a busload of people that was just unloading off of the bus. Well, of course, they were all glad to see me, especially my sister and her husband. Well, we finished our cruise and went into Paris, where we all put up at a big hotel. While there, I contracted a bad cold, and was running out of handker-chiefs. There was a big department store across the street from the hotel, and I thought that I would go over there and buy myself a dozen or so. I found the handkerchiefs, and picked out a dozen of them. The clerk took me over to the cashier. Now when traveling in a foreign country, I usually tried to keep about $150.00 of their currency on me just in case of any emergency. Well, of course the cashier wanted francs. I started counting out francs, and she kept saying more, more, more. All of a sudden, I looked at my pocketbook and I didn't have but ten francs left in it. I had $150.00 worth of francs out there, and she was still asking for more. A little mental arithmetic told me that amounted to over $25.00 a handkerchief. When I realized that, I reached inside the cage, grabbed my stack of money and pulled it out, and shoved the handkerchiefs in to her and told her that she could just keep the handkerchiefs and I would keep my money. She didn't like it too well, but there wasn't anything she could do. I went back to the hotel, got a hold of a bellboy and told him to go into the kitchen and get me a stack of big heavy napkins that they used. He went in and came back with about three dozen of them for me. Well, I used those for handkerchiefs and they worked just as well as any-thing. But, the next day I was into another department store about a mile away from the hotel, and I found some cheaper handkerchiefs there. I bought ten of them at just 5.00 apiece.

Les had booked us into the Moulin Rouge, which is a famous nightclub in Pig Alley, which is the famous red light district in Paris. We had balcony seats and it only cost us $85.00 a person. But then we were each given about a half of a bottle of champagne. We were so crowded in there, you couldn't move, and I mean that you couldn't move. If there had ever been a fire there, it would have been horrible, because we would have never been able to get out. We watched the floor show, which was really good. Everybody really enjoyed their champagne. I often wondered how much it cost the people that were eating down on the main floor. About six years later, I found out, after I had moved to Wellington. Trudie's daughter, Debbie, and her husband, Dave, had been to Paris and went to the Moulin Rouge, and they had ate supper down on the main floor, and it only cost them $200.00 a person. They had two shows a night and were always all packed. Just doing a little rough arithmetic, I figured that they were taking in over one million dollars a night there. They had to be at those prices.

On one of our trips, when we were in London, we all had tickets to the musical, Miss Saigon. When we had bought the tickets, they had charged us $85.00 apiece for them. But, when we got to the music hall, they refunded $30.00 apiece to us, so the show only cost us $55.00. But, it was well worth it.

I bought a house in Harvard as an investment. It was a two-story residence house. The tenants had been in the house for years, and had no intention of moving. I made several improvements on the house. One of which was putting in a half bathroom downstairs. When I had remodeled our apartment in Marengo, we had put in a completely new, full bathroom, and I had contracted with a plumbing firm in Harvard, and they had installed a new, oversized bathtub, a new stool, and a new sink. They furnished everything for $950.00 and did the labor. They had done a good job, their price was okay, and I was well satisfied with their work. I called them in to do the work on the house in Harvard. I never bothered to ask them for a price. I had bought the sink and the stool from them and had paid them for it. So, all they had to do was to connect it up to the water system and drain. When they finished, they mailed me a bill. When I read the bill, I just couldn't believe my eyes. It was for $1,650.00 just for labor. Well, I refused to pay it and had several arguments with them over it. Finally, I got them down to $825.00, which was way too much yet. But, I paid it, just to be done with it. Two months after I paid them, they were in bankruptcy court.

Retirement

The day my wife died is the day that I retired. For the last two weeks that she lived, well, I had help during the daytime, but at night, I was by myself taking care of her. I was up at least once every fifteen minutes during the night with her. I not only was retired, but I was just plain tired period. I had been in good relationships with all of her children except one son. As soon as she died, they no longer had any consideration for me whatsoever, except for my stepdaughter, Mary. She continued to treat me as she would her father. The four boys however hired an attorney and contested the will and held up the settlement for 1-1/2 year. I don't know for sure how much they finally got, but according to my figures, it must have been about $25,000.00 above their inheritance. I had a good attorney that I liked, and I expected him to handle the probate of her will. But, he turned it over to his partner, saying that his partner handled all of the probate business of the firm. Well, I didn't like his partner at all, but I was stuck with him. When the case come up in court, the opposing attorney got a six-week postponement. Well, six weeks later when we came into court again, there were just four people in the courtroom, the judge, two attorneys, and myself. These proceedings were supposed to be in open court for the public to hear if they wanted to. But, there were just the four of us there and the two attorneys went up to the judge's bench and held their conversation in whisper, so I couldn't hear. Every time I thought that we had reached an agreement with them, they would come up with a new point and get another postponement. This went on for a year and a half before we finally settled. To start out with, my attorney told me that he would charge me $75.00 an hour. After a couple of trips to court, he raised it to $85.00 an hour. I managed to get that in writing with his signature, and it's a good thing that I did, because a couple of months later when we were talking, he said, "Well, I'll only charge you $100.00 an hour." I said, "Like hell you will. You started out at $75.00 and went to $85.00 an hour, and I've got a paper at home with your signature on it stating $85.00 an hour," He charged $15.00 every time he wrote a letter for you, and also if he made a telephone call for you, he charged $15.00. Well, it never failed to happen, he would have his secretary to call me up and make an appointment with him, and the next day I would get a letter from him in the mail, setting up the appointment. I think my attorney agreed with everything that the boys wanted. I doubt if he objected to even one thing.

My wife had never gotten more than $250.00 a month rental for her apartments, although several times I had tried to get her to raise the rent, and just two months before she died, I raised the rent on one apartment to $300.00. I was supposed to have the use of the house throughout my lifetime. But, she had never put that in her will. And the boys thought that I ought to pay $450.00 a month rent for my apartment. Well, I put my foot down there, and told my attorney that I would pay $300.00 a month and not a penny more, period, which is what it finally cost me. When we got ready to sell the place, I called Century 21, and they sent out a woman salesman, and she wanted to know how much I wanted for the place, and I told her that if I got $60,000.00 out of it, I would be happy. This was in the afternoon, and the next afternoon, she was back, and said, "I've got a little news for you." I said, "Yes. What?" She said, "I just sold the place for $89,500.00." I said, "Wonderful." I told the attorney that I wanted that money put into an account in my name, and I wanted to sign every check that was written against it. Well, he put the money into a special account, and he was the only one that could write a check against it. I never did get an accounting or no idea what was paid out or to whom it was paid. Well, I finally settled up with the attorney, and he charged me a flat $6,000.00 for his services. I checked since with three or four different attorneys, and they all told me that they could have handled that probate for less than $2,000.00.

I have never known a girl to have as many jobs as Mary held. But every time she changes jobs, it's always a step up the ladder and for a better pay scale. Today she is an editor of a fairly prominent magazine in the Chicago area. I even hired her one summer, and she worked for three months on my paint crew. I never allowed her to do any heavy lifting, or do any ladder work, except off of a six-foot stepladder. But, she was really good at masking out windows and scraping areas that she could reach. And when she finally took another job, I really missed her on the crew. Two different times, I loaned her money to buy a car with, so she wouldn't have to get tangled up with a finance company. She promptly repaid me every penny. Her husband Jerry is quite a fellow. He started out with a large plant in Woodstock as a laborer. He stayed with the company for twenty-one years, and when he finally left, he was plant manager over the entire operation. When he was 42, he went to night school to get his college degree, because he had to have a college degree in order to get his promotion to an executive position. After 21 years, he finally quit them and took a job as general manager with a larger factory in Rockford, IL.

Of course, after we sold the house, I had to vacate it. I moved down to Newtown, IL, which was about 150 miles south of Marengo. I moved in with a widow lady named Evelyn Jones. I had become acquainted with her through a social club and lived with her for ten years. Although we slept in the same bed, there was never any sex between us, because by that time, I was completely impotent. After about a year there I became acquainted with a firm called the National Safety Associates (NSA). It was strictly a selling job and I thought it would be a good retirement job for me. I invested $5,000.00 with them and set out to try to organize a sales crew. I even bought a small Toshiba copier for $1,000.00. That area turned out to be like the area around Mendota. You had to be about a second generation resident before the people would have anything to do with you. After three years of fooling with it and spending over $10,000.00 of my own money, I had to give it up as a bad deal.

One year, Les had a trip planned through the Eastern Block countries, which consisted of Hungary, Czechoslovakia, Poland, East Germany and Berlin. Les became sick and was unable to go, but there were several of us that had joined up with another tour group and made the trip. We had an excellent tour guide. On our passage through Hungary, we never saw any houses in the country, but on the edge of every city we would see large apartment buildings, eight and ten stories high. Our tour guide told us that most of those were walk up and cold water apartments. Most of them were little three room apartments and some of them will have three generations living together in one apartment. There was a lady from Seattle, Washington, on the tour with us. I became quite well acquainted with her as she was traveling alone and so was I. Her name was Maureen. At the time she was eighty which made her four years older than I was. We paired up for the trip. I think that she was the most traveled person that I have ever met. She was a widow and her husband had owned seven large sporting goods stores through out Washington. He had loved to travel. At one time they had signed up for a tour on a freighter. It had cost them $10,000.00 apiece (or $20,000.00) for the trip. She said that she really enjoyed it, and that they actually saw more and went to more places than they would have on a modern tour liner. When we got into Krakow, Poland, we went out to visit the church of the Black Madonna, which is quite famous.

During the tour through the church of the Black Madonna, Maureen became separated from the group and was lost. When we finished the tour and got back to the bus, Maureen was nowhere to be found. I told the tour guide to take the bus and the rest of the tour group down to the restaurant where we were booked for dinner and I would stay and try to find Maureen, and after they finished dinner, they could come back for me. I went back into the church grounds and realized that I would never find her in that crowd of 10,000 by myself. There was a museum near the entrance and I went into it to see if I could find someone who could talk English. I finally found a nun who could speak English. It was so noisy in there that we almost had to shout to be heard. I took the nun outside where it wasn't quite so noisy.

I tried to tell her that we had lost a lady out of our tour group, and I wanted to get a hold of the police or security somehow, and have a search made for her. She could talk English all right but she couldn't understand it. When I told her that I was looking for a woman, she thought that I meant the Black Madonna. I started to get a little disgusted and raised my voice, when all of a sudden, I heard someone say, "I was never so glad in my life to hear your voice!" It was Maureen. She had had the same I idea that I had and was headed for the museum to find someone who could talk English and who could help her out. She hadn't seen me, but when I raised my voice, she heard it and recognized it. She told me that she had just gotten tired of the crowd in the church, and that she had stepped outside the door to get some fresh air and then found herself locked out. The door opened from the inside, but did not open from the outside. She had got hold of a priest who talked English and had asked him for directions back to the parking lot where the bus was, and when she got to the parking lot it was the wrong one. It was completely empty. There was not a single car in it. After that she just wandered around for about an hour trying to find the parking lot, then she remembered the museum at the entrance gate and had headed back for it to see if she could get some help there, then she heard my voice when I was talking to the nun. I asked her what she would have done if she had not met up with me. She said that well she had plenty of money on her, and that she would have just taken a cab from Krakow to Berlin, that she knew the hotel that the group was staying in there. We got back to the parking lot, and just as we got out into the parking lot, a cab pulled up in front of us and stopped. The tour guide got out and said, "Oh, thank God, you found her! Come on and get into the cab, they are up at the restaurant waiting for us." We went and had dinner, and then headed for Berlin. When we got up to the border between Poland and Germany, I'll never forget that border crossing, There were five lanes of semi trucks, backed up bumper to bumper for over three miles, waiting to cross the border into Germany. The tour guide told us that they inspect these trucks at the border, and that it takes an hour per truck to inspect them. They search for drugs etc. She said that sometimes it takes them three or four days to get across the border. They know that they are going to have a long wait there, so they bring about a week's supply of food with them. They have to stay with their trucks all the time because every once in a while, they will have to move up a few feet. We were in a tour bus and were a privileged vehicle. We were able to bypass all the trucks and go immediately into Germany, although we were stopped for about an hour while they searched the bus and all of our baggage.

All the way through Hungary, Czechoslovakia, Poland and Germany, we continued to see these high rise apartment buildings. Outside of Krakow, which is a large city, there was a line of these apartment houses as far as the eye could see. While we were in Krakow, we took a side trip out to Auswich, which was the infamous concentration camp, and that was very interesting to go through.

My next door neighbor, Gus, worked as a security guard for a large utility plant about ten miles out of town.

He told me that they were looking for another man or two on their crew, so I went out and applied for a job as a security guard. This was in 1995, and I had already made reservations and paid for them with the tour group from my army reunion organization to go to Belgium to celebrate the fiftieth anniversary of the Battle of the Bulge. Also, my school reunion at Delavan, Wis. I also had reservations made and paid for there. At first, the Lieutenant in charge said that he would let me know. Well, it went on for over two weeks, and I hadn't heard from them, so I went back out there again, and the Lieutenant said, "You want to much time off to start out with." I told him "I'm sorry about that, but I already had the reservations made and paid for, and I would lose too much money if I didn't go, and being a veteran yourself, you ought to appreciate the fact that I do want to go over to celebrate the fiftieth anniversary of the Battle of the Bulge." He said, "Well, alright." So he hired me. I worked two weeks and took off for two weeks to go to Europe, came back and worked a week, took off five days to go to my school reunion, then came back and settled down to work.

I worked for about a year and a half as a security guard there. In all that time, I was never properly trained for the job. There were always two of us on duty at the same time. We had a guard shack sitting right by the entrance to the plant grounds. All the trucks had to stop there and sign in with us. I would go out to check in a truck driver, and before I could get his signature on our sign in sheet, the Lieutenant would send the other guard out, and he would push me aside and take over. I often wondered why they bothered to keep me when they wouldn't let me do the work. I think the Lieutenant was just jealous of me because I could afford to make a European trip, and he was having the whole crew harass me. Even Gus my next door neighbor that was supposed to be friends with me was in on it. I had a small desk lamp that I had taken out there and used it to read by. I sat at a desk on the west side of the shack and he sat at a desk on the north side, facing the front side of shack. Actually I was sitting behind him. He kept complaining the light was bothering his eyes and would I adjust the lamp to keep it from bothering his eyes. I thought to myself, Gus you don't have eyes in the back of your head. So I said, "Sure." I reached over and tapped the light and never changed the position of the light at all. He said, "Oh, gee thanks. That is so much better." We had one large fellow on the crew, his name was Louie, and if there was ever a moron, he was the original. While we could read, we weren't allowed to play cards, or have any friends visit us, or bring any pets out to the job with us. I had the night shift once with Louie. After things had quieted down at about 10 p.m. he pulled out a deck of cards, and wanted to know if I knew how to play 500 Rummy. I told him that I did and used to play it when I was a kid. So, he dealt the cards and we started playing. I could remember the general outline of the game, but I was making errors and Louie would wait until he had scored some points off my errors, then he would tell me what I had done wrong. Despite my not having played the game for over sixty years, I managed to beat him. We played three games and I won all three of them. After we quit playing, for the next half-hour, he sat over there grumbling to himself about how he hated a poor loser. Well, I didn't say anything because I thought that if he hates a poor loser, then he must hate himself, because I had won all three games. I figured that would be the end of the card games, but no, the next night he wanted to play again. This time I won one game and he won two games. He got up and started pacing around the shack, cussing me out. He went on for 45 minutes. I don't think he ever used the same word twice. I had never heard such a filthy mouth in all my life. Then he went out to his car and brought in a small portable TV and hooked it up. He sat there watching TV for a couple of hours and never invited me to watch with him. Now, there will be more about Louie a little later on.

I was sitting at my desk one night, when I felt wet-ness down alongside of my legs, and I wondered what the devil? I haven't had any water or coffee that I could have spilled on myself. I reached down and felt of my pants leg, and both of them were sopping wet. I had wet myself and never knew that I was doing it. I didn't say anything but I finished up my shift in my wet pants. The next day I went to the Doctor for an examination. It didn't take long for him to tell me that I had sugar diabetes, and also along with the diabetes, I had an enlarged pros-trate, practically no control over my bladder, a slow heart beat, poor blood circulation and a shortness of breath. I went to the VA hospital at Danville, IL and stayed there a week until they got me straightened out. At the end of the week they took me off of the insulin and gave me a little pill to take once a day. I had my bodily functions straightened around so that I had some control over them, and I went back to work. We had two women guards working there. One of them was named Beverly, and she was a real nice person, and I liked her quite well. The other one was named Margaret, and she liked to think she was quite the hot potato. One night when I was pull-ing the night shift with Louie, Margaret came in at mid-night to relieve me. I gathered up my lunch pail, and put my coat on and headed for the door. She called out and said. "Ralph, before you go home, you go in the bath-room and clean up your piss off of the floor." Well now, she hadn't been in the shack five minutes, and hadn't been in the bathroom at all, so she had no way of know-ing whether or not there was any piss on the floor or not. I knew it wasn't mine. Without even turning around, I said, "Margaret, if there is any piss on the bathroom floor, then it has to be Louie's and if you want to go in there and clean up Louie's piss, you go ahead, because I'm not." I just went out the door. I never heard anything more about that.

In March of 1995, I had a 1987 Pontiac Grand Am and while it was a used car, it was in excellent shape.

Evelyn and I were returning from a neighboring town, when the car in front of me came to a dead stop right in the center of the lane. I saw that I was going to rear end him, so I pulled the car completely off the road onto the side of the road and came to a complete stop. The fellow in front of me heard my brakes screeching, and he took off down the highway like a scared rabbit. As it was there had recently been a small shower of rain, and while the highway was dry, the grass on the edge of the road was not. It was wet and when I came to a stop there, one rear wheel was in gravel and the other was on the wet grass. The wheel on the gravel completely stopped, and the wheel on the grass kept spinning. Well, that combination just whipped me around and shot me right across the highways and I hit a large semi tractor that was hauling half of a trailer house. It took just about three seconds to make a worthless pile of junk out of that car. Neither Evelyn nor I were hurt, But she had a head full of glass, her hair was just covered with glass. She wasn't cut or anything.

There were about eight of the northwestern states that I had never been in. And I had never seen the Grand Canyon, Yellowstone Park, Redwood Forrest, or Mount Rushmore. I had been planning a trip to go up through all of those states, and see all the natural sights, and part of western Canada. That meant I had to buy another car. I went to a farm auction, where they had advertised a Chevrolet Impala. It was a 1987 model, and had only 12,000 miles on it, and was in really beautiful condition. I bid the car in and it cost me $6,000.00. I drove it home. About the middle of May I started off on my trip. I went first to Mt. Rushmore, and it was socked up solid with fog. You couldn't see your hand in front of your face. I left there and went down through the Grand Canyon. I had intended to take a mule ride down into the bottom of the canyon But when they told me that the ride cost $200.00, and I would have to pay for my nights stay in the motel at the bottom of the canyon, I decided that it was not worth it. I took a helicopter ride instead which only cost me $85.00 and I had an hour and a half flight over the canyon, and saw so much more of the canyon than you would any other way. From the Grand Canyon I went over to Salt Lake City, as I had always wanted to see the lake, but it was about fifteen miles out of town, and I never did get out to it. From there I went up to Las Vegas and spent about an hour and a half there. I never did go inside a casino. I then went up to Yellowstone Park and saw Old Faithful. Then I went back to Mt. Rushmore. This time I had a clear day and I managed to see it. I also went over about fifteen miles to where they were working on the statue of Chief Crazy Horse.

I guess I got a little ahead of my story. For, when I started out, I first went up through Minnesota, where I stopped at St. James for a day and visited with my wife's brothers. Then I went on across Minnesota to Montana, where I went through the Wall Drugstore. Then I went on into North Dakota where I visited the little town of Spencer, then dropped down across the border into South Dakota, where I visited the little town of Spencer again. From there I went on down and went through the Badlands.

After leaving Mt. Rushmore the second time, I went on up through Idaho into Canada, and from there I went up through the mountains to Lake Louise, which is a large lake up in the mountains. There is a big glacier right off of the lake. Then I went on through the mountains into British Columbia and went on up to St. George, which is about half way up to Alaska. Then I turned and came back south to North Vancouver, where I checked into a large hotel and spent the night. The next morning I went out and couldn't find my car. It had been stolen and had all of my cloths and everything in it. I was left stranded there with just the cloths I had on to wear. However I did have my toilet articles and all of my money. I reported the theft to the Royal Canadian Mounted Police. Then I thought that I would stick around there for a couple of days to see if they picked up my car. In the meantime I went shopping for some clothes and the prices were so sky high. I just couldn't afford them. One shop advertised a sale on socks at 1/2 price I thought at least I would go and get me a clean pair of socks to wear. They only wanted $17.00 a pair for them and that was 1/2 price, the full price was $34.00. I told them they could just keep their socks.

On the fourth day, I took a ferry over to Vancouver, then another ferry up to Victoria Island, where I got onto a third sea ferry that took me down to Seattle. I had called Maureen and told her that I was going through Seattle, and that I would pay her a visit. After getting into Seattle, I spent the first day buying myself a new wardrobe. Then, I called Maureen and told her what had happened, that my car had been stolen. She came over to the hotel and picked me up, and took me back to her apartment, which was a very beautiful one. I imagine that it probably cost her at least $1,500.00 a month rent for it. However, I did not stay in the apartment with her. She had rented a two-room apartment in a motel for me, about a half a mile from her apartment. I spent a week there in Seattle with Maureen. She really made a wonderful tour guide. She had lived there all her life. At this time she was 82 and still played golf twice a week, worked out in a gym for an hour three days a week, and played a lot of bridge. She took me out to dinner one night to her country club, which is a really plush affair, so in return I took her to supper in the restaurant on top of the Needle. From Seattle I took a bus down to Portland, OR. where I attended a reunion being held by the western chapter of the 10th Armored Division Association. From there I took another bus going south, and went on down through the Redwood Forrest. I didn't get to see much of the redwoods, because it was night when we passed through it. From there I went on down to San Francisco where I had to change busses. I had about a three-hour lay over, so put my bags into a locker, and hired me a cab to take me for a drive around town. I wanted to see Fishermen's Wharf. I also wanted to take a ride on the cable cars, but it wasn't practical, so I went back to the bus depot and got on the bus again. I took it down to Los Angeles, where I was going to visit my sister and her husband. They lived out in Woodland Hills north of Los Angeles. I called my sister and told her to come pick me up at the bus station in LA She said, "Lord have mercy. I don't even know where that is at." I told her. "All I can tell you is that it is downtown somewhere." She said, "Why don't you just take the bus up here, I know they have busses running up here." I said OK. 1 went out and started to check on a bus going out to Woodland Hills, and I found out that they did have a bus running out there, but the bus depot that the bus operated out of was ten miles away, and they only had about two busses a day that went out there, and I would get out to Woodland Hills at about 4:30 p.m. Now it was 9:00 a.m. at that time, and that meant I would have to fool around on those buses for about 7-1/2 hours. I figured that it just was not worth it. I went out of the bus depot and hired a cab.

It only cost me $45.00 and at 10:30 a.m., I walked into my sister's house. I spent nine days with my sister and her husband. They really showed me around the country. They took me to Beverly Hills and Hollywood, and showed me all the other sights.

My sister's booking agent managed to get me on a Southwestern Airlines flight from Los Angeles to St. Louis for $109.00. When I got into St. Louis, I had to take a cab from the airport to the bus depot, then take a bus out to Effingham, then a cab from Effingham to Newton, and finally I was home. I immediately stated looking for another car. I found a beautiful old Cadillac in a farmer's yard about three miles outside of town. It was eight years old, but in perfect condition, inside and out. I told him to just hold it for me and I would go into town to the bank, and make arrangements to get the money. I stopped at the house first to tell Evelyn about it. I walked in the door, and she was very excited. She didn't give me a chance to say a word. She said that she had just had a call from the Royal Canadian Mounted Police. They had found my car, and wanted me to come pick it up. I got on the phone, called the RCMP, and asked them what kind of condition the car was in. They said it looked to be in pretty good condition. I told them okay, that I would come and pick the car up. I went back out to see the farmer and told him to go ahead and put the Cadillac back up for sale again. Two weeks after having completed a 12,000 mile journey, I was off on another 4,000-mile trip to pick up my car. I flew up to Carlisle, Canada and had to change planes in Salt Lake City. Our plane was delayed and I missed my connection for Carlisle. The airline put me up over night and put me into a hotel room. I had never seen the likes of it before. It was absolutely huge. It was the largest hotel room that I had ever seen. They even bought my breakfast the next morning, then boosted me up to first class for the hour and a half flight to Carlisle. When I got to Carlisle, I found out that the car was in a little town about 45 miles out of Carlisle. I took a cab out there. When I got out there and inspected the car it was in prefect condition. There was not even a dent in it. It even had a full tank of gas in it. They had driven it about 1,000 miles and abandoned it in a church parking lot. After it had sat in the lot for about two weeks, one of the Deacons had called the police and reported it. I had a spare set of keys taped to the top of the radiator. I opened up the trunk and was surprised to see all my suitcases there. In opening them, I found that they had not even been touched. There were only three things that were missing, one, my binoculars, and the second was my fuzz buster, and the third item was my camera. I paid off the towing company for the towing and storage charges and headed back home. I got back into Carlisle, and found out that the Carlisle Stampede was going to start the next day, and since I had never seen a rodeo, I thought I would get a motel room and stay for the first day of the stampede.

That morning, I left my car at the motel, took a train downtown and walked over a couple of blocks to the parade route. This was on July 8, and I stood there and almost froze to death. I was talking to a young fellow who lived in the building that we were standing in front of. He saw that I was shivering, so he went up to his apartment and came back with a chair and a blanket, so I could sit down and wrap up in the blanket. That all helped a little but not much. After another hour of shivering, I got up and said good-bye to the boy, then walked back to the train station and caught a train back to the motel. I then got in my car and headed for home. I stopped in St. James, MN to visit a couple of my wife's brothers. They told me that I would probably have to put up with them for about a week, that the Mississippi was flooding and the bridges all the way down to St. Louis were closed. I only stayed 24 hours, then I went up through Minneapolis, which was a couple hundred miles out of my way. There was one bridge there that was open, and I was able to get across the Mississippi River, I got back home without any further incidents,

In 1997, I took my next trip and it was a cruise down through the Panama Canal, which I had always wanted to see. It was in November, and I left Newton in a snowstorm, and drove into Indianapolis and parked in a long-term parking lot. I caught a flight out of there to Acapulco, where we were to board ship. When we landed in Acapulco, they loaded us onto a bus, which took us directly to the ship. All we got to see of Acapulco was the thirty-minute drive through the downtown section. My sister and her husband were on this trip with me. On the second day of the cruise we stopped in Costa Rica, and I joined a group that was going on a short bus tour of the country. They stopped at a church and took the group inside. I had been through so many churches in Europe that I didn't go inside with them. I just waited outside on the steps. After about five minutes, there was a lady that came out and stopped beside me. She said,

"I'm Trudie Peters from Wellington, Texas. Who are you?" I said, "I'm Ralph Spencer from Newton, IL." We had a real nice visit and finally the group came back out of the church, and we loaded back on the busses. She was on the first bus and I was on the second bus. I didn't see any more of her that day. The next morning I found her waiting outside of the restaurant, so we could have breakfast together. From then on for the rest of the tour we were a twosome. She had a stateroom on deck 9 at one end of the ship and my stateroom was on deck 11 at the other end of the ship. I hadn't been able to get a partner to share a stateroom with so paid an extra $600.00 to have a private stateroom. When I boarded ship they took me to the stateroom and it was a huge room with two double beds in it, and five minutes later, they brought in another old fellow and I told them, "Wait a minute. I paid $600.00 extra to have a private stateroom. What is he doing in here?" He told them the same thing, that he had paid $600.00 extra to have a private stateroom. They said, "Well, we are sorry. The ship is crowded, and we just can't give you a private stateroom." I said, "That's fine. Just refund my $600.00 then," They said, 'No, we can't do that. We don't have anything to do with the finances." I never did get my $600.00 back. My roommate was an odd fellow. He went to bed every night at 8:00 p.m. We got along fairly well, as we were rarely in the stateroom together. One afternoon Trudie was visiting me, and we were sitting on the bed having a talk, when my roommate came in, saw Trudie there and almost jumped back out the door. He looked at the door number to make sure he had the right room and started to turn and leave. We called him back in and told him he was in the right room. and that we would be out of there in just a minute. I guess that he just couldn't believe that I would have a woman in my stateroom with me.

Trudie was traveling with a group of six doctors and a pharmacist. The pharmacist was her son in law. I was with my 10th Armored group. One night she would eat supper with my group and the next night I would eat supper with her group. On the fourth day we went through the Panama Canal and spent the day in her daughter's cabin because they had a private cabin with a balcony on it. We really enjoyed the trip through the Panama Canal. The next day we docked at Colombia, South America, where a lot of people went shopping and we went sightseeing. In the evenings they always had an excellent show in the ship's theater. The shows were not movies they were all live. We really enjoyed those. One night they were having a dance. I wanted to dance, but Trudie said no she had never danced. I was sitting next to a Chinese lady, and I asked her if she would like to dance. She said no, that she didn't dance at all, but that her companion did, and was a good dancer. When her companion showed up she told her that I would like to dance with her, and she said sure. We went up onto the dance floor, and I was really surprised because she knew all of the western dances and we really had a good time.

After Colombia, we docked at Aruba. I had previously signed up for a submarine trip there at Aruba, Trudie didn't think that she could get down into the submarine or get back out of it, so she went on a short excursion trip while I took the submarine trip. I got down into the submarine, and they had stripped everything out of one compartment of the submarine, and put in a wood bench that extended the whole length of the compartment. It had a common back to it in the center, and when you sat down there, everybody had their own private porthole to look out of. I think that I enjoyed that submarine trip the most of any of our excursions. The water was crystal clear and we were down about a hundred and fifty feet and you could still see everything just as if it was broad daylight. We went past a lot of coral reefs and one sunken freighter.

We went on from Aruba to St. Francis, where Trudie and I took a side trip over to St. Johns, which we were both glad we did. Because we saw some of the most beautiful scenery that we had ever seen in our lives. We went on from there to Porto Rica, which was like Acapulco. They loaded us On busses to take us to the airport, and we got to see about a mile and a half of the shore. Of course we split up there at the airport, because Trudie was going one way and I was going another. That Christmas I went down to Skiatook, OK to spend Christmas with Trudie at her daughter's home. Of course I had met her daughter and her husband on the cruise. They took me in and treated me like one of the family. We had an enjoyable Christmas and drove on down to Wellington, Texas, where I took a good case of the flu. Trudie and her son Fred took me home. We were going to fly and when we got to the airport at Amarillo, we found out that it would be several hours before our plane would take off. They took me out and down through Palo Duro Canyon, then to supper at the Big Texan, then back to the airport. We caught our plane to St. Louis, where they rented a car and drove me out to Effingham where I had my car parked at one of my apartment houses. I got in my car and drove back to Newton, and they went back to St. Louis, where they took a motel room for the night. The next day they decided to stay in St. Louis because Trudie had never been there before. They went into a large department store and got onto an escalator to go down a story, and Trudie misjudged her step. When she got on the escalator, she fell. At the bottom her son Fred and another fellow pulled her off the escalator.

Fortunately she was not hurt bad, just shook up and a few bruises. The next day, I went to my chiropractor and got myself straightened out. About this time, Evelyn was becoming senile, and was just impossible to live with. I moved out and into one of my apartments in Effingham, which was an upstairs apartment. As I didn't have any cooking equipment Trudie boxed up a large box full of pots and pans and sent them to me by UPS. Well, I never got them, and UPS never compensated Trudie for them. They weren't worth a lot but they were of some value, and I could have really used them.

I had wanted to come down to Wellington to be with Trudie on her birthday, which was Feb. 7th, but she said no. Then on the afternoon of the 7th she called me and said, "Guess where I am?" I said, "Well, its no telling where you are at." She said, "I'm in the hospital. I had a stroke. She had some good therapists, and it wasn't to long before they had her back on her feet.

After Trudie got out of the hospital and had been home for a little while, I came back down to visit her. While I was there I bought a small house on West Ave. in Wellington. Trudie wanted to go down to Jackson, MI to see her new great-grandson, who was born six weeks prematurely and weighed only one pound and eleven ounces at birth. I decided to go along with her. At the time we got there, the baby was a little over two months old and was still in the hospital. When we got to the hospital, Trudie told them who she was and they let us in. I went right along with her and they never questioned me. They allowed us to hold the baby, and I could hold him in the palm of my hand, he was that small. Shortly after he was born, his father took his wedding ring off and slipped it over the babies hand and up as far as his elbow. His arm was that small. The doctors didn't believe he would live, but he fooled them. And today he is a very active and healthy four year old.

After visiting there for three or four days, Trudie decided to take me back up to Illinois as she had never been in that part of the country before. When we got up there I decided to ride back with her as far as Tulsa, and then take a bus back from Tulsa, which is what we did. Then I had to get busy and put my apartment houses on the market. I was lucky and managed to sell the two buildings that I had in Newton in about two weeks, and for the price I was asking. I was really happy to get rid of them. They were nothing but a headache and a big expense. Then in about a month I managed to sell one of my apartment houses in Effingham, for $55,000.00, which was my asking price, and that was all clear money, as there was no mortgage on it. The other apartment house in which I was living, I had a little trouble in selling it. Finally a fellow made me an offer for it for $45,000.00 and that was $15,000.00 under my asking price. I decided to take his offer even though I would be losing $15,000.00.

I sent Trudie $10,000.00, with which to get my house remodeled and repaired so it would be ready for me to move in when I came down. She hired a contractor out of a neighboring city and he really took me to the cleaners. Of course Trudie didn't know that. Trudie and I had met with him when I was visiting her before we went to Jackson. I had reached an agreement with him as to what work should be done. I authorized him to completely repaint the interior of the building, including all ceilings, sidewalls, and all woodwork, for the price we agreed on he was to furnish the paint. When I got down here I found that he had painted the ceiling and walls in three rooms, and the other two rooms he hadn't touched. He hadn't painted any of the woodwork. He charged $385.00 worth of paint to Trudie's account and I doubt if he used over $75.00 or $80.00 of paint all total. He had taken the cabinet doors off to paint them, and then when he put them back on, there wasn't a single one of them that would close, and he just left them that way. Trudie had paid him off before I got down there, not knowing what he was doing.

Well, as usual I'm getting ahead of my story. When I sold my last apartment house I retained the apartment that I was in for another two months as my school in Delavan, Wis. was having a reunion. It was to be my class's 64th reunion, which I wanted to attend. The reunion started on July 6, 1998, and ran for three days. Trudie flew into St. Louis, and I picked her up at the airport. We went up to Delavan for the reunion. I had made reservations at a motel about seven miles west of Delavan. When we got there the motel was out of business and closed down. Everything around Delavan was filled up. So we went over to Elkhorn, which is five miles east of Delavan and found a very nice room in a motel over there. We both enjoyed the reunion. Sunday morning, we were eating breakfast in a restaurant in Delavan and were sitting at a table for four. Two women came in and were standing there looking for a table, but the place was filled up, so we invited them to sit down with us. We introduced ourselves, and they introduced themselves. One of the women was one of my classmates. My classmate leaned over to read Trudie's name tag and she said, "Wellington, Texas, I used to room with a girl that married a man from Wellington, Texas. You know his name was Peters too. But I can't remember what her name was." Trudie said, "Was it Ursalla Barnhart?" She said, 'Yes that's what her name was." Trudie said, "Well that's my sister-in-law."

We returned back down to Effingham, and I had previously made arrangements for the rental of a moving van. I had paid them an $800.00 fee. They guaranteed me that they would have the truck delivered to my house there Tuesday morning. Well, Tuesday morning came and no truck. The truck was supposed to be there at 8 a.m., and I had waited till 9 a.m. I went up to the truck office and the woman that had rented the truck to me wasn't there. Her helper didn't know anything about it. I told him that he must have her home phone number, and that he should get on the phone and call her. He said that she was probably asleep as she had worked the night before. I told him that I didn't care if she was asleep or if she worked all night last night, I wanted her on the phone. He finally called her and woke her up, and handed me the phone. I said, "Where in the devil is my truck?" She said, "Well, you didn't want the truck until Tuesday morning." I said "Woman. this is Tuesday morning. I've got two men hired and waiting over there twiddling their thumbs waiting to load that truck. It is costing me $20.00 an hour to have them sitting there." She said, "I'll have the truck up there in about a half of an hour or forty-five minutes.'" She came in with the truck in about forty-five minutes and it was a much larger truck than what I had arranged for. I told her, "This is a much larger truck than what I wanted." She said, "I know, but the truck you wanted was rented out, and this was the one that I had, so I'm letting you have it for the same price and I'm not charging you any extra for it. Besides that, it is a diesel and you'll like it much better." Well, we had the truck loaded at about 2:00 p.m. and I was leery about driving that truck because I had never driven one that large. Well, Trudie's son was flying into St. Louis to drive the truck back for me. I told Trudie, "Let's get, in the car and drive into St. Louis to pick Fred up." Trudie said, "We will do no such thing. I'll drive that truck into St. Louis." And she did. Well, we picked up Fred and he drove the truck. As it was about 5 p.m., we had decided to ride for about an hour, then find a motel and check in for the night. At about 6 p.m., we came to a sign on the highway that said Food, Lodging, and Gas, next Exit. So we took the next exit off and drove for over 20 miles before we finally found a place to even eat supper. Well, we ate and drove another 20 miles and got back on the highway. Then we finally found a motel and pulled in for the night. Fred was cussing the truck, because he could only get about 40 miles per hour out of it. Well, he nursed the truck along until we finally got into Tulsa. He then got on the phone and called the company agent there in Tulsa, and made them give us another truck, which meant that they had to transfer everything from one truck to another. Well, Trudie's daughter and son-in-law, Beth and Randy Motsenbocker, met us in Tulsa, and Randy drove the truck from Tulsa down to Wellington. Trudie and I stayed overnight in Skiatook, then took a long route home, as we wanted to make sure they had the truck all unloaded before we got there.

After I got settled in, I contacted another local contractor, and had him to come in and straighten up the cabinet doors so they would work and shut properly, and paint the other rooms and woodwork. I had them to completely reside the house and give it a complete paint job on the outside. I had another cement contractor to come in and put in a nice wide concrete driveway for me, a new sidewalk in front of the house, and a walk from the driveway to the front door. I also had them to put on good storm windows on all of the windows, a new front door and storm door, and build a small tool shed onto the end of the house at the end of the driveway. I paid $6,500.00 for the house. and spent over $15,000.00 on the remodeling. But, I finally had a nice little home to live in.

One day, about a year later, I went over to see Trudie, and she and Fred were very excited. Fred found a cheap airfare from Los Angeles to Thailand, for $600.00 for a round trip ticket. When Fred was going to college, he had had a boy from Thailand in his class and Fred had brought him home for the Christmas holidays at one time. After that, he had spent all of his holidays here in Wellington, and had considered Trudie and her husband David as his Mama and Pop. They had kept up correspondence with him for over thirty years, and he had been asking them to come over and pay him a visit. I told them that they didn't need to think that they were going to make a trip like that and leave me sitting behind. So, I ordered out a ticket and Trudie ordered another one for her daughter La Wanda, so there were four of us that made the trip. It was the longest flight that I had ever made. We landed at the Tokyo airport in Japan where we changed planes. We were only there for about an hour and never left the airport. But, I can still say that I was in Japan. We got into Bangkok at about 8:00 p.m. and their friend met us at the airport. He was a wealthy man and bought a new ten passenger van for the occasion. When we got out, I gave him about ten minutes for him to greet the others and finally when he turned my way, I put out a hand to shake hands with him, and said that I was Ralph Spencer. Instead of shaking hands with me, he slapped my hand down and said, "Later!" He turned out to be the rudest person I had ever known. He wasn't rude to Trudie, Fred, or La Wanda, but he sure was to me. I think he was jealous and thought that I didn't have any business going with Trudie. He was having his home remodeled at the time, so we stayed in a hotel all of the time. He would pick us up in the morning and give us a guided tour around the country. He was a good host in that manner, and we really got to see a lot of the country. Since he could speak pretty good English, we had no communication problems. About the only thing that we didn't get to do there was go inside the Palace. The Queen of the Netherlands was visiting there that day, and no tourists were allowed inside the Palace, although we did get to walk around through the palace grounds and walk around the Palace. In spite of our host's rudeness, I really enjoyed the trip. Thailand is one country that I had always wanted to see and never thought that I would get to.

Trudie and I earned enough free air miles off of that trip that we could fly to Alaska and back for free. In April of the next year, we flew into Vancouver, Canada and rented a car. We drove back down into northern Washington to visit for a couple of days with some friends of hers, then back to Vancouver, where we boarded a ship for a cruise up the inside passage, which we both enjoyed, because there was some beautiful scenery there. We had visited Ketchikan, Alaska, and were out in Glacier Bay when the ship caught on fire. The fire was in the lowest deck, which is where the crew and the hired help bunked. Somebody had left a hair dryer on and left it laying on their bunk. It burned up ten cabins before they managed to get the fire out.

Trudie and I were caught without our life jackets, as we didn't think it was the real thing and only a fire drill. Within half of an hour, the announcement was made that everybody would have to evacuate the ship and get outside on the deck. We could begin to smell the smoke and

I knew that I would not be able to make it to the cabin and back. Well, everybody moved out on the outside deck and went to the life boat stations that they were assigned to. I was rather amazed because there was absolutely no panic whatsoever. Everybody was just as cool and calm as could be. We stood outside there for three hours until they finally got the fire put out. They announced that the fire was out, but everybody was to stay on deck until they could get the smoke cleared out of the ship. About twenty to twenty-five minutes later, they announced that it was ok to re-enter the ship. How they ever managed to clear the smoke out of that huge ship in less than half an hour, I'll never know, but they sure did. You couldn't even smell the smoke inside there.

Later that evening, they gave every passenger on the ship $100.00, which you could either spend in the ship stores, or take it in cash if you wanted it, plus a coupon that was good for 40% off on the next cruise we might make with the Holland American Line. We stayed aboard ship until we got into Anchorage. We saw some mighty beautiful scenery along the way, and really had a pleasant voyage after the fire was put out. From Anchorage, we took a bus up to Denali State Park, where we stayed overnight, and then took a train back down to Anchorage. It had been misty in the morning, but the mist cleared out, and we were able to see Mt. McKinley in the distance. In Anchorage, Trudie's niece, Joan, picked us up and took us to her home in Wasilla, which is about 30 miles north of Anchorage. Joan was a very good hostess and was driving us around the countryside showing us all of the local sights. But, on the second day there, I came down with the flu, so I stayed home. Of course they were both worried about me. I told them not to worry, because I had the flu before and I would outlast it. On the sixth day there, Joan took us back to the airport in Anchorage, where we caught our flight to St. Paul, MN, where we changed planes to go to Dallas, where we had to change planes again to get to Amarillo, and then had a two hour drive from Amarillo back home. Then the next day, I had Trudie to take me up to Shamrock to my chiropractor and one good treatment from him cleared up my flu.

Then, on Labor Day weekend, I flew out to Louisville, KY to go to my army reunion, which I hadn't been to in five years. Everybody was glad to see me. I really enjoyed the reunion. Monday, I took a cab back out to the airport, which was only a ten-minute drive from the hotel. I went up to the counter and handed my tickets over to a lady to get me checked in. She took my tickets and looked at them, looked up at me and said, "You know, my name is Spencer, too." I said, "Well, pleased to meet you." She said, "You know, I tell everyone that I'm a cousin to Princes D, and I told her. "Don't feel proud, I've been telling everybody the same thing. My sister who is the genealogist in the family, actually found a link between our family and Princess D's family in the early eighteenth century." She said, "You know, I am just going to upgrade you to first class." I said, "Well, I certainly won't object to that." So, for the two and a half hours that it took to fly from Louisville to Houston, I enjoyed first class passage.

I changed planes in Houston, got on board the Amarillo plane, and then we just sat there in the terminal for an hour. We were supposed to be in Amarillo at 7:30 p.m. After sitting there in the terminal for about an hour, the plane taxied out onto the runway, and when we got out to the take off point, they just pulled off to the side and sat there for another two hours before they would let us take off. There was an awful bad electrical storm between Houston and Dallas, and they would not let the pilot fly into it. Any planes going east or south were able to take off, but all traffic going north or west was halted until the storm had passed over. Finally, we got the okay to go ahead and we took off and landed in Amarillo at 10:30 p.m., only 3 hours late. Trudie was there, waiting for me, and we got home at about 1:00 a.m.

Here are a few more incidents that are out of sequence, but have just come to mind, so I'll relate them now. Shortly after I married Marie, I started saving stamps. Over the years, I put together a collection of over 40,000 used stamps. When Marie contracted Lou Gehrig's Disease, I sold the collection off for $2,000.00, as we needed the money for expenses. After Marie died, I started another collection, and when I had about 10,000 used stamps in it, I became interested in new stamps and started collecting them as well. Today I have a collection of over 60,000 stamps. About 50% of them are used, and about 50% of them are new stamps not only single but doubles, blocks, plate blocks, strips, books, and whole sheets. I haven't touched my collection now in five or six years. I have lost interest in stamp collecting and have my collection up for sale now. So, if any of you readers are stamp collectors and are interested in buying, please contact me.

Over the years, I have been involved in eighteen car accidents. In six of them, the cars were totaled out, and the other twelve were just fender-benders. One really wasn't an accident as my car caught on fire and burned up. In another one, I was a passenger in the car. However, I have been fortunate as I have never been injured and have never injured anybody. Also, I have never worn a seat belt, as I consider them to be a death trap. I know that each of the four cars that I totaled out, if I had been strapped in, I would have been injured and in the hospital or possibly killed.

After I settled up my wife's estate, with what money I cleared out of that, plus my inheritance from my aunt, I had a little over $80,000.00. I had never had money to invest out before and was leery about the stock market. When I moved in with Evelyn, she had about $60,000.00 invested in T. Rowe Price Investment Company. She had had the money invested with them for several years. She finally talked me into investing with them, too. I put $50,000.00 with them. I am no financial expert, but I kept a pretty close eye on the stock market reports, and after a year and a half, it looked to me that there was going to be a drop in the stock market in the near future, so, I pulled my $50,000.00 out. I told Evelyn that she ought to get her $60,000.00 out, too. But, she wouldn't do it. I kept after her. So finally, about six months later, she pulled her money out, and the next day, the stock market crashed. If she had left her money in there one more day, she would have lost over $30,000.00 just overnight. After that, I invested my money in apartment houses. I had two in Newton, one had four apartments in it, and the other had two small apartments in it. The other two were in Effingham. One had three apartments and the other one had two apartments. When I bought the big apartment house in Newton, I needed a $50,000.00 loan to close the deal I had $30,000.00 of my own money for a down payment, and I went to the bank and asked for a loan. They agreed to give it to me, but then they told me that I had to give them a mortgage on my one apartment in Effingham, along with the mortgage on the one that I was buying. Well, the apartment house in Effingham was mine; it was free and clear, with no mortgage. I had paid cash for it. I was not about to put a mortgage on it. So, I borrowed the $50,000.00 from Evelyn.

One day, Trudie pointed out an ad in the Amarillo paper to me. The ad stated that it would pay 10% interest, which of course, was much better than the 3-1/2 and 4% that I was getting at the bank. We made a trip to Amarillo to see about it. The fellow explained to us that it was investments in insurance. And, that there was no way possible that we could lose our money. In order to get the 10%, we had to leave it in for three years, or he had another deal where we could draw interest every three months on it, but that only paid 9%. So, I put $40,000.00 into the 10% deal, which was all the cash that I had free at that time. Trudie put $15,000.00 into the 9% deal. About 3 weeks later when I got my other

$20,000.00 clear, I went back and was going to invest that into the 10% deal, too. Trudie kept telling me to diversify and to not put all my eggs in one basket. So, I put the $20,000.00 into the 9% deal. Three months went past and we never received any interest checks. I called the broker up, and asked him about it. He said that he was sure that they would get the checks out to us, and in the meantime he sent Trudie and me our interest checks, which he paid out of his own pocket. I imagine that he was paying other investors out of his pocket the same way, and after two such payments, he just couldn't afford to do that anymore. The upshot of it all was that the big shots of the company had embezzled millions of dollars there and no one was getting the money. There was a few million left in the company coffers, but it is all tied up in the courts now. It has been three years now, and will probably be another year or two before the courts release the money, and even then, we will probably get something out of it, but it will only be about a third of what we put into it.

Well, that brings us pretty well up to date, so I guess I'll end my saga here.

The End

Pertinent Facts of my Life

1. At age 83, I finally became an author.
2. I have moved thirty-six times in my life.
3. I have worked in thirteen different factories.
4. I have painted eight factories both inside and out.
5. I have painted one huge grain elevator.
6. I have had five falls between twenty-five and thirty feet to concrete.
7. I have never had a broken bone in my life.

As a Salesman

1. I have sold magazines.
2. I have sold neckties door to door.
3. I have made and sold popcorn balls professionally.
4. I have sold newspaper subscriptions.
5. I have sold hospitalization insurance for four different companies.
6. I have sold Ware Ever Aluminum two different times.
7. I have sold Cutco Cutlery.
8. I have sold fine china.
9. I have sold hosiery.
10. I have sold food plans.
11. I have sold paint jobs.
12. I have sold roofing jobs.
13. I have sold novelties.
14. I have sold stainless steel cooking utensils
15. I have sold sterling silver.
16. I have sold barn cleaners.
17. I have sold air purifiers.
18. I have sold water purifiers.
19. I have sold furniture.
20. I have sold newspapers.
21. I have sold Fuller Brushes.

Types of Work I Have Done in my Lifetime.

1. I have been a school crossing guard.
2. I have worked in a butcher shop.
3. I have caddied.
4. I have herded turkeys.
5. I have mowed lawns.
6. I have cleaned and sharpened lawn mowers.
7. I have unloaded coal cars by hand.
8. I have worked threshing crews.
9. I have built and set concrete forms.
10. I have set metal forms.
11. I have mixed and poured concrete by hand.
12. I have done concrete finishing both by hand and by machine.
13. I have used and operated a concrete vibrator.
14. I have done reforestation,
15. I have worked on a rock crusher.
16. I have been a carpenter's helper.
17. I have been a carpenter.
18. I have done roofing.
19. I have sanded and refinished floors.
20. I have run a pressing service.
21. I have done sign painting and lettering.
22. I have taught a Red Cross first aide class.
23. I have been a hobo.
24. I have been a truck driver.
25. I have been a taxi cab driver twice.
26. I have driven jeeps.
27. I have driven tanks.
28. I have been an auto mechanic.
29. I have used an electric welder.
30. I have used an acetylene torch.
31. I have done spot welding.
32. I have planted cabbages by the thousands.

33. I have planted tomatoes by the thousands.
34. I have operated tractors.
35. I have been an air hammer operator.
36. I have installed car hoists.
37. I have roofed barns and houses.
38. I have been a spray painter.
39. I have been a brush painter.
40. I have been an interior decorator.
41. I have hung paper.
42. I have hung sheet rock.
43. I have spent eighteen months in the CCC Camp.
44. I have been a soldier.
45. I have operated large air compressors and all the air tools that go with it.
46. I have been a section hand on the railroad, laying new track.
47. I have worked on the W.P.A.
48. I have worked at the Ravenna, Ohio ordinance plant.
49. I have worked at the Plumb Brook Ordinance works, Sandusky, OH.
50. I have worked at the Lone Star Ordinance Plant, Texarkana, TX.
51. I have worked at an ordinance plant at Little Rock, Arkansas.
52. I have worked at Fort Bliss, El Paso, TX.
53. I have worked in a box factory in Houston as a sawyer & assembler.
54. I have worked in a sheet metal factory, making metal cabinets.
55. I have worked in a furniture factory in Chicago (lathe operator).
56. I have worked in another furniture factory as an upholsterer.
57. I have worked in a plating department plating car bumpers.
58. I have operated a spray booth in a factory.
59. I helped build a big air base at Deming, NM.

In the Army

60. I served in the engineering corps.
61. I served in the armored infantry.
62. I served in the armored cavalry.
63. I have qualified as expert with M1 Rifle.
64. I have qualified as expert with a 30-caliber machine gun.
65. I have qualified as expert with a 50-caliber machine gun.
66. I have qualified as expert with a 45-caliber pistol.
67. I helped build both pontoon bridges and log bridges.
68. I have helped build a 90-foot firing tower.
69. I have set up a box factory to crate the division up for overseas shipment. At this time, I was just a private, but I had 264 men under me. I probably should have had sergeant major's stripes out of it, but as it was a special duty detail, I didn't get even as much as corporal's stripes. There were only two men in the division that could give me an order, one was the second lieutenant in charge of the detail, and the other was the commanding general of the division. I had as much or more power there than most captains. Starting without even a hammer or a nail, in three months time, we turned out over 85,000 waterproof boxes.

After the Army

70. I have worked several construction jobs as carpenter and foreman.
71. I have worked in a factory running a machine that made nylon hosiery.
72. I have also operated a steam mangle stretching and pressing sweaters.
73. I have dug sewage ditches by hand with a pick and shovel.
74. I have had my own small restaurant.
75. I have had a small drive-in.
76. I have worked as a waiter.
77. I have worked as a dishwasher.
78. I have been a janitor.
79. I have been a bartender.
80. I have had my own box factory.
81. I have been a census taker.
82. I have had flying lessons, but never soloed or got my pilot's license.
83. I have been an iceman.
84. I have helped install piers in the spring and remove them in the fall.

A Few More Facts

I have traveled extensively through forty-nine states. I have never been to Hawaii, but I am planning on going some time this year. I have made six trips to Europe. I have been on a cruise through Panama Canal, and on another cruise up the Inside Passage to Alaska. I have been in twenty-nine different countries and islands.

At age 75, I contracted sugar diabetes, which also gave me an enlarged prostate, a slow heartbeat, and poor blood circulation. I have also acquired eczema and the doctors have told me that I have emphysema. I also have senile skin, a bad postnasal drip, and my balance isn't all that it should be. But, for an 83-year-old, I guess I'm in pretty good physical shape. I still walk without a cane, so I don't think that I have too much to complain about.

That's all folks.

www.ingramcontent.com/pod-product-compliance
Lightning Source LLC
Jackson TN
JSHW080101141224
75386JS00028B/802